W9-BMG-618

Defusing the High-Conflict Divorce

Publisher's Note

This publication is designed to provide accurate and authoritative information in regard to the subject matter covered. It is sold with the understanding that the publisher is not engaged in rendering psychological, medical, or other professional service.

Books in The Practical Therapist Series® *present authoritative answers to the question, "What-do-I-do-now-and-how-do-I-do-it?" in the practice of psychotherapy, bringing the wisdom and experience of expert mentors to the practicing therapist. A book, however, is no substitute for thorough professional training and adherence to ethical and legal standards. At minimum:*

- *The practitioner must be qualified to practice psychotherapy.*
- *Clients participate in psychotherapy only with informed consent.*
- *The practitioner must not "guarantee" a specific outcome.*

— Robert E. Alberti, Ph.D., Publisher

Other titles in The Practical Therapist Series®

Defusing the High-Conflict Divorce

A Treatment Guide for Working with Angry Couples

Bernard Gaulier, Ph.D.
Judith Margerum, Ph.D.
Jerome A. Price, M.A.
James Windell, M.A.

The Practical Therapist Series®

Impact Publishers®
ATASCADERO, CALIFORNIA

Copyright © 2007
by Bernard Gaulier, Judith Margerum,
Jerome A. Price, and James Windell

*All rights reserved under international and Pan-American Copyright
Conventions. No part of this book may be reproduced, stored in a retrieval system,
or transmitted in any form or by any means, digital, electronic, mechanical,
photocopying, recording or otherwise, without express written permission of the
author or publisher, except for brief quotations in critical reviews.*

ATTENTION ORGANIZATIONS AND CORPORATIONS:
This book is available at quantity discounts on bulk purchases for educational,
business, or sales promotional use. For further information, please contact
Impact Publishers, P.O. Box 6016, Atascadero, California 93423-6016. Phone:
805-466-5917, e-mail: info@impactpublishers.com

Portions of chapters 8 and 16 originally appeared in articles by Jerome Price,
M.A., in *Psychotherapy Networker* in 2005 and 2006 (www.psychotherapy
networker.org).

Library of Congress Cataloging-in-Publication Data

Defusing the high-conflict divorce : a treatment guide for working with
angry couples / Bernard Gaulier ... [et al.].
    p. ; cm.
  Includes bibliographical references and index.
  ISBN 1-886230-67-6 (alk. paper)
1. Divorce counseling. 2. Divorce therapy. 3. Interpersonal conflict. 4.
Divorced people—Psychology. I. Gaulier, Bernard.
  HQ814.D37 2007
  616.89'1562—dc22

                                                         2006028101

Impact Publishers and colophon are registered trademarks of Impact
Publishers, Inc.

Cover design by Sharon Wood Schnare, San Luis Obispo, California
Composition by UB Communications, Parsippany, New Jersey
Printed in the United States of America on acid-free paper
Published by **Impact ✍ Publishers®**
POST OFFICE BOX 6016
ATASCADERO, CALIFORNIA 93423-6016
www.impactpublishers.com

Dedications

To Laura; to Patrick, Marc and Nick.

— B. G.

To all of the families that I have worked with who allowed me to help them navigate such a major life event. And to my own co-parent and children who have shown me how important it is to put the children first.

— J. M.

To my brother Marty who got me interested in non-adversarial divorce work and to all the children hurt by feuding parents before, during, and after high-conflict divorces; particularly to those preteens and teens who think they're fighting a just battle against one of their parents when they should never have been put in the position to choose sides to begin with.

— J. P.

To Jane; and to every one of the people I've gotten to know who suffer from high-conflict divorces.

— J. W.

Contents

Acknowledgments

Writing a book involves so many more people than just the authors. Therefore, there are many people we wish to acknowledge and thank for their important — although in some cases unknown — contributions to this book.

It would be impossible to write a book about high-conflict divorce without acknowledging the seminal work of Joan B. Kelly, Judith Wallerstein, Janet Johnston, and Constance Ahrons. Throughout this book, you'll find many references to the work of these individuals. James would like to thank Joan Kelly for an interview she granted him for an article in *The Michigan Psychologist* and for a delightful lunch a few years ago when she was in Lansing, Michigan, presenting a workshop on high-conflict divorce.

Attorney J. Kim Wright, the editor of the new magazine, *The Cutting Edge*, made valuable suggestions in making sure our review of current models of alternative dispute resolution processes was accurate and complete.

Jerome feels it is important to thank Cloe Madanes for her wisdom and mentorship — particularly for her pioneering work in addressing power balance in couples and Jay Haley for his splendid teaching and sense of Zen. It's also important to acknowledge all of the attorneys we work with whom we refer to as "family friendly." These attorneys sacrifice income by doing the right thing for families and children when litigating would be ever so much more lucrative.

We would also like to thank all of the Family Division judges in Oakland County Circuit Court for their support of our work. Those judges are the Honorable James M. Alexander, Martha D. Anderson, Linda S. Hallmark, Cheryl A. Matthews, Eugene Arthur Moore, Daniel Patrick O'Brien, Elizabeth Pezzetti, and Joan E. Young. In addition, the Friend of the Court counselors in Oakland

County, the professionals who usually first come in contact with high-conflict couples, deserve special thanks and our gratitude for being so pleasant to work with. They have over and over again proved to be steadfast in maintaining a professional perspective, and a sense of humor, in a job that is extremely stressful and difficult. And that has helped relieve tension and make our jobs less stressful. We'd especially like to thank Sandra Binder, Elaine Bryant, Katharine Dopke, Judy Froemke, Brian Gallant, Beverly Green, Lori Klein-Shapiro, Jany Lee, Jody LaPointe, Suzanne Lehsten, Jane McCarron, Susan McCoy, George McGrath, Mary Kaye Neumann, Terry Oppenheim, Joseph Rzpecki, Katherine Stahl, Judith Trombley, and Lorie Willing.

Judy would like to thank F. Edward Rice, a professor at Oakland University, who first brought family therapy and systemic thinking to her attention when she was an intern in the psychology and counseling program at Oakland University. It opened the door for her to work with difficult clients and families — which she's been doing ever since.

James and Bernard would like to thank all of the Family Division judges in Oakland County, along with Pamela Davis and Lisa Langton. It would be impossible to run a high-conflict divorce program without administrative and judicial support. Also, James would like to thank Katie Schultz McCarthy, because of her contributions to the development of the ADEPT program. We started out a new program without knowing much about what we were doing, but by working together and being creative, we were able to implement a program that has become successful. Katie was succeeded by Mary Seyuin, who has been a splendid co-therapist and has continued to help tweak the ADEPT program to improve our work with high-conflict divorce couples. Furthermore, Bob Hack deserves credit for running a private ADEPT program and making his own contributions to improvements in the program.

Finally, we'd like to thank Bob Alberti and Kelly Burch at Impact Publishers for being such wonderful, patient editors. Bob gave us encouragement from the start of this project and helped us to find a voice as the four of us struggled to find a way of communicating what we wanted to say to our readers. Bob was always a reassuring presence when we needed support, and the questions and editorial comments he and Kelly offered were a tremendous help in finishing this book on schedule.

About the Authors

❖❖❖❖❖

Bernard Gaulier, Ph.D., is Director of the Court Psychological Clinic (Family Division of the Circuit Court, Oakland County, Michigan). As a forensic psychologist in the field of juvenile justice and custody disputes, he has conducted numerous assessments and helped coordinate services regarding children and family issues.

❖❖❖❖❖

Judith Margerum, Ph.D., is a clinical psychologist and Co-Director of the Michigan Family Institute. Dr. Margerum received her doctorate from the University of Detroit and has over 20 years experience working with families experiencing difficult problems. She provides professional consultation and training as well as therapy.

❖❖❖❖❖

Jerome A. Price, M.A., is the director and founder of the Michigan Family Institute. He is an internationally known brief therapist, teacher and consultant who is widely published. He is contributing author in several books, has written numerous articles, and is author of the books *Power and Compassion* and *The Right to Be the Grownup*. Price is an Approved Supervisor for the American Association for Marriage and Family Therapy.

❖❖❖❖❖

James Windell, M.A., is a court psychologist at the Oakland County (Michigan) Circuit Court where he conducts group therapy with adolescent delinquents and treats high-conflict divorce couples. He is the author of several parenting and medical books, and his most recent book is *The Fatherstyle Advantage*. He writes a syndicated parenting column.

❖❖❖❖❖

Preface

The four of us decided to write this book after discussing high-conflict divorce cases innumerable times. We frequently met for lunch and the topic of conversation inevitably came around to the difficult cases we were seeing. They were always the high-conflict divorce cases.

We frequently commiserated with each other about the frustrations of trying to bring about change in these couples, and we exchanged war stories about testifying in court about our assessments or interventions.

As we picked each other's brains in these informal consultation sessions, the thought occurred to us that perhaps we, collectively, knew enough about high-conflict divorces that we could pass on some useful tips and advice to other professionals.

Jerome Price, M.A., a family therapist, and Judith Margerum, Ph.D., a psychologist, founded the Michigan Family Institute some 21 years ago. Their clinic, based on their training in systems therapy, has specialized in working with difficult children, adolescents, and families. Because of the reputation they developed over the years, they began to get more referrals of families in which there was high conflict.

As a result of their work as well as their clinical orientation, they've creatively developed a family systems approach to treating high-conflict divorce cases that has been successful in helping many couples change the embattled nature of their relationships.

Bernard Gaulier, Ph.D., first met Jerome Price more than a decade ago when Bernard hired him to conduct a workshop for court personnel at the Oakland County Circuit Court Family Division. That encounter led to a lasting professional and personal friendship. However, as chief of the Psychological Clinic at the Family Division, Bernard has seen the same patterns observed by other court psychological clinics: the number of angry co-parents referred for psychological evaluations has increased dramatically over the past several years.

As a consequence of the increase in such assessments, the psychologists Bernard supervises have been challenged by the difficulties of making recommendations for the court concerning child custody and parenting time. Too often, Bernard and his staff have found, a psychological assessment may have provided a judge or a referee with more insight regarding a particular high-conflict divorce case, but very little resolution to the family's problems.

It was the judges in the Sixth Circuit Court Family Division who, several years ago, asked Bernard and his staff to develop a treatment program for high-conflict divorce couples; those intractable couples who seemed to consume so much of the court's time and energy. Assigning this task to James Windell, M.A., and Katie Schultz McCarthy, Ph.D., a group program was developed and implemented. This program, begun in 2000, was the ADEPT program. The acronym stands for After Divorce — Effective Parenting Together.

Treating many of the same kinds of difficult co-parents, the four of us found a bond that has led to this book. As it turned out, this book has been a labor of love for all of us as we discovered in the writing that we better defined what it is that we try to do to bring about change with high-conflict families. In addition, writing *Defusing the High-Conflict Divorce* has allowed us to better understand, and appreciate, how we each approach assessing and treating angry co-parents.

We hope that you get as much out of reading this book as we did from writing it.

Introduction

Volatile, embittered postdivorce relationships — "high-conflict divorces" — frustrate and perplex therapists, attorneys and judges. These obstinate cases have become a major concern for therapists and the courts. As a therapist, you've very likely experienced the acute frustration these difficult couples produce when you try to help them resolve the issues they present.

Ever since the divorce rate in the United States leveled off in the 1980s, it's become commonplace for about forty percent of all first marriages to end in divorce. Most of us who do clinical work have noticed that an increasing number of divorcing couples remain angry with each other long after the decree is issued. Why are there so many angry, embittered divorced mothers and fathers — *co-parents* — who continue to fight each other for months or years after their separation?

In your therapeutic role, you will be faced with many questions and concerns about such cases. Here are a few:

- ❖ How can I help them manage their anger toward each other?
- ❖ How can I encourage them to be reasonable with each other?
- ❖ How can I help them put their children first?
- ❖ How can I help them to concentrate on the issues, rather than on each other's personalities?
- ❖ How can I best use my therapeutic skills so they resolve their problems?

Defusing the High-Conflict Divorce: A Treatment Guide for Working with Angry Couples is a book that will help you answer these questions. It will give you many ideas and strategies for helping couples locked in bitter disputes. We'll address and discuss proven approaches to dealing with many of the issues clinicians typically encounter in divorce counseling. And we'll show you how to use your skills and talents to engage and successfully treat high-conflict divorces.

The book begins with a look at what happens when co-parents continue to fight after divorce. Who suffers the most? We'll look at the research and share our collective clinical experience. In chapter two, we point out why ten to twenty percent of divorces become high-conflict divorces. Is it because of personality disorders in those individuals? Is it because of mental illness? Or is it just a sign of the times? What causes some people to be unable to work through the issues of their separation and divorce? We'll examine the recent research to present an objective assessment of the causes of high-conflict divorce.

In Part II, we present six patterns you'll likely encounter in working with individuals and couples who are involved in angry conflict after the first year or two following divorce. The patterns, discussed at some length in chapters three through eight, include:

- ❖ co-parents placing their children in the middle of their arguments and fights.
- ❖ children developing a troubled relationship with one parent (including the situation called Parental Alienation Syndrome);
- ❖ one or both of the ex-partners getting remarried;
- ❖ one or both co-parents abusing substances;
- ❖ one or both co-parents being accused of mental illness;
- ❖ one co-parent being (or feeling) disempowered.

As we discuss these patterns, you'll find advice and suggestions for dealing with them that will help you to respond in clinically astute ways when you encounter them in practice.

Part III places the high-conflict divorce in the context of the legal and mental health systems in which we find these cases. Attorneys, often the first to see divorcing couples, have a unique opportunity from the beginning of a divorce to encourage or discourage future high conflict. Judges in family courts are in a similarly critical role, as are mental health professionals who do divorce counseling.

High-conflict relationships do not occur in a vacuum. They take place within a setting, a context. Embattled couples are surrounded by a family and by friends who influence their behavior. They also operate within the wider context of a legal system and, if they're referred for a psychological assessment or for counseling, the context also includes the mental health system. In this part of the book, we describe the circles of the legal system and the mental health system. In chapters nine, ten, and eleven we address concerns about how attorneys, judges, and clinicians may either escalate or defuse conflict between co-parents; these professionals can contribute to greater harmony and cooperation — or they can encourage greater conflict.

For many readers, Part IV will be the most critical section in this book. Chapters twelve through sixteen address interventions in high-conflict divorces. That, of course, is the issue that most courts and clinicians see as the bottom line concern. How do you best get involved and offer help to individuals caught up in the bitter rancor of a difficult divorce?

Chapter twelve offers an overview of the usual court and mental health approaches to education and treatment. Succeeding chapters describe parent coordination and mediation. In chapter fifteen, we describe in considerable detail the ADEPT program, an eight-week educational and psychological group treatment program with a proven track record. And in chapter sixteen, a successful systems therapy intervention developed by co-authors Jerome Price and Judith Margerum at the Michigan Family Institute is presented.

After reading this book, we hope that you will be better able to recognize patterns of dysfunction in individuals and couples who are in the midst of high-conflict divorces, and that you will see the bigger picture — how high-conflict relationships develop within the systems that surround families. And finally, it is our sincere wish that you will come away from this book with many new ideas for intervening in troubled postdivorce relationships, guiding you toward your own success in working with some of the most difficult clients you'll ever encounter.

Part I

High-Conflict Divorce:
Who Gets Hurt?
Why Does it Happen?

Who Gets Hurt When Parents Fight?

Almost every divorcing couple who ends up in family court will have traveled down an angry road littered with discord, heated arguments, and blame. For most of those couples, the disappointments and heartbreak will cause such intense emotions for a year or more following the granting of a divorce that they won't be able to deal with each other in a civil, let alone friendly, manner.

Fortunately, emotions cool down for a majority of divorced couples and they are able to work out a reasonably affable accord that allows them to raise children together (King and Heard, 1999). However, there are other families in which two or more years go by and the fighting and bickering fails to cool down. It's in these families that children are most in jeopardy. The parents in these families make up what we call the "angry twenty percent." Whether you're a psychotherapist, attorney, judge, or family counselor, you've been frustrated more than once with these angry couples who can't even end their marriage without bitter and prolonged fighting. You will very likely recognize at least one of the following angry couples:

❖ ❖ ❖ ❖ ❖

Tim and Shannon have been divorced for three years following a nine-year marriage. Shannon, a striking blond, was a stay-at-home mom with their three children throughout their marriage. Tim, a handsome tennis pro at a suburban country club, left the marriage to pursue a relationship with a younger woman with whom he was having an affair. Bitterly angry since then, Shannon is so resentful she cannot tolerate being in the same room with Tim and she blames him for all of their conflicts.

"Tim does everything he can to make my life miserable," Shannon complains. "He's supposed to pay for all dental and medical bills for the children, but he constantly finds excuses as to why he can't pay."

"I don't want to fight with her, but she's always trying to get back at me," Tim says. "I'm devoted to the children but she finds every excuse to take me back to court."

❖ ❖ ❖ ❖ ❖

Samantha and Brian carry on a love-hate relationship with each other even though they've been divorced for four years. On the one hand, they both readily admit that each loves their two children, but on the other hand, they say that each has serious faults that make it impossible for them to communicate with each other except by email.

"She makes me crazy with her always asking me for more money," Brian says. "She's a loving mom, but she wastes money that's supposed to go for raising the kids and she expects me to provide more."

"He threatens me," Samantha says about Brian, "and I'm afraid of him. He stalks me and says I'm still his wife as far as he's concerned. Over and over he's said that he will eventually win me back or else he'll try to get full physical custody of the kids and not let me see them."

In both mediation and therapy sessions, Brian and Samantha argue and threaten each other. And they can never seem to reach an agreement. At times they talk nostalgically about their previous love for each other. But they always end up vociferously blaming each other for sabotaging any peaceful resolution to their disagreements.

❖ ❖ ❖ ❖ ❖

Todd and Jennifer were together in a relationship long enough for Jennifer to get pregnant. They stopped living together by the time she was six-months pregnant although Jennifer was devastated by Todd's leaving. Since Andrea was born, Todd has insisted on being part of Andrea's life. Jennifer, however, refuses to let him spend more than an hour or so at a time with their child, who is now eighteen months old.

"She wants to cut me out of Andrea's life," Todd says. "She doesn't care that Andrea needs to know her father."

"Todd thinks I don't want him to be part of Andrea's life," Jennifer explains, "but I can't trust him. He's not dependable and he's so irresponsible. How could I allow my baby to be with someone like him?"

Jennifer and Todd have been back to court five times in the past year, Jennifer arguing that Todd is an unfit and irresponsible parent and Todd arguing for more parenting time.

❖❖❖❖❖

If these couples sound familiar to you, then you know what it's like to work with high-conflict divorce couples. And as you've discovered, not only is this frustrating but it's exhausting, stressful, and ultimately unsatisfying. High-conflict divorce couples are the people that almost nobody wants to deal with — not judges, not attorneys, not counselors, not psychotherapists. They drain the emotions of those who try to help them solve their conflicts, and they consume the resources of the courts by demanding time to air their complaints while frustrating any and all attempts by attorneys, therapists, judges, and other court personnel to help them. Those of us who work with such couples realize they badly need help, but they often leave our offices or the court just as angry and vindictive as when they came in; and then they have the nerve to blame just about everyone for their conflicts — except themselves.

More than anything, working with high-conflict divorce couples is like trying to settle an argument between two obstinate, completely irrational children. High-conflict divorce co-parents are emotional, stubbornly set in their ways, and unwilling to compromise or see the other's point of view. They say they want their conflicts resolved, but they can never accept the decisions or agreements handed down by court counselors, referees, or judges. They say they want the problems they have with their co-parent to end, but somehow their problems continue and those problems and conflicts take priority over almost everything else in their lives. They say they wish their co-parents would just stop fighting and harassing them; at the same time, both are unwilling to let the other walk peacefully out of their lives.

In *Defusing the High-Conflict Divorce: A Treatment Guide for Working with Angry Couples*, we describe high-conflict divorces, identify how couples become part of them, and explain the treatment approaches we have found to be the most effective for ending the conflict. We describe various approaches to helping high-conflict divorce couples resolve their problems, with a focus on proven successful educational and treatment programs that we have developed.

To give you a context in which to better understand high-conflict divorce couples, we discuss the history of divorce in the United States in the rest of this chapter. We take a look at the effects of divorce on children and explore what the research says about conflict after divorce and its impact on children.

❖ *A Brief History of Divorce in the United States*

Many people think that divorces started in this country in the 1960s and that before this turbulent decade U.S. couples stayed together in more or less happy marriages throughout their lives. It's easy to be seduced into thinking that the happy little family television sitcoms of the 1950s actually reflected traditional U.S. life up to the radical 1960s. However, families in the United States never much resembled Ozzie and Harriet's family — before or after the decades of the 1950s (Coontz, 1997).

In fact, separation and divorce have been normal aspects of U.S. life since 1640. But it is true that divorce rates didn't cause much concern until the 1960s. Between 1962 and 1982, divorces nearly tripled (U.S. Census Bureau, 2001; Siegel, Welsh and Senna, 2006). In 1982 the number of divorces reached a record 1.2 million a year (Bryner, 2001), and many people became concerned about the changes in U.S. families.

Social pundits as well as scientists began to seriously question what was going on in our society. What was the impact of those marital breakups on children? Was the nuclear family still viable? Did divorce cause children to become involved in delinquency and crime? What about the mental health of those who separate and divorce? Was divorce a harbinger of mental health problems for children whose parents split up?

Sociologists and psychologists began intensely studying the American family starting in the late 1960's, with particular interest in what was going on with marriage and divorce. For instance, Judith Wallerstein and Joan Kelly followed a group of sixty families in California (Wallerstein and Kelly, 1980). Constance Ahrons studied 100 California families over a period of 10 years (Ahrons, 1994). And other researchers (e.g., Hetherington, Cox and Cox, 1985; Furstenberg and Cherlin, 1991) looked specifically at what happened to the children of divorce. And other researchers looked specifically at what happened to the children of divorce across the

U.S. (Guidubaldi, et al, 1983), while others studied the children of divorce in Canada (Trovato, 1987) and Australia (Smiley, Chamberlain and Dagleish, 1987).

The results of early studies of the U.S. family began to appear in books and journals in the early 1980s. Those results pointed to poorer outcomes for kids whose parents had divorced. Many professionals suggested that broken families led to behavior and discipline problems both at home and at school (Amato and Keith, 1991a). Furthermore, studies indicated that children of divorce were more likely to have academic problems compared to children who lived in intact families, and they were more likely to suffer from depression (Cummings and Davies, 1994).

In their groundbreaking 1980 book, *Surviving the Breakup*, Wallerstein and Kelly postulated that divorce hurts children throughout the childhood and adolescent years and often into adulthood. Later research indicates that both children and adults experience adjustment problems following divorce.

Amato and Keith (1991a), for instance, found in reviewing a number of research articles that parental divorce was associated with negative outcomes for children in the areas of academic achievement, behavior, psychological adjustment, self-esteem, and social relations. When Amato and Keith looked at a number of other studies involving adults, they discovered that divorced persons, when compared to adults who had never been divorced, experienced difficulties and disorders in the following areas:

❖ Psychological well-being, with considerably more depression
❖ Family well-being, with less satisfactory marriages and a greater number of future divorces
❖ Socioeconomic well-being, with lower educational attainment and lower income
❖ Physical well-being, with less adequate health (Amato and Keith, 1991b).

Everyone Suffers

Do children or adults suffer more following divorce?

The simple answer is that indeed everyone suffers in a divorce. However, since children are in the formative years of their lives, they have the potential for more far-reaching harm. They have to form secure attachments with their parents, learn to control their behavior, negotiate peer relationships, and succeed at school — all of which make up a necessary prelude to adult life, when they must be able to form satisfactory marital relationships and find an occupation.

It's estimated that each year the parents of more than one million children go through divorce (Hetherington and Stanley-Hagan, 1999). Other estimates suggest that at least forty percent of children will experience the divorce of their parents before they reach 18 years of age (Weir, 2006).

❖ *What Causes Children to Suffer When Their Parents Divorce?*

An extensive look at the research on families who divorce shows two schools of thought about the risk posed to the children involved. One school says that children are harmed regardless of how the parents get along following divorce. The other point of view, led by more recent researchers, suggests that it isn't the divorce that hurts kids but the *conflict* during and following divorce that spells the difference in children's adjustment (Cummings and Davies, 1994; Cummings and O'Reilly, 1997; Kelly, 2000; Lamb and Kelly, 2001).

The optimistic point of view of many writers of the 1960s and 70s was that divorce was a good thing because it meant an end to parental conflict and discord. The optimists said that children would be hurt by parental bickering and disagreements but once the divorce took place, the result would be less discord and, in the long-run, children would be better off. In other words, divorce was a way of solving marital problems and children would be relieved of having to live in a family made dysfunctional by frequent fighting and tension.

As research continued into the 1990s, though, studies tried to determine what it was about divorce that hurt children. Initial studies identified three potential factors: (1) parental absence, (2) economic disadvantages, and (3) family discord both during and following divorce (Amato and Keith, 1991a).

Parental absence was cited as a factor in child maladjustment when a parent, typically the father, dropped out of a child's life. Economics were also cited as a factor in the emotional adjustment of children following a divorce because economic disadvantages accrued to many children after divorce since most children live with their mothers, who are more likely to experience a lowered socioeconomic status. However, family discord in the postdivorce period (the subject of this book) has gotten more attention than either economic or parental absence factors.

Of course, there are both practical and research reasons for this. Since you wouldn't be reading this book if you weren't concerned about high conflict after divorce, you know that your experiences tell you this is a vital factor in everyone's postdivorce adjustment. However, starting in the early 1990s, social science researchers argued that long-term studies indicated that children's problems arose mostly from marital conflict (Furstenberg and Cherlin, 1991). Some, such as Amato and Booth (1991), studied families after divorce and concluded that both divorce itself and conflict were to blame for the maladjustment of children. In an effort to learn more about the effect of conflict, children of low-conflict families were compared to children of high-conflict families. In a survey of fourteen research studies that compared intact families as either "high conflict" or "low conflict," the children in the high-conflict families had more behavior problems, more anxiety, more depression, and less self-esteem than kids in "low-conflict" families (Amato and Keith, 1991b).

Whether or not you are a therapist working with families, you may have observed that it is the inability of parents to resolve conflicts that most jeopardizes the health and well-being of children. The major stressor for children of high-conflict divorce appears to be that they grow up in families marked by chronic conflict. In some families the conflict merely continues despite the divorce. Other families may have experienced little conflict until the divorce. The conflict in these families escalates to the point that the marriage can't continue — but the conflict goes on and on, despite divorce heralding a new beginning in which parents can develop a new cooperative way of dealing with each other.

When the conflict resolution patterns of families were studied, it was found that the overall amount of conflict didn't predict how the children were doing. The way conflict was expressed turned out to be the most important factor (Camara and Resnick, 1988, 1989).

What Is It about Parental Conflict That Leads to Emotional Problems in Children?

When parents are unable to resolve conflicts, they're teaching poor social skills. Without expert teaching in conflict resolution, children don't learn how to handle conflicts. In addition, it could be what happens to parents when they fight that has such a big impact and influence on their children. For instance, it's been found in some studies that mothers who were involved in higher levels of conflict in their marriages were colder toward their children and more rejecting of them (Kline et al., 1991). These mothers were also unhappy themselves and often had poor control over their emotions.

Conversely, it may be what happens to children and teens when their parents go on fighting that may end up causing damage to kids. Some children who feel caught up in their parents' conflicts don't feel close to either parent. Such children are more likely to be depressed and anxious and to engage in reckless and law-violating behavior (Buchanan et al., 1991).

It also has been found that when children are exposed to chronic parental conflict, they're more likely to feel insecure, guilty, and helpless and to be less involved with their parents and to sense rejection from others (Cummings and Davies, 1994; Harrist and Ainslie, 1998; Johnson, LaVoie and Mahoney, 2001).

As we said at the beginning of this chapter, most couples will experience some level of discord and carry on angry arguments leading up to a divorce. For a great many, the disillusionment and anguish of a divorce will bedevil their relationship for a year or more following the granting of a divorce. It's in the families in which two or more years go by and the fighting and bickering fail to cool down that children are most in jeopardy. These are the parents who continue to fight, and aren't helped by counseling, mediation, court hearings, judicial orders, or family counselor intervention. Their disagreements drag the children into the fray in such a way that the children come to be resentful and angry themselves. They are especially angry that their parents don't act in a more mature and responsible manner (Grych and Fincham, 1993).

How Can Families Be Spared the Suffering Conflict Causes?

It's tempting to say that parents should realize that their children will suffer greatly if they continue to fight long after a separation and divorce takes place. However, chronic fighters don't *plan* to continue their conflict — it just happens. They don't even realize the ongoing conflict is damaging their kids. Even though they know that children don't respond well to their bickering, parents can't seem to stop on their own.

It's when parents are unable to stop fighting and control their conflicts that they have high-conflict divorces. And that's where this book will be helpful. In the rest of this book we describe the parents who engage in high conflict and outline the reasons for ongoing conflict and ways to disrupt this damaging cycle.

Do you find yourself wishing that John and his ex-wife, Christine, won't show up for their two o'clock appointment? Do you get a headache every time you play a message from Frank and Rebecca? Does every suggestion you make to Cynthia and David get rejected as untenable by one or the other? If these things happen to you, go on to chapter two, where we discuss why divorces become high conflict. Knowing this will give you an edge in diffusing the conflict before it gets more ingrained.

2

Why Do People Have High-Conflict Divorces?

❖❖❖❖❖

When Bridget and Don were going together, they were inseparable.

"We liked the same things," Bridget recalls. "We enjoyed snowmobiling, ice skating, and going out to dinner. He had a great sense of humor and he made me feel secure."

Don says that they were an "ideal" couple.

"She was very loving and we could talk for hours," he says. "I never felt closer to anyone else in my life."

Eight years later, after two children and a divorce, Don and Bridget are locked in a fierce custody battle over their children. While they both can recall those loving and affectionate times early in their relationship, they no longer talk to one another and their communication takes place more through their attorneys than in any other way. Who could have predicted they would get a divorce and become a high-conflict statistic?

❖❖❖❖❖

In this chapter, we will provide the latest research as well as our own clinical experience to answer the question posed by the title of this chapter: Why do people have high-conflict divorces?

Research suggests that somewhat less than twenty percent of couples who divorce continue to fight and engage in conflict after the first year or two following the termination of marriage (Buchanan and Heiges, 2001). Almost all couples who are getting a divorce do so because they can no longer get along. When two people have been in love and that once-loving relationship has deteriorated, emotions will certainly be involved. Beyond emotional reactions, arguments, conflict, and even bitterness are to be expected. However, when there are children involved, a majority of divorced couples look beyond their own hurts and resentments and begin to consider what's best for the children. They may never quite stop being angry with and resenting each other, but their emotions are neatly shelved so that the kids don't suffer.

Yet, there are those nearly twenty percent who can't do that. The big question is *why*. Why can't they let their feelings go to protect their children?

Why Do Different People React so Differently to Divorce?

First of all, there's no question that everyone responds somewhat differently to divorce. That's to be expected because people are different. Each of us has our own personality, temperament, and life experiences — all of which leads us to deal with the stress and crisis of a deteriorating marriage in a unique manner.

❖❖❖❖❖

When Eric and Deborah got a divorce after ten years of marriage, each reacted in a different way. Eric, who had been unfaithful and often detached during the marriage, was devastated. He reacted in an emotional way that surprised him as much as it did Deborah.

"I literally had never seen him cry before," Deborah said. "But here he was, calling me at all hours of the day and night sobbing about how much he loved me."

Eric said he thought that when Deborah filed for a divorce that that was really what he wanted also.

"I thought I could just walk away from her and our marriage without feeling bad," Eric said. "But I couldn't. In fact, I had no idea why I was so upset. I had feelings I didn't know I had."

Deborah, on the other hand, had been unhappy with the marriage and Eric's philandering for several years. By the time she filed for a divorce, she had worked through many of the feelings that resulted in her falling "out of love" with Eric.

"It was like he had been dead for a while, and I had learned to live without him by the time we got a divorce," Deborah explained.

❖❖❖❖❖

Two people in the same ten-year marriage, yet each responded in a different way. That's true of every couple — and individual —

who gets a divorce. It's difficult to predict how each person will feel once the marriage has officially ended. Divorce, however, can be viewed as a major crisis that can lead to trauma or growth.

Divorce as a crisis

Divorce is similar to other life events that feel like a crisis as they're developing and being experienced. One definition of a crisis is a major turning point. Another definition is a time of great trouble or difficulty. Separation and divorce definitely fit both these definitions. In fact, for most people who experience a divorce, the definitions would seem like understatement.

Typically, crises are times of feeling overwhelmed, devastated, or immobilized. After all, a crisis is a stressful event or situation. Crisis is usually not as quick as an automobile accident (although an accident could lead to a crisis); rather it's often an ongoing series of stressful events. The way individuals respond to a crisis — such as divorce with all the issues that need to be handled — will be influenced by several personal aspects. McIntosh and Deacon-Wood (2003) enumerate these factors:

❖ their personalities
❖ their coping methods
❖ their emotions
❖ their past experiences
❖ their states of health
❖ their communication skills

These factors are important in understanding why some individuals adjust to divorce relatively well while others go into an emotional tailspin from which they may never really recover.

The personality of each parent

Personality is the distinctive pattern of behaviors, thoughts, and emotions that characterizes each of us. Everyone can be described by various personality traits that are influenced by genetics (including temperament and cognitive abilities), learning (including what parents have modeled and taught), and social interaction.

Each of us has, as a result of inheritance, learning, and the influence of others, a unique set of traits that make up a distinct personality. For example, Brandon, at 25, is viewed by others as hard working, conscientious, trustworthy, tough-minded, honest, and disciplined. Sarah, age 51, is said to be caring, empathic, self-conscious, thrifty, slow to anger, and spontaneous. Ryan, 36, has been described as callous, rude, temperamental, self-centered, and domineering.

Although early socialization experiences, including identification with parents, shape personality, it also depends on the various inborn skills and limitations each of us possess. It is our personalities that help determine how we'll react to a divorce and to the stress of ongoing conflict with a former spouse.

For example, if Anita is self-effacing, placid, dependent, and passive, she is unlikely to react to a divorce with bold attempts at revenge or uncontrolled anger. More likely, no matter the cause of the divorce or the provocation, Anita will handle the stress and trauma of a divorce with her usual easygoing and passive approach. She also may need encouragement to ensure that she negotiates for a truly fair settlement.

On the other hand, Angelo is brash, outgoing, impulsive, quick tempered, and self-confident. He makes hasty decisions, holds grudges for a long time, and adheres staunchly to his particular view. Although he had an affair, he faulted Kathy, his former wife, for filing for a divorce. He chided her for taking "the easy way out" by getting a divorce and he meant to punish her for it. He frequently yelled at her, said negative things about her to their 7-year-old daughter, and threatened her with physical harm. After he'd behaved in a hostile manner, he apologized for his actions and said he wanted nothing more than to get back together with Kathy. He told her that if she gave him another chance, he was certain they could work out the problems.

There are, however, specific personality characteristics that are more likely to lead to ongoing conflict. These characteristics are rigidity, need for control, defensiveness, and reactivity.

Rigidity

People who are flexible will have an easier time adjusting to divorce. It is the rigid and inflexible who are more likely to be in a high-conflict divorce.

❖ ❖ ❖ ❖ ❖

Edward, at 43, had been married for seventeen years. An engineer who worked for the same automobile design company since he graduated from college, he frequently said he "hated" change.

Even though a supervisor had mistreated him, he put up with being disgruntled rather than change companies. And even though he realized for many years that his marriage was less than ideal, he could not tolerate the idea of divorce and the changes this would entail. During the divorce negotiations, he insisted on keeping the house exactly as it was and having the children live with him.

❖ ❖ ❖ ❖ ❖

Joyce, a woman who had been married for seven years before divorcing, was a "black and white" thinker. There was little room for shades of gray in her life. While married, she was steadfastly in favor of men and marriage. Once she was divorced, Joyce saw her former husband in a completely negative way. She had a virtual litany of his abusive and nonsupportive behaviors. She referred to him as a poor father and said she worried about him abusing the children "just like he abused me." When she was asked for details about the abuse she suffered, she couldn't be specific, but she insisted he was both an unfit husband and father. She said she had "never" loved him and knew from the beginning of the marriage that he was "no good."

❖ ❖ ❖ ❖ ❖

Co-parents who become rigid in their perceptions of their former spouse tend to view themselves as all good and the other parent as all bad. They have difficulty seeing the positive in their co-parent and often assert that their co-parent is to blame for all the problems. Such a rigid personality structure leads to an intractable approach to working out problems that leaves almost no room for negotiation or compromise in such areas as shared custody and equitable parenting times.

Some authorities in the field of high-conflict divorce (e.g., Stahl, 1999) state that the rigid stance some parents take is related to the fear that their co-parents will take advantage of or control them.

Need for control
Closely allied to rigidity is a need for control. Although, like rigidity, a need for control may be related to fear, it can also be due to mistrust or insecurity. Whatever the wellspring of the strong need for control that some co-parents have, this characteristic often goes hand-in-hand with both rigidity and possessiveness.

❖ ❖ ❖ ❖ ❖

Brett, a 24-year-old man with impulsive behavior and a short fuse, was very possessive of Katie, his co-parent. This was true both before and after their divorce, which she initiated because she could no longer tolerate "his trying to run my life and dictating what I did." On more than one occasion, Brett told Katie, "I don't care if we are divorced, you're still my wife and you will always be my wife."

❖ ❖ ❖ ❖ ❖

One of the most frequent complaints we hear from women (and many men, as well) in high-conflict divorces is that their co-parents are "control freaks" or are still trying to "run my life — just like when we were married."

Co-parents intent on gaining control over the other parent are likely to meet with resistance, and this may intensify their attempt to control. The situation with one pushing for independence and the other for control is rife for conflict. Both may see the other as unreasonable, and if one of them is rigid as well, conflict is inevitable and perhaps perpetual.

The possessiveness that the need for control engenders relates to the co-parents at times but also to the children. When co-parents with the need to control speak about their children, they will often say, "*my* child" or "*my* son" — not "*our* child." Custody battles become heated when the possessive parent insists, "I want custody of my son!" And parenting time issues are fraught with pitfalls when the possessive parent feels he is being denied time he deserves with "*his* child."

Defensiveness

One of the most frequent personality characteristics to show up in the research of high-conflict divorces is defensiveness. Several studies on divorce (Ackerman, 1995; Posthuma and Harper, 1998; Siegel, 1996; Siegel and Langford, 1998) have found that high-conflict individuals are defensive and deny personal responsibility for any of the problems, projecting much of the blame on their co-parents. Defensive individuals see themselves as the wronged party and, in addition, blame their co-parents for keeping the conflict alive. They seem to lack insight into the reasons for ongoing arguments, and any wrongdoing — even their own — is blamed on the other person.

❖ ❖ ❖ ❖ ❖

For example, Joyce, whom we introduced earlier in this chapter, was evaluated by a court psychologist to help the judge in her case make a custody decision. During the clinical interview, Joyce asked why she needed to be tested. She was not crazy, she said, and she had already told the court that her former husband was abusive. She, therefore, didn't need to be "treated like I was guilty of something."

"All the judge has to do is give me full custody," Joyce told the psychologist. When she was prompted for specifics about the alleged abuse, she incredulously asked the examiner if he didn't believe her.

"Do you think I'm lying?" she pointedly asked. On the Minnesota Multiphasic Personality Inventory — 2 (the MMPI-2), her L and K scores were elevated and her F score was low.

❖ ❖ ❖ ❖ ❖

The MMPI-2, which is one of the most widely used personality testing instruments, has several so-called validity scales. The three most relevant for our discussion are the L, K, and F scales, which were developed to give a sense of test-taking attitudes. The L scale, or Lie scale, is calculated to find out if individuals will admit to what most people admit to — basic human shortcomings. A high L score means they are reluctant to admit any faults within themselves. The F scale is used to measure the amount of distress people are experiencing. A low F score indicates individuals are unable or unwilling to admit that anything is wrong with them. The K score was developed to assess how defensive individuals are in taking the MMPI-2. In effect, the K score reveals how willing individuals are to talk about their various problems.

The high L score suggests the person is saying, "I don't do anything wrong." The low F score means the person is saying, "I don't have anything wrong with me." And the high K score indicates the person's attitude is "I resent you asking me about these things."

When individuals in high-conflict are engaged in disputes over custody, child support, and parenting time, the stakes tend to be high. As a result, when administered the MMPI-2, high-conflict people will all tend to have a defensive profile of a high L, low F, and high K.

❖ ❖ ❖ ❖ ❖

Roy was taken to court by his co-parent for a personal protection order against him. She told the judge that Roy was stalking her, driving past her apartment frequently and parking in front of her office so it was obvious to her that he was watching her. In court, however, Roy denied stalking her and said if he parked near her office it was to protect himself from her and make sure she was where she was supposed to be. "I'm the one who should have a personal protection order against *her*," Roy proclaimed to the judge. "She's mentally ill and I'm afraid she will attack me or my car." The judge, shaking his head, quickly granted them both personal protection orders and told them to keep away from each other.

❖ ❖ ❖ ❖ ❖

On the other hand, Judith, a 28-year-old car salesperson, had a more open personality along with a great deal of persistence, a positive outlook on life, and honesty. When her husband filed for a divorce after they were married for three years, her response was to take on more hours at work, join a health club, and reconnect with old friends. Adopting a positive attitude, she told a friend a few weeks after her divorce was final that although she was disappointed that the marriage didn't work out, she viewed the divorce as a "new opportunity to find the right man." When she talked to a court counselor about custody and parenting time, she was open about her faults as both a wife and parent. "I spend too much time at work," she admitted, "and my energy and enthusiasm can overpower others. I get too impatient with our son, and that's something I can say about Ken, he is a very patient father."

❖ ❖ ❖ ❖ ❖

Unlike Judith, people who are engaged in a high-conflict relationship are not only defensive but often cannot see their own faults, nor are they able to see the strengths and assets of their co-parent.

Reactivity

Co-parents involved in high conflict are more often than not more reactive than passive. Although reactivity may incorporate impulsiveness and a need to act out, people involved in high conflict often respond as much to their inner feelings as to external events. Reactive individuals are less inhibited and respond to strong emotional arousal. They are more likely to react in explosive ways rather than feeling anxious or guilt ridden. The strong emotional arousal, based on inner feelings, is usually related to emotions such as fear, anxiety, rage, and sadness. A co-parent dropping off a child late, differing philosophies about toilet training, disagreements over the clothes sent during parenting time, arguments over the amount of sleep a child needs, and other common situations that confront parents raising a child together often set off these feelings.

When interviewed or tested by a psychologist, reactive parents are frequently described as histrionic and narcissistic. Their reactions to their co-parents tend to be out of proportion to the situation.

❖ ❖ ❖ ❖ ❖

For instance, when Ricky dropped off their children thirty minutes later than scheduled, Heidi screamed at him, "You do this kind of thing on purpose to disrupt my life! You don't care about me or the children! All you care about is yourself!" On the other hand, when Heidi sent stuffed animals with the children when they went back to Ricky's house, Ricky refused to let the children take the stuffed animals to bed. "This is just your little way of trying to intrude on my time with the kids," he snapped at her when he returned the children. "You'll do anything to make sure they don't have fun with me."

❖ ❖ ❖ ❖ ❖

Daniel was a reactive parent, too. During an exchange of children at his house, he and his co-parent, Amy, got into an argument over the medication their son was supposed to take for asthma. When Amy yelled at him, accusing him of trying to "over-medicate" their son, he called the police, charging that Amy was threatening him.

❖ ❖ ❖ ❖ ❖

Because of the reactivity of some divorced co-parents, protective services departments are sometimes called in to investigate spurious allegations of abuse. Children are court ordered to be exchanged at police departments or in public places in an attempt to reduce the chances for the co-parents' reactive responses to get out of control.

Maladaptive coping methods

Research shows that immature and inappropriate coping skills increase the failure rates of couples locked in ongoing conflict (Mathis, 1998). Some of the coping styles co-parents use that doom their efforts to get along better with a former spouse include overreacting, blaming, projecting blame, attacking rather than communicating effectively, defensiveness, threatening, and involving the children in the dispute. Couples engaged in high-conflict relationships have a tendency to repeat the same behaviors, even though they don't work.

For example, in many high-conflict divorces one or the other co-parent will yell, swear, or threaten the other co-parent, even though this has never produced a positive result or led to a compromise. For these individuals, even normal conflicts with each other escalate into major events that feature exaggerated reactions, which means that virtually no resolution is possible.

Mathis (1998) found that many people engaged in postdivorce high conflict actually *enjoy* the conflict. For some, there is the wish to prolong the conflict. For those, it may be that without conflict they will feel alone or abandoned. As you might suspect, poor coping strategies cause conflict in marriages. Hopper (2001) found that high-conflict marriages are often replaced by high-conflict divorces.

❖ ❖ ❖ ❖ ❖

Deidre and Thomas were an example of this. Prior to the divorce, whenever they had a disagreement, Deidre threatened a divorce and Thomas withdrew. He would leave the house and go to a neighborhood bar to drink until he was drunk. The next day, Deidre and Thomas avoided each other without talking. When they did begin talking again, the original disagreement was never addressed. They promised each other every time that they wouldn't threaten divorce, get drunk, or stop talking; however, those patterns continued. This was so after their divorce as well.

❖ ❖ ❖ ❖ ❖

Past experiences
Past experiences play a big part in postdivorce conflict. Family relationships when growing up, traumatic events, difficulties in previous romantic relationships, and various life events can have an effect on what happens in a marriage and after a marriage has ended.

❖ ❖ ❖ ❖ ❖

For example, Barry and Jan were so angry with each other during and after their divorce that they both tried to get revenge against the other. Jan induced a male friend to slash Barry's car tires. Barry called Jan's boss and told him that the reason for the divorce was that Jan had multiple affairs with men with whom she worked. This led to Jan being fired. To retaliate, Jan tried to poison Barry's dog.

❖ ❖ ❖ ❖ ❖

Jan's anger was fueled by her childhood experiences; her father left her mother when Jan was very young. When Jan married Barry, she swore that her marriage would last forever and life would be different for her than it was for her mother. When Barry filed for a divorce, all of Jan's pent-up rage from childhood, including her anger at being abandoned by her father, were unleashed on Barry.

Barry, too, had his past experiences to contend with. Unpopular in high school, when Barry did finally begin dating, he usually fell deeply in love with girls he dated. He would then be crushed when they broke up with him. He angrily blamed girls for being shallow and fickle, but he was really angry at himself for being unpopular and unlovable. To protect himself, he would break up first. He was conflicted about marrying Jan, but she convinced him that she truly loved him and would never leave him. When Barry sensed waning interest between them after several years of marriage and three children, Barry filed for a divorce — continuing a pattern he had established after high school.

Emotions

If there's one thing you have to give individuals stuck in a high-conflict postdivorce relationship, it's that they express their emotions. Rather than holding back how they feel, they emote all over the place. As therapists, you actually want to teach them to hold their emotions in check. And as an attorney representing them in court or as the judge who has them in front of your bench, you sincerely wish they would restrain their emotional reactions and outbursts.

❖ ❖ ❖ ❖ ❖

"I hate him. He's determined to ruin my life!" shouts Gloria to her therapist.

❖ ❖ ❖ ❖ ❖

"She's so vindictive," says Harold. "She'll never change and I feel so bad for our children who have to listen to her bad mouth me."

❖❖❖❖❖

"You don't know how hard this is for me," said Burton in a high-conflict group educational program. "I want to learn to communicate with her, but you don't understand what she has said to me. I can't get past her vicious words. They keep replaying in my head."

❖❖❖❖❖

These individuals let you know exactly how they feel and the emotions that hang them up and keep them involved in bitter exchanges and ongoing conflict. These couples' threats toward each other are no secret, nor is the enmity they feel toward each other. Benjamin and Irving (2001) indicate that the couples in high conflict are emotional, impulsive, and difficult to control. This not only makes them difficult to work with in educational and therapeutic programs but leads them to continue to express their emotions whenever there's any contact between them outside of a supervised setting. They look emotionally unstable and in certain circumstances — particularly when they feel wronged or injured — they act in an emotionally unstable manner.

Communication skills

There is no question that poor communication skills are associated with high conflict. Even if you have had limited contact with high-conflict couples, you will quickly observe that they are often unable to communicate about the simplest issues. But this is not because they have borderline personality disorders as some researchers and clinicians have maintained (Johnston and Campbell, 1988).

In our experience, when you see these individuals without their co-parent present, they are perfectly reasonable and evidence adequate communication skills. In fact, if you investigate other areas of their lives, you'll find that they communicate effectively within their extended family, in social circles, and at work.

❖❖❖❖❖

Marcie sold radio ads for a local station. She was very skilled at her job and was usually the top grossing salesperson year after year for her company. She was well liked by colleagues as well as by her clients — which brought them back to the station to do business with her. However, when she and her former husband tried to solve problems, Marcie acted as if she had no communication skills at all.

❖ ❖ ❖ ❖ ❖

Jeffrey was highly skilled at his job as a defense attorney. He understood the nuances of language and could charm and disarm potentially hostile witnesses — not to mention juries. However, with his co-parent following a highly emotional divorce, he was loud and bombastic and tended to approach her with verbal attacks and threats, something he would never do with a witness in court.

❖ ❖ ❖ ❖ ❖

As Rudd (1996) indicated, many individuals involved in high-conflict divorces use aggressive communication and antisocial "compliance-gaining strategies." Such tactics antagonize their co-parents and continue an adversarial relationship. When such individuals fail to use their own feelings in "I" messages, fail to acknowledge what the other person may be feeling or expressing, fail to use basic conflict resolution strategies, and fail to engage in negotiations that lead to compromise, they are essentially using dysfunctional patterns that lead to failed communication.

Furthermore, as Retzinger and Scheff (2000) have pointed out, when co-parents use dysfunctional communication patterns they alienate each other. They then tend to deny they are doing this, which in turns sets up a conflict that cannot be easily overcome.

State of health
Both physical and mental problems can play a decisive role in how well or how poorly an individual copes with a divorce.

❖ ❖ ❖ ❖ ❖

Before Phyllis's husband divorced her after nearly twenty years of marriage, she was diagnosed with multiple sclerosis. Although it was apparent that Martin had been thinking about a divorce for a long time, he was more certain of needing to get out of the marriage when he concluded he could not spend the rest of his life caring for someone for whom he no longer felt love.

Phyllis was still reeling from the devastation she felt at having one of her worst fears confirmed — that she would become disabled and dependent. She also believed that Martin owed her his loyalty and devotion after the number of years they'd been married. She vowed she would do everything she could to make him as miserable as she felt. One way to do this was to get back at him through their children. She was resolved to hurt him and to be as disagreeable as possible.

❖ ❖ ❖ ❖ ❖

Physical illnesses and diseases play other roles in how people cope with divorce. For example, individuals with cancer or emphysema may lack the stamina or the will to fight a settlement. They may feel they are doomed anyway, so causing others discomfort is only fitting. Other times people experiencing serious illnesses may decide that it's best to give in and avoid conflict. Still others become depressed because of their illness and withdraw from conflict.

Mental health issues may represent the most serious challenge both to co-parents and to mental health counselors or legal advisors. Individuals who can be described as having personality disorders may "enjoy" the disruptions they cause — even in the lives of their children. Or they may be so egocentric that they fail to appreciate the unhappiness or harm they're causing others.

Most frustrating are those people with serious mental illnesses. They may be so impaired because of delusions or hallucinations that they're unable to handle conflict or discussions in rational ways.

❖ ❖ ❖ ❖ ❖

Kristine stalked her former husband while accusing him of various sexual crimes against her, her children, and his neighbors. She frequently called the police to report a sexual offense, and the police department in her city no longer took her complaints seriously and stopped investigating them. This convinced her that her co-parent was in a conspiracy with the police department against her.

❖ ❖ ❖ ❖ ❖

Karl, the 42-year-old father of two small girls, told his therapist that he had photographs that he would show him to prove that his former wife had sexually molested their daughters. When the therapist asked to see the photos, he announced that he had decided to put them on his website for the entire world to see. The therapist could not find the photos even when he located Karl's crude website.

❖ ❖ ❖ ❖ ❖

In situations like those involving Karl and Kristine, the co-parent's bizarre behavior leads the court to limit contact with the children for safety reasons. The mentally ill parent then becomes more disturbed in reaction to a perceived slight or a perceived conspiracy, and she or he goes about causing more trouble for everyone, including the children.

Working with individuals like Kristine and Karl is very difficult for their co-parents and frustrating for therapists, attorneys, and courts alike. While it isn't possible to say they won't benefit from successful postdivorce programs, having people with such problems in a program may cause disruption and benefit no one.

As indicated, some researchers and clinicians have said that they view many people in a high-conflict divorce as suffering from antisocial personality disorder or having a borderline personality. Janet Johnston and Linda Campbell, directors of the Center for the Family in Transition in Corte Madera, California, studied eighty families. One of their findings (Johnston and Campbell, 1988) was that two-thirds of the parents received a diagnosis of personality disorder. Johnston and Campbell (1988) went on to write that they thought that the core problem was narcissistic vulnerability. Divorce, they postulated — with its implications of failure, loss, rejection, and unworthiness — was a tremendous blow to the ego of these individuals. Initiating and winning a custody battle, for instance, was a way to save face, to compensate for humiliation and an injured self-image (Ellis, 2000).

Ehrenberg and his colleagues (Ehrenberg, Hunter, and Elterman, 1996) proposed that individuals with narcissistic personality traits are prone to highly conflicted relationships because they are dependent on admiration and attention from their partners. Under the stress of marital breakup, these needy people feel particularly deprived of soothing and admiration, and they turn to the children, as well as to others, to meet these needs.

❖ *Can We Predict High-Conflict Divorces?*

Given what we have just said about individuals in high-conflict divorces, it would seem that we should be able to make some predictive statements about which individuals and which couples are likely to be high conflict. Indeed, in some instances, we can predict. However, knowing the factors we have listed in this chapter and the personality characteristics associated with high-conflict divorce does not increase our ability to make consistent predictions. In other words, we cannot yet predict who will make a relatively quick and healthy adjustment versus who won't get over the pain of being abandoned.

If better predictions were possible, that would help judges and attorneys recommend interventions for the most vulnerable co-parents so treatment could begin before they become enmeshed in destructive battles that hurt everyone in the family. Nonetheless, the descriptions of the personality characteristics and other factors in this chapter will guide you to begin appropriate intervention approaches. You should keep in mind that educational, treatment, and intervention approaches that fail to take these important factors into consideration will likely be much less successful than those that do.

Do Sociocultural Factors Contribute to High-Conflict Divorce?

Just as there are no particular personality characteristics that help us predict who will have a high-conflict divorce, a couple's race is also not a determinant of their susceptibility to a high-conflict postdivorce relationship.

While it is a statistical fact that African-Americans had higher divorce rates throughout the 1990s than did whites and Hispanics (McLoyd, Cauce, Takeuchi, and Wilson, 2000), that did not apparently translate into higher conflict. In fact, no consistent racial differences have been found in how couples manage conflict in general (Adelmann, Chadwick, and Baerger, 1996; Sistler and Moore, 1996; Mackey and O'Brien, 1998).

Indeed, based on our own collective experience as well as a review of the research, no socioeconomic, income, ethnic, religious, or racial differences appear to influence whether a couple has a high-conflict or a low-conflict divorce (Johnston, 1994).

To Sum Up What We Know About High-Conflict Divorce

In general, it may be said that individuals who are rigid, inflexible, engage in black and white thinking, are controlling and possessive, and are very reactive are more likely to become engaged in high conflict following divorce. In addition, if the individuals have antisocial personality disorders prior to the divorce or if they were in a high-conflict marriage, they are at greater risk of high conflict following divorce. Finally, if they are very self-centered and are not getting their needs met after divorce, you can look for them to use conflict and the children to satisfy their needs.

In the next section, we describe various patterns you will likely encounter in co-parents who have high conflict in their relationships. We begin in the next chapter with an examination of the pattern in which children are placed in the middle between battling co-parents. In particular, we describe several situations in which parents entangle children in the co-parents' conflicts.

Part II ❖

Patterns of Dysfunction in High-Conflict Divorces

Pattern 1: Children in the Middle

I n this section, we describe six patterns of parents and co-parents you are likely to encounter in high-conflict divorces. While in chapter two we discussed some of the personality characteristics of high-conflict co-parents, we look beyond individual personality traits in these six chapters. Here we will talk about patterns of how parents interact with one another and how they interact with the institutions we represent as helping professionals.

Co-parents who feel victimized and powerless, who are alienated from one or more of their children, who have substance abuse problems, or who are accused of being mentally ill represent some of the predictable patterns you are likely to see when working with high-conflict postdivorce couples. This section of the book will give more details about six such patterns so that you recognize them when you encounter them and so you will have increased skills to deal with these patterns in the most appropriate ways.

Divorced, With Children

It's relatively easy when you get a divorce if you have no children — you can just walk away. When you divorce and there are just the two of you, any lingering emotional turmoil associated with the divorce can begin to heal once the divorce papers are signed and all the possessions and financial assets are divided. You can choose never to see each other again because what once bound you together can be quickly dissolved. You don't have to learn how to get along better, how to resolve conflicts, or how to negotiate.

Not so when you have children. No matter how much pain and suffering the disintegration of the marriage has caused, you are forever bound together by your children. As co-parents you continue to see each other, and you must communicate in some fashion.

However, when hurt feelings and anger continue to fester, there is often serious interference with your attempts to communicate and to be effective co-parents (Fincham, Grych and Osborne, 1994). Often, too, this is when you are likely to drag the children into the middle of your communication disputes, your emotional problems, and your nasty battles. And this is when children are put at risk of suffering emotional damage (Amato and Keith, 1991; Zill, Morrison and Coiro, 1993).

❖ *Helping Children Adjust to Divorce*

Difficult as divorce is for the adults, it's equally or more difficult for the children. No matter what age children are when their parents divorce, they'll experience distress (Wallerstein and Lewis, 1998; Buchanan and Heiges, 2001; McIntosh, 2003). Divorce forces many changes in children's life — changes over which they usually have no control and very little understanding. The changes that may most affect kids usually have to do with the daily routines and the structures that once brought order and consistency to their lives: coming home from school to the place that was once considered home, the school containing all their friends, the family finances that provide security, the amount of time they spend with each parent, and the caretakers who watch them while their parents are working.

Will these changes bring about serious adjustment problems in a particular child? Or will the child make a fairly smooth and rapid transition to new life circumstances?

Those questions are best answered when a myriad of factors are considered, including the child's temperament, personality and age, relationship with each parent, and ability to understand the divorce's impact on her life. Furthermore, how a particular child reacts to a divorce will depend, in large order, on how her parents are coping with the divorce. Show us a couple who has worked out an amiable parting of the marital ways and are getting on with their lives, and we'll show you two parents whose children are probably adjusting just fine.

The more reactive the parents have been during the divorce, however, the more reactive children of all ages are likely to be. When the worst case scenario occurs, that is, when parents are engaged in a prolonged, persistent battle over various issues, the more distressed and upset the children will be.

❖ *How Parents Involve Children in Their Divorce*

There are several situations in which children at different ages and stages become entangled in their parents' divorces. The most frequent and common situations include

- ❖ When parents exaggerate minor incidents
- ❖ When highly enmeshed parents have been overly attuned to their children's emotional and physical well-being
- ❖ When parents give children too much information about the reasons for the divorce and their own emotional states
- ❖ When distressed parents require the care of their children
- ❖ When parents allow their children to manipulate them
- ❖ When parents use children as pawns in the divorce

When parents exaggerate minor incidents
A familiar pattern in high-conflict divorces occurs when one parent accuses the other of being abusive or endangering the children. It's not unusual, even in a low-conflict divorce, for one co-parent to become concerned about the other parent's discipline or behaviors with and toward the children.

❖❖❖❖❖

After Diane divorced Jerry, she was depressed and had a very high anxiety level. She worried about her finances because she had never worked a full-time job before and because Jerry was frequently late making his child support payments. Their three children were all under 6 years of age, and at times Diane felt overwhelmed caring for them. One day, when she was worried about paying the rent on her apartment, her children were misbehaving and she exploded in rage at them.

Having trouble getting them to go to their rooms, she slapped Cynthia, age 5, and twisted 4-year-old Gregory's arm. The next weekend, the children told their father what had happened. Jerry was incensed and told Diane he ought to call protective services to investigate her abusing the children.

❖❖❖❖❖

Like many parents recently divorced, Diane was highly stressed and she hadn't yet established new patterns of discipline. Without these new patterns of discipline, parents are more likely to overreact to their children's misbehavior. If a parent blows out of proportion a single incident of the other parent yelling at or grabbing a child, he can set off a highly negative and escalating pattern without really meaning to. If, however, one parent is looking for an excuse to be hostile or vengeful toward the other, she can use such an incident to "prove" that the co-parent is incompetent. Such incidents can be utilized as opening moves in a dangerous game of putting the kids squarely in the middle of the adults' inability to smooth out their differences.

Parents who are overly concerned about their children have a more difficult time tolerating the child's grief and sense of loss. During the best of divorces, people may be overwhelmed by circumstances and have increased fears regarding their children. Many parents initially experience some guilt about the divorce and the effect it is having on their children but are able to understand that their children will be able to cope. When parents are unable to tolerate the child's distress, they need to search for a solution to the problem. Often in their searches for a solution, they blame the co-parents or the parenting time schedule.

For example, younger children and infants cry during exchanges for a variety of reasons, including separation issues, difficulty with change, or their reactions to tension between parents. Because younger children can't verbalize their discomfort, parents must guess at the cause. It is easy to misinterpret crying at the exchange to mean children are afraid, being hurt, or are not bonded to the parent they are going to.

Normally, once a routine is established, children will become accustomed to exchanges. It's our job to help parents make the same adjustment to new patterns and schedules. If parents decide that there's a problem, they'll see everything that occurs in relation to that problem. When co-parents are looking for a reason to blame the other parent, they may accuse the other of not responding quickly enough to the infant's crying, not knowing how to change diapers, not holding the child correctly, or not talking in the correct tone of voice.

When highly enmeshed parents have been overly attuned to their children's emotional and physical well-being

Highly enmeshed parents, those who actually experience what they believe their children are feeling, will have a great deal of difficulty tolerating their children's reaction to divorce. Those parents will often project their angry or fearful feelings from the failed marriage onto their children and unwittingly cause their children to actually have those feelings. Parent and child amplify each other's distress.

❖ ❖ ❖ ❖ ❖

Melissa and George were referred for therapy by a court counselor after Melissa petitioned the court to suspend all of George's parenting time with their 11-year-old daughter, Jordan. Melissa told the therapist in the very first session that she couldn't possibly bring Jordan to the office for a session with her father.

"Jordan feels too hurt by what her father did to have to be in the same room with him," Melissa told the therapist.

Melissa described Jordan as being angry with her father for his disregard for both Melissa and Jordan in having an affair during the marriage and then filing for a divorce. George indicated his love for Jordan and said that he believed Melissa was turning her against him.

After several meetings and some reduction of tensions between Melissa and George, the therapist persuaded Melissa to bring Jordan in to meet with the therapist and her father. However, Jordan was very emotional in the waiting room, proclaiming that she'd call the police if she had to be in the same room with her father.

With Melissa in the office, the therapist calmed Jordan down. However, as the meeting time with George approached, Jordan became more agitated and angry. Melissa began speaking in a little-girl voice, telling the therapist (and Jordan) why her daughter felt such pain and discomfort. Each statement Melissa made, the therapist was convinced, matched with Melissa's own feelings about George.

For instance, Melissa said, "Jordan's just too scared of his controlling nature," which was what Melissa had previously told the therapist was one of her own biggest complaints about George. As Melissa became more upset and tearful, Jordan also became more angry and aggressive until the mutual escalation resulted in canceling the joint session with George. Of course, George was irate and used his next appointment with the therapist as an opportunity to berate Melissa as a controlling and vindictive woman.

❖ ❖ ❖ ❖ ❖

Melissa epitomizes the overly involved parent who has difficulty seeing herself and her child as separate individuals. Because the parent is enmeshed in her child's emotional life, her child has a difficult time reacting to the divorce and to the conflicts her parents have in her own way. Children like Jordan take on one of their parents' feelings and react as if the feelings were their own.

When parents give children too much information about the reasons for the divorce and their own emotional states

The older the child, the more likely he will seek an understanding about why his parents divorced and who is to blame. If children are able to obtain specifics about a parent's wrongdoing, they will inevitably take sides with the parent who feels most hurt. If you are involved with a family where children have been given too much information, you have an opportunity to head off an impending emotional car wreck.

To avoid this potential wreck, you must use every ounce of your persuasive abilities to convince both parents to refrain from discussing adult issues with the children. Adult issues that you should help co-parents avoid disclosing to the children include substance abuse, sexual aberrations (such as viewing pornography or going to prostitutes), affairs, psychiatric diagnoses, and the parents' emotional and personality states. If both parents fail to make it clear to their child that these are adult issues that a child should not struggle with or be privy to, the child's emotional distress can escalate significantly over time. To help parents avoid disclosing too much, it may be important to establish certain rules and procedures for how your clients talk to their children about adult issues. For instance, you might suggest that when a child says, "Daddy said that you always spend all of his money," the parents' response can be, "I will discuss that with Daddy and we will work it out so you don't have to worry about it." Or, if the child says, "Mom's boyfriend said that the reason you guys got a divorce was because you're an alcoholic," the parental response could be, "Moms and Dads often say things after a divorce that are upsetting to children. I'll have a talk with your mom and her boyfriend so that we decide if it's something that you need to worry about." Furthermore, you might have a maxim for divorced co-parents that helps them to know how to handle situations in which they might be tempted to give too much information to their child. That maxim could be: When an adult issue is raised by a child that seems inappropriate for parent-child discussion, the parental response should be to say, "Both of us love you very much and we don't want you to worry about such things. When adults get divorced, they sometimes have hurt feelings and those hurt feelings sometimes make us say mean things about each other. However, your father (or mother) and I will talk about this so that we try harder not to say things about each other in front of you that will cause you to be worried or upset."

❖ ❖ ❖ ❖ ❖

For instance, 14-year-old Bobbie was angry at his mother for divorcing his father. Bobbie asked his mother why she'd divorced his dad. His mother felt caught between defending her actions and protecting her child emotionally. She settled on telling him about his father's obsession with pornography because she felt he deserved to know "the truth."

However, once Bobbie heard this, he felt differently about his father and saw him as a "sick pervert." This knowledge also confused Bobbie, and he wondered if he had inherited some sick traits from his father and worried that maybe he was a pervert "just like my dad."

❖ ❖ ❖ ❖ ❖

As a professional, you must be cautious in your guidance to parents of what they can or should tell their children about themselves or the other parent. The "truths" and the information children can handle depend heavily on their age and maturity levels. After all, we don't tell our children everything about sex the first time they ask. We tell them a 6-year-old's version when they're 6 and an 11-year-old's version when they're 11.

Teens may blame one parent for causing the family home to be sold because the other parent wanted to keep the home and told them that they would continue to live in it. Adolescents have a keen sense of fairness and justice and are likely to side with the parent that appears to be the weakest and most wronged. The problem with a teen aligning with the parent he sees as the underdog is that the adolescent lacks the judgment and experience necessary to assess what is a very complex situation. Not only is an adolescent likely to have limited and one-sided information to base his decision on, but he is also presented with a dilemma in which he may find it difficult to continue to love both his parents.

Parents frequently defend themselves to therapists and attorneys by denying they ever asked their child to take sides. However, a dad doesn't have to be specific to demonstrate to his child that his life was destroyed by his ex-wife.

It's more important to protect children's relationships with both parents than to tell them the graphic details of the marriage or the reason for the divorce. Sometimes, "We just weren't getting along" or "We were arguing too much" is all of the truth that's necessary or helpful to children.

When distressed parents require the care of their children

During and after divorce, one or both parents may become depressed or anxious or develop other emotional symptoms. A sensitive child will step in to soothe or protect that parent. This protection may take healthy forms such as comforting, listening more carefully to instructions or commands, or simply helping more around the house or taking care of younger siblings.

However, in families in which there is high conflict following divorce, children may adopt more adult-like roles. This can be encouraged or promoted by one of the parents. Or, a parent may be too distressed or depressed to do anything other than allow a more mature or responsible child to take over a more adult-oriented role.

❖ ❖ ❖ ❖ ❖

Belinda was depressed after her divorce, and when she and her former husband continued to argue about child custody and parenting-time issues, Belinda's depression worsened. Many days she spent the whole day in bed. This left the responsibilities of running the household to her 8-year-old daughter Jo Ellen.

Jo Ellen was an excellent student who was well liked by her classmates and her teacher. At home, she was meticulous about keeping her room clean and making sure she got herself up, fed, and dressed each morning. As Belinda became more depressed and dysfunctional, Jo Ellen took on many duties Belinda had previously carried out. The girl made sure the house was tidy each day after school, vacuuming and washing the dishes. She prepared meals and took them to her mother's bedroom.

After doing her homework, she would sit on her mother's bed listening to Belinda talk about her unhappiness and how distressed she was with Jo Ellen's father. Jo Ellen tried not to take sides, although she always agreed with whatever her mother said because she realized to do otherwise would cause her mother more sadness.

Although she saw her father every other weekend, she made excuses as to why she couldn't stay overnight with him so that her mother wouldn't be alone overnight. She covered for her mother, making up activities they did together so that her father was unaware of the huge role Jo Ellen played in caring for Belinda and the household.

❖❖❖❖❖

Jo Ellen provides the quintessential example of the young child who is forced to grow up very quickly because she has to care for a dysfunctional parent. Not only is a child like Jo Ellen very good at this role, but she hides the extent to which she really runs the household. In the long run, Jo Ellen and Belinda, and perhaps Jo Ellen's father, will pay a price for this role reversal. Jo Ellen will not only resent her mother for allowing her to take over the "mother" role, but she will be resistant to giving up the power and control she has inherited. If Belinda gets help and becomes less depressed, Jo Ellen is very likely to oppose efforts on her mother's part to resume her proper role as parent. Likewise, after running her own life for any length of time, Jo Ellen will resent intrusion into that life by either her mother or father.

Another way that children are allowed to assume too much power and control is when they are expected to provide support and "therapy" to a parent who is suffering from the effects of conflict following a divorce. Scott provides an example of this.

❖❖❖❖❖

Scott, age 12, lives with his father, Barry, who has been divorced for three years from Scott's mother, Gabrielle. His parents agreed that since Scott's mother needed to go back to college to complete a nursing degree, he would be better off living with his father. Scott and his father had always been close, and they liked many of the same things.

Barry and Gabrielle agreed on where Scott should live — but not on much else. Barry insisted that Gabrielle pay child support even though she was going back to college to complete her degree to get a job to support herself. She wanted time with Scott every weekend and at least one night during the week although Barry was opposed to this. As they battled over these issues with frequent trips to the court for hearings, Barry became more and more upset.

He started drinking in the evenings right after he got home from work and made Scott listen to his harangues about Gabrielle. Scott felt sorry for his father, who characterized himself to Scott as a hapless victim. This led to Scott taking an active stand against his mother, whom he perceived as the perpetrator of injustice against his father. Scott's protectiveness of Barry often took the form of Scott getting into arguments with Gabrielle. She saw Scott as judging her because he felt that she was wrong in wanting to see him regularly and in resisting paying child support.

"You don't know how rough it is on dad," Scott would say to her. Beyond arguments and his condemnation of her, Scott contrived ways to chastise her and provide consequences to her. For instance, he would purposely miss time they had scheduled together, avoid telling her about events at school, and make excuses as to why he should stay home with his dad.

Scott became the child avenger of his father's wrongs at the hands of Gabrielle. This is another kind of reversal in which a child taking on the role of a parent leads to kids becoming progressively more adult-like in their speech and actions.

❖ ❖ ❖ ❖ ❖

As professionals, our job is to help children go back to living the simpler existence as the children they really are without being embroiled in parental politics. Children like Jo Ellen and Scott often develop emotional symptoms, and sometimes their academic success begins to wane (Hetherington and Stanley-Hagan, 1999). They may be quite successful in their pseudoparental roles, but their social lives with peers will always suffer.

When parents allow their children to manipulate them

A child of divorce has many opportunities to experience newfound power at a time when that child is emotionally vulnerable. Having two parents who are now at odds allows children to be the primary source of communication between parents who won't speak to each other. As the verbal intermediary between parents, a child has the option of distorting information to her benefit if she wishes. As long as the distortion creates a picture that impugns one parent, the other parent will believe it. In high-conflict divorces, children have a place they can always appeal for sympathy if they aren't happy with the actions or decisions of either parent. That place, of course, is the other parent.

❖ ❖ ❖ ❖ ❖

Brittany, who is 15, was having parenting time with her mother for the weekend. She wanted to stay overnight at the house of a friend her mother hadn't met. Brittany assured her that her father already met the parents and the friend and had said it was a safe place to be. In fact, her father didn't know this family either, yet Brittany got to go because she knew her parents would never speak to each other to confirm the truth or falsity of her story.

❖ ❖ ❖ ❖ ❖

Brittany's story illustrates a very mild example of the kinds and severity of manipulations that children and teens might resort to when co-parents are not communicating. A far more serious example concerns 13-year-old Derek:

❖ ❖ ❖ ❖ ❖

Derek's parents had been divorced for only a year. However, their anger and hostility toward each other seemed not to have dissipated at all during that year. They were determined to hurt each other by any means possible, and each tried to recruit Derek to their side.

Derek quickly figured out during that year that it was beneficial to him to appear to support whichever parent he was with at the time. He also discovered that telling lies about the parent who wasn't there made him an especially valuable ally in his parents' feuds with each other.

For instance, if Derek didn't finish his homework when he was with his father for the weekend, he told his mother his dad wouldn't help him with it. Furthermore, Derek told his mother that his father also kept him too busy working at his dad's condo for Derek to actually have time to complete his schoolwork. That was the kind of ammunition his mother needed to call her former husband and accuse him of selfishly neglecting their son. The fact that her co-parent denied the accusations only strengthened her belief that it was true. Derek could, as a result, avoid doing his schoolwork.

When Derek was with his dad, he complained that his mother never let him watch sports on television. His father, who valued sports in a child's life, made sure that Derek watched sports during his weekend visits and frequently got tickets to big games so he and Derek could attend together.

Derek could be secure in the knowledge that his parents were unable to talk rationally with each other, and he could get away with almost any lie he told.

❖❖❖❖❖

As long as co-parents only want to believe the negative stories their children report about each other, kids can get away with manipulations that result in more privileges, fewer responsibilities, and greater freedom to pursue their interests.

Younger children, too, quickly become aware of how to communicate effectively to manipulate their parents. If they don't feel like going to school, they find out that saying they want to stay home doesn't work, but having a stomachache allows them to miss a day of school. Similarly, mom and dad might lecture you if you tell them the entire story about why another child was mean to you, but they'll comfort you if you leave out the part about how you started it. These normal kinds of manipulation become more of a problem in the high-conflict divorce where parents are already looking for the other parent's faults.

When the child comes home from parenting time and says "Daddy is mean" or "Mommy didn't feed me," the parent doesn't let the statement go, as she might have when they were married. Nor does she casually call the other parent to find out what really happened. When parents hear these kinds of comments, they question their child about why daddy is mean or why mommy didn't feed her. When the child says, "I don't know," parents may dig deeper for answers because they believe the child is hiding something important. If a child is questioned long enough, she comes to understand that this is a very important situation and that the interrogation will not end until she comes up with an acceptable answer. Once a youngster finds that "telling" on mommy or daddy is important, she will repeat it and it will become an important part of the relationship with the "concerned" parent. The child finds that even though she may have become involved inadvertently in the parents' fights, she may also relish this new role because she gets lots of sympathy and individual time with the parent.

When parents use children as pawns in the divorce
Distressed and angry parents may use their child as a pawn in the divorce, and this may occur both wittingly and unwittingly. Under

normal circumstances parents ask children to pass messages to the co-parent such as, "Remember to tell your dad that you have to go to band practice at ten o'clock on Saturday" or "Tell your mom that your science project has to be completed by Sunday night." Such communications aren't inherently evil or damaging. However, in high-conflict divorces, parents may use such communications to avoid talking to each other or to pass on controversial information that is likely to fuel further conflict.

For example, when parents are fighting about child support and finances, one parent may tell the child just before being picked up for parenting time, "Tell your dad that his child support is late and if it isn't here by next Wednesday, I'm taking him back to court."

When children are placed in the middle as carriers of this kind of provocative message, they are enlisted in the fight to do each parent's dirty work. This isn't fair to the child and it puts him in the position of being the "bad guy" delivering unwelcome messages. Usually, children hate this role and resist delivering upsetting messages or learn to "forget" to tell the intended parent to avoid an ugly scene.

But it's a Catch-22 situation for children. If they faithfully deliver the message as requested, the parent who gets it will be angry and that may ruin the child's visit time. If the child "forgets" or only delivers a partial message, the other parent may be angry with him for forgetting or lying.

Sometimes, children are fed information that a parent is certain the child will repeat to the other parent. The first parent knows that when this information gets to the other parent it will create upset and turmoil.

❖ ❖ ❖ ❖ ❖

Just before leaving for his mother's house for the weekend, Mitch's dad strategically mentioned that he had set the date for his wedding to Betsy and it was on his mother's weekend. This communication was particularly toxic because Betsy was the woman that Mitch's father had left his mother to be with. While Mitch's father didn't direct him to tell his mother about the wedding plans and scheduling dilemma, his father knew Mitch wouldn't be able to resist telling his mother as soon as possible. Because of his mother's jealousy and anger, she reacted with expected rage. She railed indirectly at Mitch's father for the next several days for having an affair, getting remarried so quickly, and intentionally scheduling his wedding during her parenting time. Mitch felt guilty for telling his mother, but he also knew he had to break the news of his father's remarriage at some point.

Mitch, as he got older, figured out that his parents used him to report upsetting news and events to each of his parents. Over time, he vowed never to tell them anything and when asked if he had would say, "I forgot." He knew he didn't forget, but he didn't know what else to say.

❖❖❖❖❖

Teenagers are no different than other children in the sense that they love both of their parents. One of the more common problems, even in less conflicted divorces, is when parents tell their teens that they are old enough to decide where they want to live. In very cooperative situations with healthy teenagers, this sometimes works. However, for the most part, the responsibility to choose between parents should not be given to children of any age. It is an adult decision and too big a burden to place on any child. There is no way to eliminate the concern about betraying and hurting the feelings of the parent the child doesn't want to live with. It's unfair of the adults to place a decision they don't want to make on young people.

Giving them decision-making power also leaves adolescents with the ability to change their minds at any time about where they want to live. If they have a fight with the parent they're living with, teens can change alliances and go to the other parent. Because parents have left the decision up to the youth, they may not be clear about when and how changes in residence should be made. Parents may not set limits or may back down so that the teenager doesn't choose to go live with the other parent. What often happens in these cases is that teenagers become so abusive and demanding over time that the parent is more than happy when the child impulsively decides to leave. We've begun seeing court cases in which *both* parents file motions demanding that the other one take their out-of-control teenager!

As long as co-parents use their children as innocent pawns in their battle, children feel the emotional tug of war between being faithful, helpful children and being used by their parents to keep the fires of battle burning. Children come to resent being pawns and react with withdrawal, passive defiance, or outright hostility to their parents. Children learn, as they grow and become savvier, that their parents should talk directly to each other — and not use their kids.

Each of these six ways that parents place children and adolescents in the middle of high-conflict divorces can take a serious toll on a child. Until these families are confronted in treatment, they may continue to place their children at risk for school failure, parental abuse, or depression. Recognizing the potential damage to the children, you might insist that your client seriously examines the stress they are placing on their children by entangling them in conflicts that should be resolved between the co-parents.

However, breaking the pattern of dragging kids into the middle of divorce conflicts is not easy for therapists. You must actively promote cooperation, new patterns of interaction, and a better understanding of the potential damage to children when they are caught in the middle. In future chapters, especially in chapters eight, fifteen and sixteen, you'll find ideas and techniques for working with parents that will help you to minimize placing children in the middle.

4

Pattern 2: Parents Claiming
Parental Alienation Syndrome

In high-conflict divorces, when conflict between divorced couples is prolonged and bitter, co-parents may stop at nothing to hurt each other. This means co-parents engaged in hostile and ongoing disputes frequently involve their children in their attempts to humiliate, punish, or exact revenge from each other. Included in such attempts are efforts to turn the children against the other parent. The condition created when a parent has succeeded in alienating the children from the other parent has been referred to as Parental Alienation Syndrome (Johnston and Campbell, 1988; Gardner, 1989).

❖❖❖❖❖

Kevin won primary custody of Heather when she was 11 because Heather's mother, Ellen, was admittedly alcoholic and she agreed at the time that she couldn't provide the stability and level of care Kevin could for Heather.

Offended by Ellen's drinking during the marriage, Kevin often said negative things to Heather about her mother. He told her he was concerned about her safety when she went on weekend visits with her mother, referred openly to Ellen as a drunk, and told Heather to call him at any time if Ellen was drinking when Heather was with her. To be sure she got the message, Kevin gave Heather her first cell phone for the express purpose of calling him if she felt she was in danger while with her mother.

By the time she was 13, Heather refused to visit her mother, even though Ellen insisted she was attending AA and had been sober for a year. Kevin thwarted Ellen's efforts to secure regular parenting time with Heather. Ellen's motions to the court requesting increased visits resulted in the court ordering a psychological evaluation for Ellen and requiring her and Heather to go to a family therapist.

Despite counseling sessions, Heather refused to visit her mother, talk with her in therapy, accept phone calls from her, or even read the birthday cards Ellen sent her. The family therapist characterized this as Parental Alienation Syndrome.

❖❖❖❖❖

Parental Alienation Syndrome

Parental Alienation Syndrome is a term coined by child psychiatrist Richard Gardner (1987). Gardner saw it as a pattern of hostility, alienation, and cognitive distortion usually directed toward the noncustodial parent. He observed that ninety percent of the time it was mothers who exhibited this behavior in an effort to alienate the child from the noncustodial father (Gardner, 1987).

In one study with eighty families, Johnston and Campbell (1988) found that between thirty-five and forty percent of the children age 7 to 14 in high-conflict families experienced some degree of parental alignment. While the phenomenon of children being aligned with one parent and alienated from the other parent has been observed by many — if not all — who work with high-conflict divorce families, few studies, aside from Johnston and Campbell's have indicated what percentage of cases fall into this category (Ellis, 2000).

Nonetheless, since 1987, the term Parental Alienation Syndrome has become widely known and used by courts and clinicians (Ellis, 2000). However, it isn't universally accepted. In particular, clinicians have objected to the designation of this phenomenon as a syndrome. "Parental Alienation Syndrome," for example, is not recognized by the American Psychiatric Association because no research has established specific DSM criteria for a diagnosis of this condition as a syndrome (Ellis, 2000). A syndrome, by general consensus, has specific characteristics, an established pattern, and a prognosis. Parental Alienation Syndrome hasn't been well researched, and none of the above criteria has been found to describe it (Warshak, 2001).

On the other hand, many parents do try to undermine a child's love or caring for the other parent. Also, a great many parents, especially in high-conflict divorces, make false allegations against their co-parents and succeed in alienating a child from the other parent. While parents may be guilty of such cruelty, this set of behaviors doesn't constitute a disease or a syndrome. In addition, because we've found each case to be so different, we can't justify calling it a syndrome.

When a label — whether syndrome, condition, or disease — is given to people, we all have a tendency to accept it at face value, and this leads us to begin to explain a set of behaviors by that label. In effect, then, when speaking of the phenomenon of one parent having turned a child against the other parent, it could be said that "the child has Parental Alienation Syndrome." However, when we start *explaining* behaviors by their psychiatric designation, we stop trying to *understand* them. We believe that the tendency to explain things by their label is unfortunate and can prevent us from seeing each case or family as unique.

Why not to diagnose

The Problem of Parental Alienation Nevertheless Does Exist

Although we can't call it a syndrome, one parent alienating one child (or more) from a co-parent still is a problem. At one time or another, all of us — and that includes everyone from counselors and therapists to judges — have dealt with high-conflict divorces in which a child is alienated from a parent. When a parent is alienated from one or more of his children, that parent believes he has been wronged. When parents feel wronged, they seek relief. Consequently, parental alienation cases result in appearances before judges, attempts at reconciliation by friend-of-the-court counselors and mediators, motions filed in courts by attorneys, efforts at mediation and resolution by therapists, and, unfortunately, considerable heartache for the parents who have lost a relationship with their children.

Although parental alienation in most instances isn't related to serious mental illness, some parents use poor judgment in communicating with their children. When upset by a divorce, parents in a high-conflict relationship will do some of the following:

- ❖ Speak negatively about the other parent
- ❖ Portray the other parent as a "bad" parent
- ❖ Scare their children into thinking or believing negative things about the other parent
- ❖ Exaggerate incidents so they appear more serious than they are

Because many parents angered or embittered by a divorce have an ax to grind with their co-parents, they will do anything in their power to hurt the other parent. They know that one effective way to hurt their co-parents is to deprive them of their children. Either consciously or unconsciously, they attempt to "program" their children to hate the other parent. As part of this programming effort, they may make false or misleading allegations of sexual abuse or of physical or emotional abuse.

❖ ❖ ❖ ❖ ❖

Dolores felt abandoned and rejected when Paul had an affair and then filed for a divorce. Dolores objected to the joint custody arrangement that was decided by the court in the divorce decree. Although she reluctantly abided by it, she began to sabotage their parenting time arrangement soon after Paul married the younger woman with whom he had an affair.

When their two children, Nicole and Michael, spent time with their father, Dolores asked many questions about what happened during their time with him and his wife. One day, when Michael, age 5, told his mother that he took a shower with his father, Dolores was livid. She questioned Michael about the details of the shower and concluded that Paul had inappropriately touched Michael by washing Michael's genitals.

Dolores filed a children's protective services complaint and felt justified in refusing to allow the children to go with their father for the next scheduled visits. She called Paul a "pervert" in front of the children and asked Nicole, age 7, repeatedly if Michael or his wife had ever touched her inappropriately.

When the children's protective service agency found no basis for taking action against Paul, Dolores was angrier and more determined to "protect" her children from their father. The court ordered Paul's parenting time be resumed, but before the visits Dolores talked to Nicole and Michael about what they should "be careful" about. She told them not to let him touch them or to make them feel uncomfortable. She told them to call her immediately if anything "bad" happened. Within a few weeks, the children were anxious about going on the visits with their father. When Dolores asked them if they "wanted" to visit their father, they both said they preferred to stay home with her. Dolores was convinced that this was their way of saying they were afraid of being abused by Paul.

❖ ❖ ❖ ❖ ❖

As can be seen in this case, Nicole and Michael did not have a "syndrome" or a "childhood disorder." It's doubtful that they shared a belief system with their mother, as is seen in some parental alienation cases. More likely, Nicole and Michael wanted to get along with their mother and found it easier to do so when they told her what she wanted to hear. They still loved their father and wanted to spend time with him. But it made their life easier if they told their mother that they didn't want to spend time with him.

Joan Kelly and Janet Johnston (2001) reformulated Gardner's Parental Alienation Syndrome. In their reformulation, they wrote that the indiscriminate use of Parental Alienation Syndrome terminology has led to widespread confusion and misunderstanding in judicial, legal, and psychological circles. Their alternative way of looking at the concept focused more on the alienated child than the supposedly alienating parent. Specifically, Kelly and Johnston stated that there are many reasons for children to be estranged from one of their parents and only one reason relates to an attempt by one parent to drive a wedge between the other parent and their child.

Furthermore, Kelly and Johnston (2001) wrote that there is a continuum of distanced relationships between children and their parents following separation or divorce. This continuum ranges from the child who is allied with one parent through children who are estranged (to one degree or another) from a parent to — at the extreme — children who are alienated from one parent. The alienated children, Kelly and Johnston indicate, express strong resentment of one parent and completely resist contact with that parent.

❖ *Parental Alienation May Mimic Folie à Deux*

Nicole and Michael still loved their father and didn't always believe what their mother said about him. This isn't always true, however. In some instances there's a shared belief system between one parent and, usually, one child. In that respect, it resembles *folie à deux*. In the DSM-IV (American Psychiatric Association, 1994), *folie à deux* is described as a shared psychotic disorder in which a delusion develops in an individual who is involved in a close relationship with another person who already has a psychotic disorder.

❖ ❖ ❖ ❖

Fourteen-year-old Stephanie echoed her mother's beliefs about Stephanie's father. Stephanie said he abused her because he once gave her a spanking. She also said that he was "cruel" because he sent her to her room for a time-out after she'd been aggressive with her 4-year-old stepbrother. She and her mother both believed that he and his wife were "devil worshippers" because they did not go to church as Stephanie and her mother did. Furthermore, they both believed that Stephanie's father and stepmother intended to sacrifice her in a satanic ritual. Stephanie testified in court that she thought she would be killed if she spent time with her father and his wife; therefore, she refused to visit him or to talk to him on the telephone. Although Stephanie saw a therapist, no amount of counseling or reasoning shook her attitudes and beliefs — which were identical to her mother's.

❖ ❖ ❖ ❖

Children Face a Loyalty Dilemma
❖

When one parent says disparaging things about the other, the children face a loyalty dilemma. Whose side should they take? Most children love both of their parents, but they may be unsure which one to give their allegiance and loyalty to considering the negative comments one or both parents make about each other.

Because it serves an emotional need for many parents to express their unhappiness and dissatisfaction toward the other parent, they often don't hesitate to say negative things about their co-parents in front of or directly to their children. But parents fail to take into consideration that children take what an adult says (especially when that adult is a parent) in a literal way. What such parents say is at best insensitive and at worst malicious, self-serving, and harmful to their children.

If children are to be spared having to face such a loyalty dilemma, their parents must take the developmental level of the child into consideration when communicating with them about the other parent.

After divorce, it's common for parents to begin treating one or more of their children in an adult-like manner. They hold discussions with the children that replace the discussions they used to have with their partners. Adult-like communication with children is perhaps the most damaging technique used by parents trying to discourage their children's relationship with the other parent.

When a 5-year-old comes home and tells one parent that the other parent screamed at him, the parent must make a critical choice about how to respond. An alienating parent may say, "That's because your mommy is bipolar with a serious mental illness." The more mature and age-appropriate response would be, "Yes, honey, I know mommy can have a bad temper sometimes, but you know she loves you."

When an adolescent asks her mother why her parents got a divorce, it's again time to make a tough decision. An alienating response would be, "I left him because he always lacked self-control and went around screwing other women the whole time we were married." Obviously, details about a parent's sexual behavior aren't appropriate information for a budding teenager. However, the mother in this situation might have said, "We hadn't been getting along for a long time and we didn't love each other the way we used to." When the daughter asks about the young woman dad moved in with so soon after the divorce, a healthy response to a young teen might be, "I know it's hard for you to understand why dad made the choices he made, but when you're older you won't find it so confusing." If a child is younger a parent can simply say, "That's adult stuff that you don't need to worry about."

❖ *The Goal in Understanding the Pattern*

The concept of Parental Alienation Syndrome has been accepted as part of the lexicon of high-conflict divorce. For that reason although we don't agree that it is a syndrome per se, we are including it as a recognizable and important pattern of behaviors frequently associated with the highly contested postdivorce relationship. This set of behaviors can occur when one parent "alienates" a child against the other parent by influencing that child to believe that the other parent is a "bad" parent. But, as Kelly and Johnston say, kids may become distant from one of their parents for various other reasons. Often, this may relate more to that parent's behavior than anything the other parent has said or done.

❖ ❖ ❖ ❖ ❖

When her father started dating a woman not much older than Charlene, who was 16, she began to make excuses as to why she wasn't available to spend time with him. Charlene told her mother and her friends that she couldn't believe her father could divorce her mother and then start sleeping with a 19-year-old "girl."

"That's the last straw," she declared at one point. "I love my dad, but I really don't like the way he runs his life. It's like he's slapping my mother in the face, the way he acts!"

❖ ❖ ❖ ❖ ❖

Our purpose in this chapter is to call attention to the occurrence of alienated children and teens and to offer readers a better understanding of how alienation fits into the pattern of many high-conflict divorces. Children, caught between two warring parents, will frequently be involved in a custody dispute or a parenting time conflict. Just as often, parents are so caught up in the battle and the effort to "beat" the other parent that they lose sight of the fact that they are hurting their children and perhaps even contributing to driving their children away from a close relationship with them.

Such a situation may not justify, as Gardner (1998) recommends, that all contact with the alienating parent be cut off. But it does require that you address the alienating behaviors in treatment.

❖ How Can Parental Alienation Be Addressed?

It is our experience that parental alienation is very difficult to treat. In more severe cases, children or adolescents may be so entrenched in their beliefs about one parent that they won't give these up — even when they are presented with evidence that their beliefs and opinions are inaccurate.

In mild alienation cases, we recommend that you discourage both parents from speaking negatively about each other in front of the children. In a mild alienation situation, the children must still have parenting times with the parent about whom negative things are said. And even if the parenting time visits are turbulent, we still recommend in most cases that parenting time continue. This might mean, in some families, that the parents be court-ordered to avoid all statements about the other parent.

When alienation occurs at a more moderate level, the treatment approach will center on helping the alienating parent change the distorted view of the other parent. In moderate cases, the children are expressing reluctance to visit the other parent, and the alienating parent may refuse parenting time or try to block it. A *parent coordinator* may be most helpful in this kind of case. As we will discuss in chapter twelve, a parent coordinator is a therapist appointed by the court to facilitate communication between parents in high conflict and to settle disputes.

It's important that every effort be made to allow the children to maintain a relationship with both parents. In extreme cases, when one parent seems bent on destroying the relationship between the children and the other parent, the courts may consider removing a child from the alienating parent. However, they are then faced with a decision as to where the child will live and for how long because the child already hates his other parent so avidly that living with the alienated parent may be impossible. Severe cases require long-term therapy to help the alienating parent develop a balanced adult perspective in dealing with the children and the ex-spouse. The alienating parent is often suffering from a serious emotional overinvolvement with the children, and the treatment must help with the extreme separation anxiety associated with letting the children visit their other parent.

One recent innovative approach provides residential treatment to the alienated parent and child (Glod, 2002). In this approach, the alienated parent and child will live in a residential clinic for two weeks to two months. The clinical staff keeps them separate at first, then gradually reintroduces the parent and child to each other in therapy, addresses specific issues between parent and child, and provides a service that can best be described as "reprogramming."

Residential programs that reunify parents and children offer the therapist a viable option for breaking the pattern of alienation. The treatment itself can create a fresh start for the parent and child. In addition, the idea of the alienated parent spending time residentially with the troubled child may act as a "therapeutic ordeal" (Haley, 1984), motivating the alienating parent to change his behavior and communications to avoid another placement that would be a painful separation.

Regardless of the level of severity, the appointment of a parent coordinator may help to protect the interests of the child as well as to provide objective information to the court. A special guardian (called a *guardian ad litem* in some states) can look out for the child and determine if the parents are keeping their word and refraining from speaking negatively about each other to the child. In some cases, if one or both parents are being sufficiently destructive, the guardian ad litem may be granted binding decision-making authority by the court.

Finally, keep in mind that children do have minds of their own. A parent may have done little or nothing to contribute to the child's distancing himself from the other parent. In this kind of situation, the child may benefit from a therapeutic intervention. In fact, the child and the alienated parent will often need to be in treatment together. Not only do they need to talk openly about the reasons the child feels estranged and alienated, but the same parent should have the opportunity to develop some insight into how she may have helped bring about the alienation and what she could do to change her own behavior.

❖ *Summing It Up*

It is clear that children benefit most from healthy relationships with both parents. That is the ideal. But the ideal is not always possible. Sometimes children are alienated from one of their parents. Parental Alienation Syndrome (though technically not a "syndrome" at all) is an all-too-real condition in the lives of many divorced families. The sensitive therapist will carefully assess the sources of a child's alienation, and attempt to intervene to bring the parent and child into a positive relationship — even if that relationship is limited. Such therapeutic interventions will likely involve the cooperation of both parents and the child, although extreme cases may require court intervention.

"Success" with children and parents who are alienated must be measured in small increments, but if time and circumstances allow, the effort is certainly worthwhile.

Pattern 3: Parents Who Remarry

Getting a divorce, dealing with all of the emotions and turmoil that go with the breakup of a marriage, and, on top of all that, working out the kinks in the relationship with your former spouse isn't easy. The difficulties in resolving the relationship with your ex-partner so that the two of you can co-parent together are compounded when one or both of you remarries before you've straightened out the complexities and ambiguities of being former spouses.

Remarriage or cohabitating with a new love interest doesn't have to cause more intense conflict, however. Carlos and Nora's case offers an example.

❖❖❖❖❖

Ana Lucia was 10 years old when her parents, Carlos and Nora, divorced after fourteen years of marriage. The marriage had been deteriorating for years, and after Nora got some therapy and earned a master's degree in police administration, she was ready to start a new life. That's when she filed for a divorce.

Prior to filing, Nora had frequently tried to convince Carlos to go to marriage counseling with her. Carlos refused, yet when he was served with divorce papers, he was shocked that Nora would end their marriage.

"Have you thought about what this will do to our daughter?" he asked many times, appealing to her strong maternal bond with Ana Lucia. Nora had indeed thought a great deal about the potential consequences for Ana Lucia, and nothing Carlos said could dissuade her from following through with the divorce.

Within two years, Nora was remarried and Carlos was dating a woman who was interested in being a good stepmother for Ana Lucia. Although they had some heated conflicts in the first year following divorce, Nora and Carlos were able to work out a congenial relationship that kept life stable for Ana Lucia. Three years after the divorce, Nora and her husband relocated, so that Ana Lucia would live close to both her parents, making parenting time and school simpler for her. Carlos agreed that the move was a good idea.

❖❖❖❖❖

Nora and Carlos worked diligently — and successfully — along with their partners, to provide a stable, pleasant family life for Ana Lucia. It's not always so easy. Many couples are not able to resolve their relationship problems quite so congenially.

❖❖❖❖❖

For at least two years prior to their divorce, Jackson and Donna had gradually become more distant. Then Donna learned that Jackson was having an affair with Coral, a woman who lived in their neighborhood. Unable to accept or forgive his unfaithfulness, Donna filed for a divorce. During and immediately after the divorce, both Jackson and Donna believed they could maintain a cordial relationship for the sake of their two children.

Several months after the divorce was final, Jackson began living with Coral. "I didn't really bear her a lot of ill will," Donna said. "I knew that the reason Jackson had an affair with her was because our relationship had broken down. We both shared some responsibility for that."

Soon afterward, Jackson and Coral were married. And then other things began to change. "The first thing I noticed was that he and I would have shorter phone conversations," Donna said. "He became more hostile toward me. Finally, he began communicating through the kids, although we'd agreed we'd never do this."

Jackson admitted he felt pressure from both sides. "I knew Donna expected me to talk with her frequently about the kids and I wanted to do that," he said. "However, Coral was jealous of my conversations with Donna and she kept pressuring me to stop talking to her. I felt I had no choice if I wanted to keep my marriage peaceful." It was almost like the affair had never ended.

❖❖❖❖❖

For some co-parenting couples, remarriage can lead to greater stability and fewer stresses on the co-parenting relationship. In these divorces, both sides have indicated they have moved on with their lives and there's less guilt about reasons for the divorce. This lessening of tension and guilt paves the way for a freer and more open relationship that allows both mother and father a guilt-free ability to relate to each other as parents — rather than as ex-spouses or potential suitors.

However, this is not the case for every couple, as we just saw with Jackson and Donna. What often happens in high-conflict situations is that remarriage provides new impetus for anger and resentment. When there is increased hostility and subsequent conflict, there are at least six reasons for this:

❖ The new partner or spouse is threatened
❖ A new partner provides new resources
❖ Remarriage unbalances the system
❖ There is concern about the welfare of the child
❖ There is a new competitor for the role of parent
❖ There is concern that the child won't be able to adjust to a new stepparent

❖ A New Partner Is a Direct Threat

One important reason for new or renewed hostility following a remarriage is that one or both co-parents are still emotionally attached to the previous spouse. The entrance of a new figure in the struggle is threatening, and one or both may redouble the anger and resentment.

❖❖❖❖❖

Gary and Michelle had been married for eleven years. As Gary became increasingly absorbed in the landscape business he was starting, he spent more and more time away from home. While Michelle tried to understand his efforts at earning more money and being successful in a business, she also resented his time away from her and their three children. After four years of struggle, sacrifice, and loneliness, Michelle filed for a divorce. She later said that she thought that by filing for a divorce Gary would "see the light" and change — and their marriage could resume.

Although Gary told Michelle that he still loved her and vowed he would always love her, he quickly fell in love with Christa; they married within a year. Michelle told Gary he was being "too hasty" and she told him it was a bad idea for him to fall in love and remarry so quickly. "You don't know anything about *this woman* and she may be out to take advantage of you," Michelle said.

Michelle continued to feel this way and she couldn't get by her suspiciousness and inability to trust Christa as the stepmother of their children. Michelle refused to talk to her and insisted that Christa not be in the car when Gary came to pick up the children for his parenting time. Michelle's unwillingness to accept Christa led to frequent arguments with Gary. "This is absolutely ridiculous," Gary said to Michelle. "Christa is my wife and she has every right to be in my car when I pick up the kids."

"I don't care," Michelle countered. "I don't know her and I can't trust her and I don't want her around my house. If you bring Christa with you, I'm not letting the children go with you."

In counseling, the therapist suggested to Michelle that she might be holding out some hope that she and Gary would one day get back together and that accepting Christa as a competent stepparent would be giving up this dream. She denied this and continued to find reasons she couldn't accept Christa as a legitimate figure in the lives of her children.

Like many co-parents following a divorce, Michelle was still very much involved in her previous marriage, and she was threatened by the new woman in her former husband's life. Her inability to let go of Gary led to ongoing conflict between them.

❖❖❖❖❖

In a later chapter, we'll discuss in more detail how to solve the problem of a couple being emotionally married despite being legally divorced.

❖ *A New Partner Provides New Resources*

A second reason new relationships might fuel conflicts is that a new marriage or partnership may provide additional emotional strength or financial resources to continue a legal battle or to fight harder. In effect, the new spouse provides "reinforcements" for the war. Although new spouses get embroiled in the situation, they believe they're supporting a just cause. This was the case with Roger and Anne.

❖❖❖❖❖

After Anne was divorced from Roger she began to see herself as a victim. Roger, an engineer with an automobile company, had more money and hired a very expensive attorney who seemed able to persuade the court to side with any motion he filed regarding parenting time or child support. As a result, Anne felt as if she was being bullied by both Roger and his attorney. She wasn't working and was dependent on child support and alimony (which would last until she remarried). Anne felt she had no voice and no way of fighting back because of her financial need.

As it happened, however, Anne met a lawyer at a singles dance at her church and they fell in love. Sam was also recently divorced and he said he wanted to protect her from her ex. With Sam and the power of his law firm behind her, Anne could finally stand up for herself against Roger. "I finally felt I could say no to him when he tried to take advantage of me," Anne said. "I wasn't going to let him dictate when he would see the children or take them out of town the way he used to. For the first time, I had some power."

Although Roger was amused by her new-found feistiness at first, he grew irritated at her demands and her willingness to confront him and tell him no. "She had all this new power," Roger said, "and I suddenly felt like the victim. I wasn't going to let her push me around, though. I was willing to go to court as often as she wanted to."

Anne and Sam said they were just trying to get what Anne was entitled to as a parent. "I wasn't going to let her ex take advantage of her anymore," Sam declared.

❖❖❖❖❖

Sam brought resources to Anne that she never had before. She no longer had to be passive in dealing with Roger. She could fight back, and she was willing to fight because Sam was there to back her up.

❖ *Remarriage Unbalances the System*

A third reason a new marriage or partnership can lead to increased hostilities is that a remarriage unbalances the system. Each may feel comfortable with the balance when they are both divorced and unmarried. When one of them remarries, however, the power that one gains by having a new partner often leads to conflict.

❖❖❖❖❖

Miles and Holly had an unhappy marriage that featured bickering and arguments — often in front of their two young sons. They both agreed that a divorce was the best solution. With both living the single life during the first two years following their divorce, Holly and Miles saw themselves as better off. They also viewed their situations as roughly equal. They had a fifty-fifty custody arrangement for the boys, both lived in an apartment, and they were able to discuss issues with only minor arguments. They cooperated well, and their co-parenting arrangement was in balance — until Holly met Ken and shortly afterward became engaged.

Although Miles and Holly tried to carry on their rather amiable relationship after the engagement, Miles began to make sarcastic remarks about Holly and her fiancé, both to her and to their sons. One day, in a phone argument over summer camp for their sons, Miles said that Holly and her "boyfriend" could perhaps afford summer camp, but since he was alone he couldn't. "Ken's not my 'boyfriend,'" Holly said angrily, "he's my fiancé and we're going to be married. Besides, that has nothing to do with the problem of paying for Louis to go to summer camp."

"It has everything to do with it," Miles said, just as irately. "You just want Louis to go to camp to prove that you and your boyfriend have more money than I have. You don't care how these things affect me. I'm the one who's struggling all alone to make ends meet."

"I'm sorry if I have someone in my life and you don't," Holly replied. "It's not my fault you're all alone."

"You never did care about me," Miles shouted. "I've always felt alone and abandoned."

Miles could keep his feelings of loneliness, depression, and abandonment under control as long as both he and Holly were single and unattached. But with Holly getting engaged, the system became unbalanced; Miles' buried feelings bubbled to the surface and spilled over into his discussions and arguments with Holly.

❖ ❖ ❖ ❖ ❖

For many co-parents following separation and divorce, feelings are controlled as long as things seem equitable. When one co-parent unbalances the system, however, feelings intrude on the relationship and interfere with the ability to parent.

There Is Concern about the Welfare of the Child

When a new person enters the life of a co-parent, there may be concern about the effect of this new relationship on the child.

This concern can be legitimate, as when the new individual uses drugs in front of the child. Or it may be more of an emotional issue, such as when the co-parent suspects the other parent is displaying affection too openly in front of the child. On occasion, it can be a matter of morality or religion.

❖ ❖ ❖ ❖ ❖

After Pilar's divorce from Antonio, they were both angry. They blamed each other for the divorce and each thought the other hadn't tried hard enough to make a go of the marriage. In the second year following the divorce, however, they began to avoid the blaming and resentments, and they concentrated on making life as normal as possible for their son and daughter.

When Antonio started dating Linda, Pilar was very concerned about whether they were sleeping together on the weekends when the children were at Antonio's house. "That's none of your business," Antonio retorted, when Pilar asked him about their sexual behavior on the weekends.

"I think it is my business," Pilar responded. "I don't want them exposed to you sleeping with every woman you date. I want them to know what is morally right."

"I don't sleep with every woman I date," Antonio said indignantly. "Linda is a special woman and I love her. And I should tell you, because you'll find out soon enough, Linda is going to move into my house."

"Before you're married?" Pilar asked.

"Yes," Antonio said. "We may get married someday, but not yet."

"Then you can forget about seeing the kids," Pilar said. "I don't want them around a woman like that."

"You have no right to dictate what goes on in my house," Antonio said. "Linda happens to be a good woman who will be very good for the children."

"No way!" Pilar shouted. "She'll never spend time with my children."

"They're my children, too," Antonio said. "And they will spend time with us! And that's that!"

From that point on, Pilar harbored ill feelings toward Linda and always viewed her as an immoral woman who would somehow damage the children if she were around them. Antonio insisted on his parenting time and went to court several times to challenge Pilar's attempts to keep the children from spending time with Linda and him.

Although the court supported Antonio's right to his parenting time, Pilar did not calm down or feel more accepting of Linda.

❖❖❖❖❖

Many co-parents have moral, religious, or other reasons for attempting to block a friend, romantic partner, or stepparent from being involved with their children. With Pilar, the issue was her view of the moral issues.

❖❖❖❖❖

With Christopher and Jenna, the issue was the behavior of Christopher's new wife, Arianna. "She's a drug user and will corrupt my children," Jenna said. She had found out that Christopher and Arianna occasionally smoked marijuana. Christopher said this was occasional and never when the children were present. That didn't dissuade Jenna from believing that Christopher's new wife was a drug user who would influence the children to believe using drugs was okay.

❖❖❖❖❖

We've found in working with high-conflict divorces that the issue is often exaggerated and may not be based on a realistic appraisal of the situation. However, for one co-parent, the issue becomes such a major concern that he's willing to fight, expending energy and money to block the children's access to this new partner or stepparent. Professionals who work with co-parents battling in such situations must weigh the potential damage of drug use (or cohabitatation without marriage, or changing religions, or whatever may be the issue of concern) against the emotional damage caused by increased fighting between a child's parents. The right course is not always easy to determine.

❖ *A Competitor for the Role of Parent*

A fifth reason remarriage leads to a deterioration of co-parenting relationships is that a new partner to one of the parents may be viewed as a competitor for the role of parent. The fears that underlie this reason for harm to the relationship are reflected in thoughts and statements such as, "She'll take my child away," or, "My son will love him more than he loves me."

❖❖❖❖❖

Loren had a distant, but amiable relationship with his former wife, Rasheena. Loren enjoyed spending time with his son and daughter, although his work as a salesman often required him to work on weekends. When Rasheena was dating, Loren thought that would be positive because Rasheena seemed happier and asked him for extra money less often.

However, when Rasheena told Loren she was getting married, he was surprised to learn that her fiancé was a child psychologist. "Is he going to tell us all how to be better parents?" Loren quipped.

Rasheena and her new husband both enjoyed the children and wanted to spend as much time as possible with them. Previously, Loren would call at the last minute if he had a day off or could free up a weekend to spend with the kids. Now, however, Rasheena and her new husband planned out-of-town trips on the weekends; they often had plans to take the children to special places, which the kids enjoyed.

Loren complained that the children were never available for him.

"You're right." Rasheena told him. "We can't put our life on hold waiting for you to get time off. We like to keep the children busy with new adventures."

"But that's not fair," complained Loren. "I'm entitled to my time with the kids. I feel like I'm being excluded from their lives by The Psychologist. I suppose they like him better than they like me." Loren was threatened by Rasheena's new husband, who was now playing a bigger role in his children's lives than he was.

❖❖❖❖❖

On the other hand, there are families in which a new stepparent enters the picture and the co-parent exaggerates a threat that really isn't there.

❖❖❖❖❖

Elizabeth was very close to her three children. When her co-parent, Al, married Janet, he became stepfather to Janet's two children as well. When Elizabeth's three kids went for their weekend visits to their dad's house, Elizabeth worried about how Janet would treat them. At first she worried that Janet would be too busy with her own children and wouldn't pay any attention to Elizabeth's.

After a few weeks, Elizabeth got a sense that Janet was able to balance the needs of her own children and those of Elizabeth's as well. However, when Elizabeth's children reported that Janet was a great cook and a skilled seamstress, Elizabeth developed new concerns.

"What did you do this weekend?" Elizabeth asked her children when they came home from their time with their father.

"We had a great dinner on Saturday night," 11-year-old Denny told his mother. "Janet made lasagna, my favorite dinner in the whole world!"

"That's nice," Elizabeth responded weakly.

"And look what she made me," 9-year-old Karen chipped in. "She sewed me a new top that I can wear to school!"

"Did you thank her?" Elizabeth asked.

"Of course, Mom," Karen said. "But she's awesome!"

When the children were outside playing, Elizabeth called Al on his cell phone and complained that Janet was trying to take her kids away from her.

"Of course, she's not trying to do that," he said. "She just likes them and has fun doing things for them."

"I feel so inadequate," Elizabeth said. "Tell her to stop trying so hard to win them over."

Although she had been reassured by her co-parent, Elizabeth continued to feel threatened and thought of ways she could undermine Janet's influence in her children's life.

❖❖❖❖❖

If parents like Elizabeth and Loren continue to feel threatened, they may begin to speak disparagingly of the stepparent or begin to interfere in the co-parenting time arrangement. Such actions, of course, lead to serious disputes and trips to court.

Concern That the Child Won't Be Able to Adjust to a New Stepparent

Finally, the last reason that remarriage leads to greater conflict is that one parent may exaggerate children's normal difficulties adjusting to a new parent figure in their lives. Overly concerned about the child's ability (or inability) to cope with a stepparent, a co-parent may use this concern as a reason to decrease visits or change custody. It is normal for children to take time to become comfortable with a new adult in their lives. Sometimes, though, one of the co-parents has more difficulty than the child. This was true of Helen.

❖❖❖❖❖

Helen, the mother of two children, ages 4 and 6, had no objections to the children having weekend overnight visits with their father on alternating weekends. However, when he remarried, Helen saw things differently.

"I can't let Marcus and Ruth stay overnight any more," Helen announced to her co-parent Perry soon after he was remarried.

"Why not?" Perry asked.

"They won't be able to understand who Mary Kaye is," Helen said referring to Perry's wife. "They'll be confused."

"There's nothing to be confused about," Perry said. "They know Mary Kaye and they understand she is my wife. They like her and accept her."

"I don't agree," Helen said. "They're my children and I think I understand how they feel better than anyone. And I think it will be too confusing for them. When they get used to your wife, I'll let them come and visit. But until they become adjusted to her, I'm keeping them at home with me."

"You can't do that," Perry said angrily. "These are my children, too, and I have a court order that says they can spend every other weekend with me."

"Court orders can be changed," Helen said. She subsequently had her attorney file a motion in court requesting that the original parenting time order be changed on the basis that she thought her children would be confused and upset by having a new stepparent in their lives.

The court disagreed with Helen and the original order was maintained, allowing Perry to have the children at his house every other weekend. Helen found excuses and reasons to interfere with Perry's time with Marcus and Ruth. It was more than two years before she came to accept that Mary Kaye was a legitimate force in the children's lives.

❖❖❖❖❖

Although, as seen with Helen, the surface reason given for interrupting parenting time is a concern that the children may not be able to adjust to a new stepparent, this is at times a cover for the co-parent's own fears that the children may love the stepparent more than her or him. At other times, the concern about adjustment is a way for individuals to justify their anger or jealousy related to their co-parents' success in a new relationship.

❖ Remarriage Meltdowns

While the six causes of remarriage meltdowns we've discussed in this chapter often lead to deterioration in the co-parenting relationship, remarriage is only one of six patterns we have examined in the chapters in this section. In a great many high-conflict divorces, you will find one or more of these patterns responsible for the significant conflict between co-parents. The importance of identifying these patterns as you try to understand the reasons for ongoing conflict is that they help you shape an intervention approach that has a better chance of working. However, each of them will require skillful intervention on the part of the therapist.

Therapists are encouraged to raise these possible concerns with the client early — prior to the co-parent getting remarried. It is important to increase the insight co-parents may have about their feelings toward a new person in the lives of their children and/or their former spouse. By confronting these feelings and helping the client to understand and deal with them before the situation develops, greater conflict may be avoided.

Pattern 4: Substance-Abusing Parents

T he fourth pattern you are likely to see among high-conflict co-parents is the substance-abusing parent. In fact, the role of substance abuse — or at least frequent accusations of substance abuse — is a recurrent theme in the conflicts reported by high-conflict couples (Johnston and Campbell, 1988). Some researchers have found that pervasive mistrust about the other parent's ability to care for the children adequately is one of the primary features of high-conflict as opposed to low-conflict divorces (Maccoby and Mnookin, 1992).

A study published in the *Family and Conciliation Court Review* of 1,669 mediation sessions conducted in California family courts found that parents expressed serious concerns about their co-parent's ability to parent. Although the greatest concerns related to child neglect and physical or sexual abuse, thirty-six percent of these parents had serious doubts about the other parent because of substance abuse (Depner et al., 1992).

Unfortunately, there have not been adequate studies of either the extent of substance abuse or the extent of emotional or personality dysfunction of people involved in high-conflict divorce. Early research from the 1980s did suggest that co-parents involved in high conflict following divorce were more likely to have severe psychopathology, personality disorders, and domestic abuse problems (Hauser, 1985; Kressel, Jaffe, N., et al., 1980). These studies further indicated that about one-fourth of the high-conflict parents studied may have had substance abuse problems. At about the same time, a self-report study indicated that the use of alcohol and drugs by high-conflict couples may not differ from that in the general population, which is usually estimated at about ten percent (Derogatis and Spencer, 1982).

According to Wallerstein and Kelly (1980), based on their studies of divorced parents, about twenty percent of noncustodial parents, usually fathers, are significantly dysfunctional. This dysfunction may include physical abuse, serious emotional illness, or alcohol and drug abuse.

We see no question, based on our experience, that there are many dysfunctional co-parents who are involved in high-conflict divorces. There is also no question that a certain number of high-conflict co-parents are substance abusers. The numbers, however, may be both underreported and overreported. We are aware that this is contradictory. However, it is difficult to adequately estimate the number of substance abusers in high-conflict treatment programs for two reasons. Substance abuse gets *underreported* during some marriages because it's likely that both parents were abusing substances. This leads to a tacit code of silence after the marriage has ended. Neither co-parent is willing to talk openly about the other's substance abuse (even though they may be hurling other accusations back and forth) because if *he* reports *her* substance abuse, *she* is likely to retaliate by talking about *his* substance abuse.

The second reason, related to *overreporting*, is that an accusation of substance abuse is a way for an angry co-parent to exact revenge or discharge hostility toward her co-parent. It is very difficult for the clinician to arrive at an accurate picture of how much substance abuse is actually going on, because one parent may have a great deal invested in portraying her co-parent in the worst possible light. By claiming that the other parent is unfit or poses a substantial safety risk to the children she can "get even" with her co-parent for perceived injustices. Although in reality the level of alcohol or drug use has not increased, a parent may use this to try to reduce the other's parenting time or to gain physical custody.

❖❖❖❖❖

When he was married to Pamela, Owen often had one or two beers when he got home from work in the evening and was often home alone with the children. His pattern of drinking continued after the divorce. However, Pamela made this a major issue in her arguments that Owen was an unfit parent who should not share equally in the physical custody of their two children. Owen was open about his drinking, which he characterized as "occasional."

He said that one or two beers a night did not prevent him from being a good father.

❖❖❖❖❖

Some Parents Do Pose Risks to Their Children

There are co-parents who do have addiction problems and who do represent serious risks for children.

❖❖❖❖❖

Leroy, the father of 4-year-old Jamar, was an alcoholic who had two drunk-driving convictions. Nevertheless, he still had his driver's license and insisted that he didn't drink when he had parenting time with Jamar. Leticia, his co-parent, said that he seemed drunk on more than one occasion when he came to pick up Jamar. She said she was terrified that he would have an accident with their child in his car. She asked the court in numerous motions to order Leroy to go for alcoholism treatment and to have regular drug screenings.

❖❖❖❖❖

This kind of situation, where it's unclear whether or not a child is in jeopardy, places every professional involved in the case in a quandary. If you ignore this alleged threat, the children may be in real danger. If you accept the claims at face value, you may anger and alienate one co-parent so that he won't cooperate with you further. Accusations and denials of substance abuse may just be ways for either parent to get his or her way.

Substance Abuse Is Rarely the Main Cause of High-Conflict Divorce

There is likely to be alcohol or drug use in some — if not many — high-conflict divorces. It should be pointed out, if it is not clear already, that drug addiction or alcoholism alone rarely causes high conflict. It's often an exacerbating condition, but it is rarely the primary reason a couple continues to have high levels of conflict.

❖❖❖❖❖

Shirley divorced Fred because he was addicted to cocaine and lost his job because of his addiction. He tried to be a good father following their divorce, but would often go weeks or months without having contact with their twin girls. When he did want to spend time with the girls, he would contact Shirley and she would work out a time for him to pick them up. She had indications that he was still a cocaine user, yet she allowed him opportunities to see the girls. She refused to let him take the girls in the car if she suspected he was high, but she would let him come in her home to play with the twins. Despite being angry at Fred for his drug use, Shirley mediated this situation nicely, resulting in a low-conflict divorce.

❖❖❖❖❖

When there are serious substance abuse problems or long-term addictions, often there is no way to hide these problems. They will be apparent not only to both co-parents but to the court and mental health clinicians as well. Parents with a serious substance abuse problem, like Fred, are more likely to drop out of the parenting picture, either temporarily or permanently. They may also have had visits from a child protection agency or lost their parental rights because of addiction.

❖ ## *Mistrust*

In the beginning of this chapter, we mentioned the problem of pervasive mistrust. Not being trusted is a significant problem for the former substance abuser who has made a legitimate attempt to end his addiction. The co-parent in recovery (and perhaps now abstaining from drug or alcohol use and abuse) may be perpetually mistrusted by the other parent. Knowing the seriousness of the substance abuse, the non-substance-abusing parent may have difficulty believing the co-parent will ever be sober or drug free and thus is unwilling to give her a chance to prove herself as a parent. This can then lead the recovering co-parent to feel angry, resentful, and victimized.

❖❖❖❖❖

Janice was drinking heavily in the year before her marriage to Mark ended. During the divorce, she went to AA and to a psychologist. She stopped drinking, joined a church, and continued to go to AA because she found the group meetings helpful.

Based on her experiences and having "found salvation," she was obsessively convinced that any alcohol or drug use by her co-parent would have serious ramifications for their children. Although Mark was a social user of moderate amounts of marijuana, Janice saw this as evidence that he had significant "psychological issues" and that if he were to be around their children he would promote drug use.

Janice spent thousands of dollars in attorney fees trying to convince the court that Mark was an addict in denial who did not deserve to be allowed parenting time. Mark viewed himself as a hapless victim of her new-found "religion of sobriety."

❖ ❖ ❖ ❖ ❖

How Dangerous Is Each Pattern of Substance Abuse?

We've categorized the levels of substance use and abuse to help conceptualize the dangers to children.

- ❖ Level One: Abstainer
- ❖ Level Two: Occasional or social abuser
- ❖ Level Three: Heavy user
- ❖ Level Four: Chronic abuser or addict

Level One: Abstainer
The abstainers are the parents who have never used either alcohol or drugs or have been successful in their recovery. Although they don't present a danger to children, they may be overly rigid in their views of others who are moderate or light users. They can be judgmental and vindictive in their condemnation of others' use of drugs or alcohol. This can lead to high levels of conflict with their co-parents who may believe that their own use of alcohol or drugs is within normal recreational bounds.

Level Two: Occasional or social user
These parents may not have a substance abuse problem. Like many people, they may drink without experiencing a significant change in mood or behavior. At times, say at a party, they may have too much too drink, and their use may at times exacerbate some existing traits.

❖ ❖ ❖ ❖ ❖

Arthur drinks when stressed. Although this may only be a few times a year, he becomes belligerent, hostile, and abusive. He pushed and hit Isabel, his former wife, once when he was drinking. She described him as an alcoholic, although he saw himself as simply an occasional drinker.

❖ ❖ ❖ ❖ ❖

The social user may also be like Hugh, who became despondent after his divorce from Susan. When he drank, he tended to drink to excess and call Susan, weepy and maudlin, telling her how much he loved her and missed her. She assumed Hugh was drinking regularly and was frequently drunk. But Hugh worked regularly, was considered a responsible and productive employee, and kept his depression hidden from most people in his life.

❖ ❖ ❖ ❖ ❖

Isabel and Susan, since they no longer lived with their former spouses, based their judgments of Arthur and Hugh on past information, brief contacts, and fears. They may be right or wrong to be concerned, but it will take further investigation to figure out how worried they should be and how risky the fathers' involvement is with their children.

Level Three: Heavy user

Heavy drug or alcohol users use several times a week. They may be on the verge of an addiction, or their drug or alcohol use may interfere with parts of their lives. Substance abuse may have been a direct cause of the divorce, and it often contributes to the conflict after divorce. It is the heavy user who is most likely to put the children at risk and to be abusive.

❖ ❖ ❖ ❖ ❖

Mary came to a therapy group for co-parents in a high-conflict divorce. She was quiet and appeared to be cooperative and willing to make things better with her co-parent. However, while analyzing her written homework assignment after the third session, the group leaders noted that her handwriting was barely legible. They confronted her privately the next week and could smell alcohol on her breath. She was told that she could not continue to drink and attend the group. She said she would stop, and for three weeks there was noticeable improvement. However, she slurred words and acted erratically in a subsequent group session and was ordered to return to court to discuss treatment for her alcohol use. Her return to court was necessary because, despite her efforts, she clearly couldn't stop drinking. In view of her difficulty controlling her drinking, it appeared that her co-parent's concerns about the safety of their children were well-founded.

❖ ❖ ❖ ❖ ❖

Level Four: Chronic abuser or addict

Chronic abusers or addicts use daily, may not be able to hold a responsible job, continue to use despite experiencing negative consequences for their use, such as DUI's, and may spend a lot of time in bars or with using friends. They have definite problems in some areas of their lives, including with their co-parents, over their use of drugs or alcohol, endangering the children, and/or failure to pay child support.

❖ ❖ ❖ ❖ ❖

Larry was an example of the chronic abuser who showed up to participate in a high-conflict divorce treatment group. In the second session of this group program he dominated the conversation with issues important only to him. He threatened other people in the group and was seductive with a female group facilitator. When confronted about his behavior the next day, he apologized profusely and admitted he had a serious drug problem. He knew he needed treatment and promised to get it. He nevertheless came to the next group meeting just as belligerent and unsteady. His co-parent said she was regularly frightened about his abusiveness both to her and the children. In view of her reports and his pattern of verbal abusiveness followed by abject remorse, Larry was exhibiting symptoms of chronic drug abuse. The leaders felt they had no choice but to send him back to court with a recommendation that he be ordered into a substance abuse program.

❖ ❖ ❖ ❖ ❖

Parents with an addiction, like Larry, must be referred back to the court with recommendations about treatment and with questions about whether they should have any contact with their children or if those contacts should only be under supervision. They frequently need to be told by a judge that they must not, under the threat of a severe court penalty, drive a vehicle with their children while they are under the influence of drugs or alcohol.

❖ Which Comes First: Substance Abuse Treatment or Relationship Treatment?

Substance-abusing parents in high-conflict divorces, in our experience, commonly abuse alcohol, marijuana, cocaine, heroin, methamphetamine, and prescription drugs. Their abuse may have started long before the divorce or it may be a way of coping with divorce. Either way, the therapist must ask whether these parents need substance abuse treatment before they enter a high-conflict treatment environment or whether their participation in high-conflict treatment will alleviate the substance abuse problem.

When the issue is substance abuse, the problem gets seriously entwined in the postdivorce conflict. Arguments may occur over whether the parent is still abusing drugs or alcohol or whether he is endangering the children. It takes a good substance abuse evaluation to untangle this situation and answer these questions.

When it's clear that substance abuse is the primary issue, the substance abuse should be addressed first. When substance abuse is a secondary issue, you should proceed with efforts to improve communication and the relationship between co-parents in hopes that the alcohol or drug use will improve as the relationship does.

❖ A Caution to Professionals

It's often difficult to separate issues of morality from issues of human behavior. Some people, including both co-parents and the professionals who work with them, believe that the use of alcohol and drugs demonstrates poor character. To some professionals, for instance, any use of alcohol or drugs by a parent will be viewed as detrimental to children (Marlatt, Blume and Parks, 2001). We don't subscribe to this point of view.

We take what we hope is a more realistic and pragmatic perspective. In effect, we prefer to look at the data and the behavior. If a parent's use of alcohol or drugs does not result in negative consequences for the user or poses no threat to the children, we don't regard it as an issue in the high-conflict divorce. Our point of view is similar to the approach of therapists who use Harm Reduction Therapy. Harm Reduction Therapy is a compassionate and pragmatic approach to substance abuse which does not view continued use of substance as a moral failure or an impediment to continued substance abuse treatment services (Parks, Anderson and Marlatt, 2000; Marlatt, Blume and Parks, 2001).

It's clear, however, that differences of values will always separate people and will always separate professionals. Those differences of values may lead to divorce at times and may contribute to high-conflict relationships. Differences in values may also lead therapists, lawyers, and other professionals to fight legal battles that are based solely on their personal or religious beliefs. We ask the question, "Does a parent's behavior objectively put a child at risk?" If a parent's behavior poses a threat, then it's a legitimate issue to confront in treatment or court. If the objective information available says that the behavior isn't a danger, then it's not a reasonable justification for interfering with the other parent's parenting time.

The caution for professionals is this: You need to be aware of your own personal beliefs, your attitudes, and your values so that they don't strongly color your ability to work with co-parents who engage in high conflict. If you decide that your values and beliefs are interfering with your ability to be objective with some co-parents, then it's important that you avoid working with those individuals.

Pattern 5: Accusations of Mental Illness

I f you have a bitter and prolonged dispute with your former spouse and this dispute endures for several years, this proves you're mentally ill, right?

Not necessarily. According to the research literature (see chapter two), few parents in high-conflict postdivorce relationships are mentally ill. If that's so, however, why do so many co-parents make accusations of mental illness?

Consider this high-conflict divorce relationship:

❖ ❖ ❖ ❖ ❖

"She's crazy!" Victor said to his therapist. "Do you know what she's done now? She said she's going to take our children and move to another state and change her name so I'll never see my children again. She's got to be crazy to be thinking that kind of stuff!"

❖ ❖ ❖ ❖ ❖

Or, think about this situation between Marshall and LaToya:

❖ ❖ ❖ ❖ ❖

"He keeps threatening to quit his job so he won't have to pay me any child support," said LaToya to a friend. "He never was very stable. Once he was taking medication because he was bipolar. So I think he must be mentally ill, don't you agree?"

❖ ❖ ❖ ❖ ❖

Or, this type of accusation may sound familiar:

❖ ❖ ❖ ❖ ❖

"My ex is really sick!" said Cassandra. "He poisoned our neighbor's dog and he enjoys hunting and killing animals. He threatened to kill my kitten after we got a divorce. I think he really would. In my mind, he is a very sick individual."

❖❖❖❖❖

As you might suspect, these kinds of accusations are made because individuals who are locked in a fierce battle with their co-parents view each other through a lens with highly emotional filters. Yet, with these kinds of allegations flying around, what should the professional think? And, more importantly, how should the professional intervene?

In this chapter, we examine how allegations of mental illness affect the high-conflict divorce situation and how accusations of mental illness constitute a familiar pattern in hotly contested divorces.

❖ What Is Mental Illness?

As a trained professional, you probably already have a good sense of what a serious mental illness is. However, just to be sure we are all using a common definition, we will review how mental illness is described in the Diagnostic and Statistical Manual of Mental Disorders-IV (DSM-IV).

The DSM-IV is, of course, the bible of psychiatric nomenclature and diagnoses, and it says (American Psychiatric Association, 1994, p. xxi) that a mental illness is "...a clinically significant behavioral or psychological syndrome or pattern that occurs in an individual and that is associated with present distress (e.g., a painful symptom) or disability (i.e., impairment in one or more important areas of functioning) or with a significantly increased risk of suffering death, pain, disability, or an important loss of freedom." The DSM-IV (p. xxii) also addresses what is not included as a mental disorder by adding that "Neither deviant behavior (e.g., political, religious, or sexual) nor conflicts that are primarily between the individual and society are mental disorders unless the deviance or conflict is a symptom of a dysfunction in the individual, as described above."

When you look at mental illness in the context of divorce, you need to look at the symptoms as they relate to the parent-child relationship. That is to say, you must consider a parent's ability to care for her child, to keep her child safe, and to change potentially damaging interactions. Beyond these issues, as a professional, it's important to look at the context of the symptoms and how much the current conflict is maintaining or escalating those symptoms. The anxiety, stress, and intense emotions generated by ongoing conflict, unresolved relationships, and fear of loss can cause parents as well as children to regress to damaging behaviors that may have been previously conquered or managed.

A small percentage of parents may be competently diagnosed with symptoms of bipolar, schizophrenic, abusive, or obsessive-compulsive conditions, and there may be very real issues of safety that concern the other parent. As discussed in a previous chapter, substance abuse must be assessed based on danger rather than diagnosis. The same holds for mental illness.

Some circumstances, of course, are obvious signs that a parent is emotionally incapable of handling the demands of parenthood in the best interests of the child(ren):

❖ extreme manic behavior, such as driving an infant around all night long at high rates of speed;
❖ depression so great that he can't attend to his crying infant;
❖ hallucinations, so as not to be able to attend to reality;
❖ paranoia, such that she doesn't allow her child to attend school or play with friends;
❖ physical and/or mental abusiveness to the child(ren).

Once again, it seems apparent to us that although there are abusive and neglectful parents, the number of parents who are truly mentally ill and are, as a result, unable to adequately care for their children is small. Rarely does mental illness, in and of itself, cause high conflict. However, a serious mental illness can contribute to high conflict when a parent has recovered and a return of parenting time is being considered.

❖ ❖ ❖ ❖ ❖

Brenda and Jack had a 3-year-old daughter, Sabrina, when Brenda had her "emotional breakdown." She began to hear voices that were telling her to hurt Sabrina and herself. Brenda told Jack about her auditory hallucinations, and she voluntarily began treatment that started with a brief inpatient stay. Upon discharge, Brenda remained in intensive treatment but did not care for Sabrina alone. However, Brenda thought she was much better because she seldom had the auditory hallucinations and she felt less depressed.

The marriage continued for a short time until Jack decided that he wanted a divorce. At the time of the divorce, Brenda felt it was reasonable to agree to supervised visits, with the understanding that, as her condition improved, she would gain unsupervised parenting time. After a year of treatment, her psychiatrist agreed that Brenda wasn't a threat to Sabrina and should have unsupervised parenting time.

Jack, however, became more and more concerned about his former wife's mental status and began to fight for continuation of Brenda's supervised parenting time. Sabrina was also seeing a therapist who supported Jack's fears and reported that Sabrina was frightened of Brenda. Sabrina reported to her child therapist things that her mother had done or said to her. Jack had begun to question Sabrina closely after every visit and Sabrina became attuned to what her father was looking for.

For example, she told her father that she was afraid when her mother didn't watch her while she went down the slide at the park and that she was upset because her mother sometimes forgot to feed her.

Although Brenda's psychiatrist asserted that she did not pose a threat to Sabrina, Jack continued in the belief that his ex-wife was mentally ill and a danger to their daughter. He unknowingly transmitted his fears to Sabrina in a variety of nonverbal ways. The court continued to order protective measures, such as supervised parenting time, to protect Sabrina from danger while her mother continued in treatment.

❖ ❖ ❖ ❖ ❖

It isn't unusual for a parent to resist the change to unsupervised parenting time. However, resistance caused by a parent's unfounded fears isn't a good reason to keep children from having a more normal interaction with their mother or father. Jack, as is typical, sought out other therapists and a lawyer to support him in denying Brenda unsupervised parenting time. This kind of effort often leads to anxiety and tension in the child, as happened with Sabrina. The anxiety observed by Sabrina's therapist led him to conclude that Sabrina was experiencing emotional problems caused by contact with her "mentally ill" mother.

In this kind of situation, concerned co-parents may resist allowing parenting time even when court ordered for the other parents' parenting time. They may, as Jack did on occasion, interfere with visitation by scheduling activities during the other parent's time or telling the child about fun activities at home that she will miss if she goes with her other parent. Or they may simply lie and insist the child is too ill to visit with the co-parent.

❖ The Problem of Labeling

As soon as one parent labels the other "mentally ill," conflict is likely to escalate, since the next step is for the accusing parent to alter, deny, or limit parenting time. The accused parent is then likely to become more reactive, feeling unjustifiably attacked or maligned. This type of circular reactivity is common in high-conflict divorces and can eventually make both parents appear disturbed.

During divorce, people begin to re-evaluate their marriages and everything that their partners did or said throughout their years together. One partner may decide that behavior that was previously viewed as annoying or difficult really constituted mental illness. Behavior that resulted from marital problems may also be viewed, after the fact, as proof of mental illness.

Divorced parents are likely to have had very different views of parenting even while married, and the parent who was stricter may be viewed as rigid and controlling. Those parents may have been more likely to yell at the children, especially if they felt the other parent was too lenient. The lenient parent becomes even more lenient and the strict parent then becomes unduly strict. Thus conflict with the children increases, allowing either parent to accuse the other of being an unfit parent. The parent who yells at a child can become the "verbally abusive" parent, and the parent who slaps a child becomes a "physically abusive parent." The more lenient parent may become "negligent."

A parent who was depressed during the marriage yet still parented properly may be accused after the divorce of being too depressed to parent. A parent who was neat and tidy might be viewed later as obsessive-compulsive. Those who had affairs might be accused of having narcissistic personality disorder because they "care more about themselves than their children." A forgetful parent might be accused of having attention deficit disorder. The fact that there is conflict is itself often construed as a problem of impulse control or intermittent explosive disorder. Diagnoses and labeling then create more problems by reinforcing one parent's fears that the other is out of control.

As mentioned in previous chapters, feelings escalate during a divorce and often result in people saying and doing things they would not do or say under normal circumstances. A small number of situations result in physical and verbal altercations that never occurred previously. This does not qualify as an abusive family situation. Although there are circumstances where there has been a history of violence and the parent and child require various levels of safety, you need to be careful to assess whether violence is a family pattern or an abnormal, but understandable, reaction to a highly stressful situation: the divorce itself.

❖ *Traits Become Problems*

Some personality traits (narcissism, dependency, and paranoia, for example) can escalate under pressure and look like serious mental illness. Narcissism may escalate into a belief that, "I am the only one who can truly take care of the children." Such an individual is likely to believe that the other parent isn't capable of knowing what their children need. The narcissistic parent may react by criticizing his co-parent and telling her how to do things. If the accusing parent can get an ally, such as a therapist, family member, or attorney, this will escalate the conflict further.

❖❖❖❖❖

While they were married, Bill relied on Martha as the primary caregiver for their three children. Even though he had not criticized her parenting abilities during the marriage, after the divorce Bill described her as unfit. Based on what he was told by a therapist, Bill complained that Martha was narcissistic and bipolar, and that the children weren't safe with her. He alleged that Martha left the children alone in the car several times, both before and after the divorce, and that she had even "lost" one of the children at a fair several years before. Bill asserted that Martha didn't care about the children's feelings, since she hadn't supported certain of their activities, such as football.

Martha had a very different explanation of the incidents that she remembered and had her own accusations of Bill having "left" the children unsupervised in questionable situations. Martha's major concern was that Bill was controlling of the children's lives and that he put the children in the middle of their conflicts by signing the kids up for expensive and time-consuming activities without consulting Martha ahead of time.

❖ ❖ ❖ ❖ ❖

If you're experienced in working with troubled divorces, you will recognize these accusations as typical of many high-conflict divorces.

❖ *Who Decides Mental Illness?*

Who decides if the parent is mentally ill and his ability to parent is impaired? Do divorcing spouses decide if their partners are mentally ill? Do the lawyers decide if their clients' exes are mentally ill? Does the individual's personal therapist decide if the other parent is mentally ill?

Mental illness should not be decided by a co-parent, an attorney, or a judge — although everyone can have an opinion. Only a qualified mental health professional who has done a thorough clinical examination should diagnose mental illness. A child's or a co-parent's therapist, who may have met the parent in question only once — or perhaps not at all — may not ethically give an opinion about that person's psychological characteristics (American Psychological Association, 2002, sec.9.01b). If we accept the guidelines for proper diagnosis that are set forth in ethical standards of every psychotherapy profession, we effectively rule out a large percentage of claims that someone is mentally ill.

When a co-parent has been in psychotherapy and has taken a psychiatric medication, there is some justification to say that person experienced some psychological problems. Unless a mental health professional has had recent contact with that individual, however, she cannot make statements about his or her current mental state. Therapists who make pronouncements based on someone else's observations are acting unethically, and doing a disservice to the individual as well as to the profession.

If a parent has a legitimate concern about the co-parent's ability to raise children, an assessment by a qualified mental health professional is in order. When parenting time continues to be highly contested, and when it's unclear whether an individual's problems are due to mental illness or to reactivity to a dysfunctional system, a psychological evaluation is appropriate. A psychological evaluation allows an unbiased third party to assess all family members, and psychological tests can be used to assess emotional instability. Psychological evaluations will be discussed in more detail in chapter ten.

❖ When Mental Illness Is Real

In the real world, children do sometimes live alone with parents who are mentally ill. However, even parents with significant mental health problems are important to their children. If a mentally ill parent takes recommended medication and is in therapy, she may function quite well as a parent. Sometimes it even happens that the mental illness is contained well enough that it doesn't have much impact on the family or child.

Often, children have been living with both parents until the time of the divorce. The mentally ill parent may have cared for the children, tended to their needs, and participated in family life. The parent who accuses her co-parent of being mentally ill as part of the postdivorce conflict may forget or just ignore the fact that the other parent behaved as a fully functioning parent for years. The children may have been left alone with the parent for hours or days without question until the divorce occurs. The accusing parent may justify her new concern based on having been there to supervise the situation in the past and feeling she now has no control if the children are not with her.

❖❖❖❖❖

Crystal was a stay-at-home mom who knew her husband, Cassidy, was not stable. After a divorce, Crystal wanted to balance their children's need for a father with her concerns about his mental health and erratic behavior. Prior to the divorce, Crystal could supervise and control the extent to which the children were with their father. After the divorce, she could no longer do this.

"I was afraid for the safety of our children," Crystal said, "because I couldn't trust Cassidy's judgment. He always thought he was fine and in control, but I knew he wasn't."

Crystal was not able to persuade the court to order supervised visits, but she was able to limit Cassidy's parenting time.

❖❖❖❖❖

Mental illness is certainly a factor in determining what type and amount of parenting time a parent will have. It's important to look at whether the mental health problem creates any danger for the child, whether the parent is able to care for the child adequately, and whether the parent has the ability to maintain or establish emotional ties with the child.

❖ ❖ ❖ ❖ ❖

Denise was a full-time mother, while Alejandro worked long hours. Denise had always been moody, forgetful, and disorganized, but she was also very close to her children. She had seen a psychiatrist and for periods of time took antidepressant medication as well as medication for attention deficit hyperactivity disorder. With the divorce, initiated by Alejandro, Denise had more frequent mood swings, became much more disorganized, and threatened suicide. The court ordered supervised parenting time for Denise until her moods and depression were stabilized.

❖ ❖ ❖ ❖ ❖

When a parent is assessed with mental illness, we need to determine which limitations are appropriate while maintaining the parent-child relationship and what the parent needs to do to return to a higher level of parental involvement.

❖ ❖ ❖ ❖ ❖

Jonathon was diagnosed as a schizophrenic prior to his divorce from Frieda. He was hospitalized on two different occasions, and each time was released after taking antipsychotic medications. He was close to his two sons and wanted to maintain relationships with them, which Frieda supported. Because of her concerns, the court ordered that he must regularly take his medication and see a psychiatrist for periodic medication reviews in order to continue to have parenting time with his boys. Furthermore, a guardian ad litem was appointed by the court to represent the interests of the boys. The guardian ad litem talked with the boys and the parents regularly to make sure that Jonathon was behaving appropriately with his sons.

❖ ❖ ❖ ❖ ❖

As we'll discuss in chapter eight, limiting parenting time without the expectation of improvement disempowers parents and makes it less likely their behaviors will improve. It's important to be very clear about what mentally ill co-parents need to do to regain a significant relationship with their children.

❖ ❖ ❖ ❖ ❖

At the time of his divorce, Ted was diagnosed with bipolar disorder and placed on medication. He was immature and explosive, and his ex-wife, Allyson, had a restraining order against him due to threats he had made to her and incidents of violence in the community. He began the divorce with supervised visitation with his 2-year-old son, Jamie.

Although immature and lacking understanding of young children, Ted was loving and attentive with Jamie. His therapist made it clear to Ted frequently that for him to have unsupervised parenting time he must show self-control and not be verbally explosive, physically threatening, or inappropriate with Allyson, with Jamie, or with anyone involved with the court. Slowly, Ted came to see how his behavior was directly related to decisions made by the court in regard to his parenting time. He even became more sensitive to Jamie's needs and feelings and less angry with Allyson.

Over a period of two years, Ted was able to move from supervised parenting time to unsupervised weekends and vacation time with Jamie. Allyson fought against the unsupervised parenting time and her comfort level was increased only when she began to realize that Ted's time with Jamie went well and Jamie was enjoying himself. If Allyson had been allowed to make the decision based on her comfort level in the beginning, unsupervised parenting time never would have occurred. His desire to be a good father caused him to rethink how he behaved in front of Jamie.

❖ ❖ ❖ ❖ ❖

When Both Parents Have Significant Psychological Disorders

At times, both parents may be found to have a mental illness. After accusations by both parents that the other parent is mentally unstable, it may turn out that each of the co-parents has significant personality disorders or psychiatric problems that are causing stress in the children. Indeed, it's rare to find one parent with severe mental illness or personality problems and the other without some significant deficits. Often, when both parents have difficulties, one may act out in a way that is more observable or that puts the children in the middle.

❖❖❖❖❖

Joe and Sue had disagreements from the time they decided to end their marriage. They made accusations of physical and verbal abuse against each other, and Children's Protective Services was called several times regarding suspected abuse and neglect of their two children. Psychological evaluations indicated that both parents had significant psychological problems.

Sue had borderline traits and was highly histrionic. Joe was described as having a personality disorder and was extremely rigid. Sue and Joe accused each other of lying and stealing. Joe was manipulative and placed the children in the middle of their conflicts by sharing financial information with them. Sue had difficulty tolerating the children's anger and became angry and disconnected from them at times.

Sue initially looked more disturbed because she was highly reactive with professionals. However, as time went on, both Joe and Sue were behaving very inappropriately. If their "craziness" had been contained between the two of them, it wouldn't have been as serious an issue, but they often dragged the children into the middle, causing them to suffer emotional distress. For their health and safety, the children were placed with an aunt and uncle who could provide a more stable home environment.

❖❖❖❖❖

❖ Advice for Professionals

When you are working with co-parents in high-conflict divorces, you need to make sure you don't jump to conclusions based on the intensity of your client's complaints. Just because your client has decided that her co-parent is mentally ill and dangerous to their children doesn't make it so.

Co-parents in high conflict often spend a great deal of time obsessing about the other parent and going over every bad moment between them. High-conflict co-parents often become very single minded, focusing on those events that support their conclusion and ignoring the behaviors that indicate that the co-parent is caring and capable. Your client may relate incidents to you out of context so that the co-parent's behavior sounds absolutely inappropriate.

But you must remember that this is only one point of view and that there is another view that could completely alter your assessment of the situation.

❖❖❖❖❖

Listening to all viewpoints was important in 14-year-old Jane's case. Jane had not seen her mother for a year because she, her father, and her therapist had decided that her mother was violent, had a mood disorder, and displayed significant anger management problems. Jane initially related to her therapist that her mother once assaulted her for no reason. Because of her parents' inability to communicate, her father believed his daughter, as did the therapist.

Everyone agreed that Jane should no longer see her mother after this incident. Her mother, however, told a different story. She explained that Jane had wanted to have a friend spend the night at her mother's house. Her mother explained that this wasn't possible because the family already had other plans. Jane got very angry and began swearing at her mother and calling her names.

Jane's mother told her to go to her room and calm down. Jane continued to swear at her and began pushing her mother. Her mother slapped her and told her she was not allowed to speak to her in such a crude manner and she certainly wasn't allowed to push her. Jane ran to her room and called her father who came over to pick her up without even speaking with her mother. Jane's therapist heard Jane's and her father's descriptions of what happened and sided with Jane and her father.

Only a court order eventually brought Jane and her mother together in a different therapeutic setting with a new therapist — one who was able to see everyone's role in the problem and focus on healthy relationships.

❖❖❖❖❖

The mother in this situation may have been abusive, controlling, and rigid, as Jane described her over and over again. However, the problem was that Jane had become entrapped by her exaggerations and couldn't take them back once they had become the source of serious actions and conclusions by her father, her therapist, and the Children's Protective Services investigator.

Keep in mind that your own experiences and beliefs about parenting children, how families should interact, and mental illness will enter into how you view the rights of parents who may be diagnosed with mental illness. It's important to be aware of your own biases so that you can try to maintain your objectivity. There are three assumptions that have been found to be prevalent among people who are responsible for making decisions about custody and parenting time. These assumptions are:

1. A mental health diagnosis predicts inadequate parenting or a risk for child maltreatment;
2. A mental health diagnosis means that a parent will be less able to benefit from parenting interventions;
3. A mental health diagnosis means that the parent is forever unfit to be an adequate parent (Benjet, Azar and Kuersten-Hogan, 2003).

If you subscribe to one or more of these beliefs, you may take action without looking at the entire picture. Making any of the above three assumptions may influence your judgment and lead you to be unduly biased in the evaluation of a particular parent's fitness. However, recent research, focusing on the parenting capacities of mentally ill parents, has shown that there is no evidence that mentally ill parents are more prone to violence, neglect or maltreatment, than are other parents (Benjet, Azar and Kuersten-Hogan, 2003; Nicholson, Sweeney and Geller, 1998). Parents with mental illnesses vary, just like mothers and fathers without psychiatric diagnoses, in their parenting abilities (Nicholson, Sweeney and Geller, 1998).

❖❖❖❖

LuEllen had been hospitalized with a major depressive episode. After a short hospital stay, psychiatric treatment and medication, she returned home to continue to parent her 9-year-old daughter, Alesha.

LuEllen had little patience for stress, and even having to wait in the pediatrician's office was an upsetting and irritating experience for her. And, as before her illness, LuEllen was inconsistent in her interactions with Alesha. Sometimes she emphasized the rules, while at other times she allowed Alesha to break the rules without experiencing any consequences.

❖❖❖❖

Randolph, on the other hand, had been diagnosed with schizophrenia. He had a psychotic break resulting in hospitalization, a day treatment program, and a parent education program. Before treatment, he was an aloof and distant parent from his 4-year-old twin daughters. In the parent education program at the hospital, he learned about child development and how to play with children. On some days, he was asked to bring his children to the parent education program so he could be observed in the nursery playing with his kids. Then he received feedback from the parent trainers about how he could improve play with his daughters.

Randolph was diligent about learning to be a better parent, and both he and the parent trainers agreed that he was much more involved with his girls. And it was agreed that he received much more satisfaction from his role as a father.

❖❖❖❖❖

As Randolph illustrates, parents with major psychiatric disorders have been found to be amenable to being taught parenting skills (Waldo, Roath, Levine and Freedman, 1987). Interestingly, parents who have been diagnosed with a mental health disorder who have received parenting instruction have improved treatment compliance and fewer rehospitalizations (Waldo, Roath, Levine and Freedman, 1987).

The most important question for you to ask yourself when assessing mental illness in high-conflict divorces is this: "What needs to be done so that the children can have the best possible relationship with both parents?" Instead of always considering how a child can be removed and shielded from the parent with a psychiatric disorder, bear in mind what we wrote earlier in this chapter: children are better off having relationships with both parents — even if one (or both) has significant mental disorders. How you try to maintain and enhance parent-child relationships despite the challenges has the potential for profound consequences for the family in the future.

A 1998 study of 42 mentally ill mothers who had been hospitalized looked at the stresses and rewards of parenting after they returned home to resume their parenting responsibilities. It was found that while these mothers acknowledged that raising children was stressful for them, it was also learned that these parents were willing to get help for themselves if they believed this action would benefit their children (Nicholson, Sweeney and Geller, 1998).

Parents diagnosed with a mental illness share similar desires with other parents. That is, they want to raise their children and enjoy family life (Benjet, Azar and Kuersten-Hogan, 2003). And with medication and treatment, most mentally ill individuals these days can function quite well in a supportive family setting, even if there has been a divorce. Your position should be unequivocal: The healthiest possible outcome for children is to have secure and significant relationships with both parents.

8

Pattern 6: Disempowered Parents

❖ ❖ ❖ ❖ ❖

Lauren cited James's explosive temper as her main reason for
divorcing him. He was arrogant, loud, and expected to always
get his way. James had a poor relationship with his parents. They
felt he didn't live up to his potential, and in response to their
criticism he started having frequent outbursts of fury toward
them as a teenager. Lauren was frightened James would hurt her.
She had a personal protection order in place and refused to be in
the same room with him. He had broken things, had threatened
her, and frequently came too close to her when he was angry. She
organized the police, community, and preschool personnel to
document James's angry, aggressive acts. James had once
screamed at a traffic control department parking attendant who
was giving him a parking ticket, and the police had been called
more than once during his angry tirades at home and in public.
To Lauren — and others — James was a scary person; she was
even able to obtain a letter from a police officer stating that
James was the most frightening person he'd ever dealt with.

❖ ❖ ❖ ❖ ❖

As always, the innocent one in the struggle — in this case,
Lauren — is the more sympathetic character. However,
the more undesirable person in a divorce is often the person who
most needs our support and help. That person has become
disoriented and unfocused, resulting in foolish and aggressive
behaviors leading both the ex-spouse and the court to punish him
with restrictions on seeing his children, with financial sanctions,
and even with time in jail for contempt of court. Yet, if this parent
is to rise up, be a competent parent to his children, and do his part

in enabling his children to have normal childhoods, we must find a way to empower that parent.

❖❖❖❖❖

James and Lauren married in their mid-twenties, stayed married for six years, and had one child, Madison, who was 3 years old when the divorce started. They were both very attractive and had loved being seen by others in the company of such a beautiful partner. Lauren had been intrigued by how sure of himself James was. James had been intrigued by her physical beauty. Their marriage was turbulent from the beginning. Their sexual relationship was incredible until they unexpectedly conceived Madison. As Lauren's perfect body swelled, James became less interested in her. Once the baby came, Lauren became maternal and less exciting, focusing more on the baby than on James. Despite the return of her body to its previous beauty, they argued more and made love less. Lauren's parents became a frequent fixture in their household once they had a grandchild, leaving James on the outside looking in. His family, despite their disapproval of his lack of business success, provided him with endless financial support. This support, however, underscored for both James and Lauren his own lack of accomplishment. In addition, his bad temper, which had been a problem throughout his teens, got worse as he grew more distant from Lauren and Madison.

❖❖❖❖❖

Cloe Madanes (1981) proposed years ago that, in marriage or divorce, the partner who has the least power will develop problem behaviors, thereby equalizing power in a dysfunctional way. In Madanes's theory, the person gains power by being troubled in ways that inconvenience others and that no one can directly stop. Symptoms of a disempowered parent include psychiatric problems, substance abuse, aggression, and employment troubles. The more extreme the symptoms, the more likely it is that this parent has dramatically less power both in the divorce and in his life in general. The extremity of his bad behavior is inversely proportional to the amount of power the disempowered parent has.

It's critical that we differentiate a genuinely dangerous or mentally ill parent from a relatively normal person whose bad behavior has escalated because of being disenfranchised from co-parent, children, and friends. The following characteristics are typical of a disenfranchised parent:

❖ Will be unsuccessful at his job

❖ Will have a conflicted relationship with his family of origin

❖ Will have friends willing to attest to his normality

❖ Will show commitment to his children and a true desire for a good relationship with them. (This doesn't necessarily mean that the relationship between him and his children is wonderful. Sometimes he contributes to a deteriorated relationship.)

❖ Will seem self-righteous rather than malicious to the therapist

❖ Will escalate his troubled behavior initially when the court takes a punitive position

In high-conflict cases where one parent is disempowered, the disempowered co-parent is angry about nearly everything and the other is frightened by his behavior and aggressive reactions. Negotiations over child custody and financial settlements typically fail due to each parent's anger at or fear of the other. Therefore, the case goes to court for an evidentiary hearing where prolonged testimony is taken in which each party brings witnesses and evidence designed to impugn the credibility of his or her co-parent. The court is asked to make a logical legal decision about custody and finances. However, the couple's fear and anger leads them to defy court orders by withholding monies, interfering with visitation, and/or disrupting phone conversations between the other parent and their children. Co-parents in these situations become progressively more manipulative despite court orders specifying solutions to the co-parenting struggles.

As the legal situation gets worse, the court sees one out-of-control individual who may appear untrustworthy to care for his children. The empowered parent may subtly interfere with the disempowered parent in provocative ways, but the behavior of the disempowered parent is so blatant that the other parent simply has to say, "See? Now you know how he is." Faced with these outbursts, the court has little choice but to find the parent who is acting crazy unfit. That parent feels vilified, while the other parent feels the court isn't taking serious enough action to stop the disempowered parent's destructive behavior. Both are correct.

❖ ❖ ❖ ❖ ❖

As many parents do in such situations, Lauren assumed that James would behave toward his daughter the same way he'd behaved toward her. Both secured aggressive attorneys with their parents' money and filed motion after motion. He wanted more visitation time. She wanted his time supervised. The child support wasn't acceptable. She wouldn't allow him his time on the phone with Madison because he was angry or insulting. The list went on and on, with the court hearing these complaints every two or three months.

The court restricted James to supervised visitation with Madison at the premises of a domestic violence program. He was allowed to see her for only one hour at a time, only three times a week. He would see his daughter in a playroom with a supervising social worker in the room. On one occasion, he blew up at the social worker, swearing and yelling at her. The social worker and her supervisor refused to deal with him further because they were frightened by his angry verbal behavior — exactly the kind of behavior that led the court to give him supervised visitations in the first place.

❖❖❖❖❖

As in many cases that involve an aggressive parent, the court took action intended to protect both the custodial parent (Lauren) and the child (Madison). Lauren prevailed based on the evidence. Her goal was to maintain the restrictions on James's involvement with her and Madison as long as possible. This position seemed reasonable in view of how scary James could be.

The court is caught in a paradox in which it feels compelled by the disempowered parent's foolish behavior to make decisions that disenfranchise this parent further and, thereby, contribute to the escalation of his emotional symptoms. Yet the court's only other option would be to fly in the face of evidence that the other co-parent and the children must be protected from a potentially dangerous person.

Although courts ordinarily decide who will prevail in such a struggle, in James and Lauren's situation the court saw the increasing animosity and litigation as a serious problem. The judge decided that this couple must learn to deal properly with each other and that the court was not the place to accomplish that. Therefore, the judge referred them to a parent coordinator, Dr. Medeiros, to carry out James's supervised parenting time with Madison.

However, healing this damaged set of relationships — between the dueling co-parents, with each of their parents in the background fueling the conflict, and between the court and this high-conflict family — required that Dr. Medeiros carry out a series of steps to help James to rise to the challenge to be successful and reputable in his dealings with his ex-wife and daughter.

- ❖ Step One: Getting the whole story
- ❖ Step Two: Assessing dangerousness carefully
- ❖ Step Three: Advocating for the disempowered parent
- ❖ Step Four: Guiding the disempowered parent
- ❖ Step Five: Soothing the anxieties of the co-parent
- ❖ Step Six: Using the court to create a balanced perspective

Step One: Getting the whole story

❖❖❖❖❖

Lauren and James were scheduled for interviews and viewed their interviews with Dr. Medeiros as a new opportunity to again convince an arbiter of their points of view. James came to his first meeting with Dr. Medeiros speaking loudly and self-righteously. Lauren came to her interview with a folder of letters and documents intended to prove James's dangerousness. When looked at objectively, James had very little going for him, and it seemed as if someone ought to try to help him learn to get his foot out of his mouth and deal with this entire situation with patience. Dr. Medeiros's position from the outset was that the child deserved both parents if at all possible. Child protection laws typically don't allow interference with parental rights unless it can be demonstrated that there is danger to the child (Child Abuse Prevention and Treatment Act, 2003). Although James had been loud, inflammatory, defiant, and even threatening at times, he hadn't actually *done* anything dangerous.

❖❖❖❖❖

The first and most difficult step in treating high-conflict couples is convincing both parties that you will be objective. You can do this by listening carefully during the first meeting and avoiding any challenges to either person's position. It helps if you provide assurances of safety during the sessions and even in the waiting room in order to reduce everyone's anxiety about meeting together at the same office. You can make sure co-parents leave the office at different times to avoid them meeting outside the building, if necessary.

Although you can't accept either person's position without question, you can sympathize with both about the difficult spot they've found themselves in. In that way, when you need to take a position for one person, you won't endanger the relationship with the other parent too badly. Each parent will be determined to convince you that the other is a demon. At this early stage, it is critical to wonder with each party whether the co-parent has any redeeming value. Sometimes therapists and even attorneys suggest logical reasons the other parent might feel as he or she does, thus hoping for an understanding response from the other.

When a previous therapist had tried this, both Lauren and James reacted with visceral angry responses and refused to consider that they both might have good reasons for their positions. This intractability is one of the defining features of a true high-conflict divorce and co-parenting situation.

Finally, in step one it is important to assess the different fronts on which the case may need to be handled. Critical players in many high-conflict cases include therapists (particularly the child's therapist), in-laws, attorneys, and other parties who have taken it upon themselves to call you requesting an opportunity to give input. Meeting with some of these people may be necessary to gain their cooperation or, in some instances, to make informed recommendations to the court asking the court to block interference by these people.

Step Two: Assessing dangerousness carefully

Before deciding how to improve the role of the misbehaving parent in his child's life, it's critical to accurately assess that parent's true capacity for dangerousness. After all, his dangerousness was the factor that most concerned the court. An excellent way to gain first-hand knowledge of his behavior, as was done with James, is to move the supervised visitation to your own office, where you can supervise his interactions with his child and intervene in problematic behaviors.

❖ ❖ ❖ ❖ ❖

Rather than just looking at how James acted toward other adults, Dr. Medeiros was concerned about the way he acted with his child. With James, his level of self-control in dealing with Madison provided information on his dangerousness to her. What Dr.

Medeiros observed was that James's main problem was that he hadn't mastered knowing when to keep his mouth shut. He regularly made two primary errors in his time with his daughter. First, he commented about the adult processes with remarks such as, "The court should let me spend more time with you" and "Your mother doesn't think we should be alone together." James believed he was explaining what Madison should know, although to others he appeared to be looking for sympathy or trying to sway a very young child over to his side in a struggle.

His second error was trying to get his needs met through Madison. For instance, he asked questions such as "Do you know how much Daddy loves you?" or made statements like "Daddy loves you and misses you. It's not fun to be away from you" multiple times during each play session while also inundating her with requests for kisses and hugs. He became frustrated when she predictably became withholding and oppositional in an age-appropriate way.

Although such communications were unhealthy, they were not dangerous. Dr. Medeiros spent time with James before and after each session discussing these developmental issues. Because of these discussions, Madison's response to her father improved. As that interaction got better, James gained trust in Dr. Medeiros's expertise and began to listen to his opinions and suggestions. As James learned these skills with Madison, Dr. Medeiros taught him how to apply them to his interactions with Lauren, and his communication with Lauren improved as well.

Ultimately, Dr. Medeiros had to answer the all-important question of whether James was a direct physical threat to Lauren or Madison. True, he had made threatening phone calls to Lauren, and the police had come when he refused to leave the house during arguments in the past. Lauren and her attorneys had convincing evidence and had persuaded the court to limit James's involvement with his daughter. His explosive outbursts, along with his willingness to defy court orders by taking his daughter where he wished and setting his own times had helped convince the court of his dangerousness; but had he ever caused injury to Lauren or Madison through violence or negligence? This assessment had to be based on evidence that could be supported, and it required Dr. Medeiros to speak with arresting officers and witnesses of reported acts of aggression.

❖ ❖ ❖ ❖ ❖

In the typical high-conflict case, there are frequent exaggerated accusations by both parties against the other. Therefore, you must use your clinical judgment to assess the believability of each claim.

Although James was clearly immature, his behavior fit that of a disempowered parent and didn't cross the line into dangerousness. As he alienated himself from other people, he had also been alienated by others from his role as a parent. As he became more emotionally distressed, he made progressively worse decisions.

If you think that the disempowered parent might be dangerous, you must support the court's restrictions. Meanwhile, you can still help that parent come to understand what he must do to stop his dangerous or potentially dangerous behaviors. If the disempowered parent is truly dangerous, it's critical that you not give him false hope of increased parenting time.

Step Three: Advocating for the disempowered parent

High-conflict divorce cases, like the one Lauren and James presented to the court at first, typically hang around in courts and mental health systems for years and in the process exhaust judges and therapists alike. The participants seem relentless and appear to have boundless energy and almost unlimited money to spend trying to defeat each other. Such cases seem impossible to resolve.

Yet, with clear understanding of the dynamics underlying many high-conflict divorces, it's possible to help change what seems like an irreparable situation. The key is to understand how power is balanced in high-conflict divorce couples like James and Lauren. By using a family therapy model and approach, Dr. Medeiros was able to understand the balance of power and then to help create a more healthy balance.

Intervention requires finding a way to advocate for the disempowered parent regarding something he finds important. In this way you can gain enough trust to get that parent to listen to your feedback. With James, Dr. Medeiros advocated for small changes such as his being able to speak with Madison on the phone more often while consistently holding him to the highest standard of appropriate behavior. Dr. Medeiros made it clear to James that he believed James could make the right choices about how to behave. If he didn't behave appropriately after Dr. Medeiros was able to get the court to grant more freedom with Madison, then he would have no sympathy when James complained in the future.

In fact, Dr. Medeiros complained to James that his "stupid behavior" might endanger Dr. Medeiros's reputation.

There were opportunities to advocate further for James as he made progress. James's increased privileges included permitting him to take Madison to the restroom, letting them run in the hall, and allowing James's mother and sister to attend a supervised visit in the office. Despite enraged responses by Lauren and her attorney, Dr. Medeiros experimented with these small, reasonable changes. Although these were small steps, they meant a lot to James, who had previously been seen as too dangerous to take his daughter to the bathroom.

Once you've demonstrated faith in the disempowered parent, you must also hold that parent to a higher standard of behavior than anyone previously has. With each increase in time and freedom with his child, Dr. Medeiros placed increased demands on James for mature behavior and self-control. As the disempowered parent's self-control improves, you can advocate for greater increases in parenting time and reduced levels of supervision.

Step Four: Guiding the disempowered parent

It is important to assess whether the disempowered parent can be trusted to make an agreement and stick to it. If the court granted one hour alone with his daughter, would he stick to an hour and no more or would he take her out of state for a week, or even kidnap her? Dr. Medeiros tested James's ability to stick to an agreement by insisting that he do difficult things that he didn't want to do. For example, he asked James to make a gift for Lauren for Mother's Day with Madison during one of the visits and gather needed materials during his own time. Dr. Medeiros also insisted he follow court orders to the letter, and his compliance was noted over several months.

The work with the disempowered co-parent must go on over many months — often replete with times of improvement as well as times of relapse — before the situation becomes steady enough to get the court to consider greater freedom for the individual. That was certainly true for James.

❖ ❖ ❖ ❖ ❖

Dr. Medeiros helped James become more patient and cooperative by simultaneously being supportive and confrontational with him.

He provided James with compassion and power in equal doses. In one sense, Dr. Medeiros was reparenting James through a turbulent adolescence by giving him what all adolescents need — both structure and caring. As a result, James's self-control steadily improved.

Next, Dr. Medeiros convinced both Lauren and the court to agree to have James enroll Madison in a little kids' gym class. There he could enjoy his daughter in a more open setting. A teacher would always be present at the class, thereby providing an informal sort of supervision. Lauren dropped Madison off and picked her up right outside the school. Such situations can be suggested by any professional as a way to improve parent-child relationships while still making sure the child is safe.

Dr. Medeiros had to testify in court and undergo strenuous cross-examination by Lauren's attorney before the court agreed to proceed with this recommendation.

❖❖❖❖❖

Step Five: Soothing the anxieties of the co-parent

❖❖❖❖❖

As Lauren faced greater separation from Madison, her worries had to be laid to rest or at least decreased. She had to be helped to see James's relationship with Madison as Dr. Medeiros was seeing it. To that end, Dr. Medeiros asked James to agree to let Lauren come randomly and watch from behind a one-way mirror to see him play with Madison at Dr. Medeiros's office and see that he was playful and appropriate with her. He wasn't to know when Lauren might be there.

Reducing Lauren's anxiety also required limiting the input of other people, such as her parents, who aggravated her fears. After Lauren's mother called Dr. Medeiros threatening a lawsuit (not to mention a complaint to the state licensing board), he explained to Lauren how poorly it reflected on her that her parents didn't feel they could trust her to handle her own family situation without interference. As she came to see parental intervention as an insult to her and a message to the court that she might not be competent, Lauren began restricting her parents' involvement in the case. She listened to her parents' inflammatory input less and acted less fearful in her dealings with James.

As with any fear cycle, the avoidance of the feared stimulus increases the fear. This was so in this situation. Therefore, Dr. Medeiros insisted that Lauren and James interact in his waiting room and say things like, "Oh look, there's mommy (or daddy)." Dr. Medeiros also conducted joint sessions in which they were instructed to speak respectfully to each other while practicing staying off the subject of their mutual history.

It wasn't necessary in this case, but it is often necessary to have meetings with both attorneys to receive their input and try to put their minds at ease about the safety of the process. Family attorneys are more likely than litigators to be relaxed and reassure their clients. However, sometimes attorneys might feel they are in danger of losing a client if they encourage a frightened client to relax and work with the situation.

Step Six: Using the court to create a balanced perspective
In high-conflict divorce cases, you will often have to encourage the court to set boundaries about how a case will be treated. A series of court hearings late in the case may be necessary as one co-parent becomes frightened and tries to block the other parent's involvement. Balance is achieved when the court clearly delineates what will constitute violation of its orders and which behaviors are interpersonal problems that must be worked out in counseling or therapy.

❖ ❖ ❖ ❖ ❖

For instance, as James gained a few hours a week of unsupervised time with Madison, he did things that many parents do at some time. He left Madison sleeping in her car seat where he could see her outside the window of a small shop he was going into. Lauren's private investigator documented this event on videotape and she went back to court to interrupt James's parenting time. At this point Dr. Medeiros had to trade on the court's trust in him to defuse exaggerated claims of danger.

Meanwhile, Dr. Medeiros coached James privately that he was pressing his luck by risking any situation that could be construed as negligent. He had to understand that if he did something truly dangerous or negligent, Dr. Medeiros would support Lauren's and the court's actions as appropriate but would still be there to help him do what was necessary to regain trust.

It took several hearings for Lauren to accept that she could not eliminate James's unsupervised involvement with Madison.

She also required several individual sessions with Dr. Medeiros to convince her that, despite Dr. Medeiros's position that father and daughter should be reunited, he understood why she found James frightening and why there would be continued monitoring of Madison's welfare.

❖ ❖ ❖ ❖ ❖

Dr. Medeiros used the court to force a stable cycle of interaction between Lauren and James that could continue long enough for each parent to see that the other wouldn't do anything to intentionally sabotage the process. Dr. Medeiros modeled this by speaking well of each parent to the other as they were being asked to do.

❖ Our Power — Helping the Disempowered Parent

In this chapter, we've discussed a type of treatment case that few therapists, attorneys, or courts wish to handle. Clients in postdivorce crisis are often anxiety ridden, verbally abusive to the people trying to help them, intractable, and generally anxiety provoking for everyone concerned. Both co-parents have generally developed a pattern of unloading their fears and anxieties on anyone who will listen. This tendency to unload causes a high burnout rate among therapists or causes them to become hardened and lacking in compassion. It's difficult to maintain therapeutic benevolence and belief in both sides. Therapists and everyone else often try to figure out who is the more troubled person, rather than actively working toward reunification of the whole family.

If you take one side over the other, it will be less stressful. On the other hand, if you take the more compassionate view with the intent of healing relationships, you will find yourself in the crossfire, you will be very stressed, and you will share the co-parent's fears and anxieties.

The ultimate purpose of your work with high-conflict divorce parents is to help the children of these high-conflict parents maintain a positive relationship with both parents — no matter how difficult the process is for you. If you are working with high-conflict divorces and you believe in keeping families connected, you must be able to recognize a pattern of disempowerment. That will necessarily require you to take risks to accomplish the long-term goal of helping children have the best possible relationship with their parents. At the same time, taking on these risks will ultimately enable you to help co-parents nurture and benefit their children.

Often we're expected to decide who the children live with full time or what parenting time arrangements should be made. As a therapist you will find yourself trying to treat a divorced couple within an atmosphere in which "fitness" is still the main consideration.

As a therapist, you may be asked to decide if either parent is harmful to the children. When faced with these kinds of questions, we all look to someone else — an attorney, a court counselor, a clinical psychologist, a psychiatrist, or a judge — to help us find out what the "truth" is. When we are the person others turn to for that truth, for a recommendation, or for therapeutic intervention, we are placed in a position of great power. Underlying this power is an awesome responsibility to try to understand what *is* happening in a high-conflict divorce vs. what *seems to be* happening. The task of understanding requires moving beyond simple conceptualizations of "good and bad" or "right and wrong." In some cases there's clearly a "bad guy," but more often there's no clear culprit.

❖ *The Next Section of This Book*

In part III, we show the context in which high-conflict postdivorce relationships develop. Often, highly contested divorces and prolonged and rancorous disputes are fueled by the adversarial aspects of our justice system. In this next section you will see how psychologists and the mental health system either contribute to maintaining high-conflict divorce or help resolve high conflict.

Part III

Understanding the Context of High-Conflict Divorce

I n part III we will discuss how the court system — by which we mean family court policies, judges, and attorneys — affects divorces and may contribute to the high conflict we see in a significant number of postdivorce relationships. Our court system is designed to be adversarial, and while this may lead to the discovery of truth in criminal trials as opposing lawyers battle against each other, it is not helpful when it comes to divorce.

Furthermore, in this third part of the book we will also look at how psychologists and therapists are brought into the conflict between divorcing co-parents and the role they play in either reducing or promoting conflict.

9

Dysfunction in the Court System: Attorneys and Judges

As a therapist or a family counselor, you may prefer to treat clients in your office, avoiding the anxiety and complications of dealing with the legal system. However, if you think that you can treat high-conflict divorce couples without dealing with attorneys and judges, then you are fooling yourself. When it comes to dealing with the angry couples with high-conflict relationships, you cannot afford to be an ivory tower clinician.

In part, this chapter will suggest ways that attorneys and judges can play a greater role in reducing the high conflict that plagues so many divorcing families these days. But suggestions are offered for you as well, so that the legal system can continue to make progress in the way it deals with high-conflict divorces. Furthermore, our goal in this chapter is to help you better understand the legal system and the role played by attorneys and judges in high-conflict divorces.

❖ The First Contact with the System

❖❖❖❖❖

Nida knew exactly what kind of attorney she wanted, and she had no difficulty finding Marlene, whose phone book ad described her as "aggressive, hard line, and demanding — a lawyer who will protect your rights as a divorcing woman."

When Nida walked into Marlene's office for her first appointment, she was feeling hurt and scared. However, she was also angry at her husband, Khaled, and she was determined to hurt him — just as he had hurt her. When she started talking to Marlene, Nida heard exactly what she wanted to hear.

"If you follow my advice," Marlene said, "we can file quickly and get the upper hand. I can get you most of what you want."

In further conversations with Marlene, Nida found she couldn't answer many questions about the family finances. Her lack of knowledge about the finances confirmed her belief about how controlling Khaled had always been, and this just increased her anger.

Marlene explained to her that, given the interrogatories, requests for documents, and depositions that might be necessary if the case went to court, the divorce would be expensive. Nida immediately wrote Marlene a check for six thousand dollars — money that was supposed to go toward buying a car for their 16-year-old son. Nida left Marlene's office after the first appointment more resentful and more determined to get back at Khaled.

Khaled was furious when he was served with divorce papers at work in front of his colleagues. After reading that Nida was asking for full custody of the children and that she had frozen all the accounts, he concluded that she had hired a "shark" for an attorney. He was shocked and afraid because of all the stories he had heard about men losing everything. Khaled soon found his own attorney to respond in a similarly aggressive manner to the divorce. Thus, the stage was set for an expensive, prolonged, and damaging conflict.

❖❖❖❖❖

Clearly, attorneys have an important impact on how divorce is played out. Attorneys are usually involved right at the beginning when the family is in chaos and most susceptible to influence, good or bad. Many family law attorneys mean well; they wish to reduce conflict and help their clients come to a quick and equitable resolution in the divorce. But, there are other attorneys who revel in being seen as aggressive. Marlene was just such an attorney.

This kind of adversarial approach is the crux of the judicial system and works well in some situations — even for many divorcing families. When the dissolution of a marriage is couched as a win-lose proposition, it can be a disastrous beginning for the potential high-conflict family. The battle lines between co-parents are drawn, and the children are almost sure to suffer.

Far too often, both attorneys and co-parents view the actions of the court as providing punishment for one side for "bad" behavior. Indeed, this may make sense in criminal cases where guilt can be assessed, but affairs, alcoholism, or poorly matched personalities are not punishable crimes. Yet in divorce, punishments or rewards might be sought through loss of property, possessions, finances, or parenting time. In the case of divorce with children, when one parent is financially or emotionally devastated, the children lose as well because one of the most important people in their lives has been harmed.

❖ The First Meeting with an Attorney

The first meeting between a person intent on divorce and an attorney can be pivotal. This was certainly true for Nida in her first appointment with Marlene. If Marlene had counseled Nida to take a less aggressive approach, Nida's divorce from Khaled might have proceeded more smoothly and with less hostility.

People are often intimidated by the legal process and fearful of the uncertainties of divorce and the changes to come in their lives. Divorce with children leaves people feeling vulnerable due to a variety of issues, including anticipated or actual loss of the children or time with them, financial stress, and the prospect of a more complicated family system. The sense of powerlessness that goes along with divorce often leaves people willing to grasp at any opportunity given to them to feel they are in control of their situations. Well-meaning friends and family members give advice based on their immediate desire to protect their loved one and to hurt the other party, without thought for the larger picture. Individuals who wish to hurt their co-parents are usually able to find an attorney who will help them. And it is at this point when the responsibility of the divorce lawyer comes into play.

When lawyers approach divorce cases where minor children are involved from the framework of win-lose, it encourages co-parents to find fault with each other rather than to cooperate.

❖❖❖❖❖

When Elisa had her first appointment with an attorney to talk about filing for a divorce, she told him that she wished to have physical custody of the children. She related various incidents when she believed Mario, her husband, had been unfaithful to her and showed disregard for the welfare of their two children.

The attorney advised her to write down all the times she could recall when Mario had done things that, in her opinion, were inconsistent with good parenting. "We can use this when we need to argue that you deserve full physical custody," he said.

Elisa's attorney did not ask about what might be in the best interests of the children. He listened to Elisa's point of view and indicated he would help her gain physical custody. He did not seem concerned about whether this approach might potentially be harmful to the children.

❖❖❖❖❖

When attorneys advise divorce clients to gather evidence against the other parent or to remove money from bank accounts, they're advocating actions that are sure to increase hostility between parents. When hostility between co-parents increases, their parenting ability decreases — especially if one parent has to move to a new residence (Stolberg, A. L., Camplair, C., Currier, C. and Wells, M.J., 1987; Fincham, Grych and Osborne, 1994).

❖❖❖❖❖

At her first meeting with an attorney, LaVonda told him that her husband of twelve years was physically abusive to her and was often argumentative. Without substantiating any of these claims, the attorney advised LaVonda to file for a protective order to have her husband, Duane, removed from the home. The attorney also advised her to stop talking to Duane in order to cut down on arguments between them. Although these recommendations were calculated to reduce the stress for LaVonda, they were not designed to help the children or to solve the issues that led to conflict between Duane and LaVonda.

❖❖❖❖❖

Attorneys Can Be a Positive Influence for Co-parents

❖ Attorneys can create a foundation for reason and fairness amidst the tumultuous emotions of divorce. Most divorcing individuals are good people who are temporarily wounded but are willing to respond to a rational approach in the beginning of the divorce process if their attorneys model this kind of approach. If the lawyer, however, sets the stage for a divorce war, even a rational adult may succumb to an unreasonable approach to the divorce. The conflict thus set into motion by a lawyer who thinks in terms of win-lose may not stop when the divorce is final but could continue well into the postdivorce years. Judgments concerning children remain modifiable throughout a child's minority, which gives parents many years of opportunities to engage in disagreements.

❖ *Focus on Fault*

When parents are angry about their marriage or their divorce, it's natural for them to want to blame the other parent, and even to punish that person. If the attorney gets sucked into the tragic story of the divorce and allows blame and punishment to rule the agenda, reasonable resolution won't occur. It's easy for the attorney (or any helping professional) to fall into the trap of giving the client a sense of power that will become a clarion call for battle throughout the divorce.

The mother who gave up her career to stay home with the kids and dedicated her life to home and family is likely to feel she deserves to get more parenting time than her co-parent. He, on the other hand, may feel that he deserves the bigger share, as he worked hard for the money while his wife stayed home and "spent every penny of it." The "good mother" may want to protect the children from the co-parent whom she sees as morally deficient, lacking parenting skills, or never having spent time with the children (or with her) before the divorce. The "hard-working father" may contend that he wasn't allowed to tuck the kids into bed, make decisions about them, or spend time with them because he was always doing other things his wife asked him to do.

Who is at fault in these situations? Who deserves more? Determining fault isn't going to bring resolution to the real issue. In fact, that was a major reason for most states, beginning in the 1970s, to pass no-fault divorce legislation (Nakoenezny, Shull, and Rodgers, 1995). The goal of no-fault divorce laws was to simplify the divorce process and reduce both conflict and cost. That didn't happen, perhaps because it's been so easy for lawyers and courts to sympathize with the pain experienced by a client who was abused, whose partner had an affair, or who has been denied pleasant experiences with the children. However, there are always two sides to the story and enough distress to go around. It may, for some attorneys, be more comfortable to deal with a parent who is righteously angry rather than a miserable and depressed client who is struggling to cope with the many facets of loss and anxiety generated by divorce.

❖ *The Best Interest of the Client*

The attorney's role is to look out for the best interests of her client. But what are the best interests of the client? One client may seek out an attorney who will help her settle her divorce with fairness and justice for both parties. Another client may come to an attorney seeking to take everything she can get financially and materially from the spouse. If the attorney sees the best interests of his client as handling the divorce in exactly the way the client wishes to have it handled, the lawyer may strive to be fair or may fight ruthlessly for everything the client wants. And he may take either approach with little regard for the potential impact on the children.

Some clients tell their attorneys that their children are complaining that they don't like the other parent and that the child shouldn't be separated from the parent who is in the lawyer's office. This parent may be seeking validation for this point of view, and the attorney may buy into the need to validate these complaints in the interest of respecting the child's feelings.

Furthermore, what a client sees as being in her best interests may well be short-sighted or patently inadvisable for the children. Co-parents who wish to take full physical custody, restrict the other parent's parenting time, or demand an unreasonable amount of child support may be reacting based on their emotional needs — not on what is objectively best for the children.

While many attorneys will let their clients know that their demands are unreasonable, there are others who are less concerned about the children and are more concerned with accommodating the angry parent-client.

❖ *The Aggressive Attorney and the Passive Client*

❖❖❖❖❖

June was a middle-aged, stay-at-home mother who, since the kids had been born, had only worked part time at the school. She and Walt had few fights or arguments during the marriage, and their friends truly expected that June and Walt would always be together. However, one day Walt told June that he had been unhappy for a long time and couldn't go on being married. June was very surprised as she never suspected Walt would ever wish to end their marriage.

When June entered the attorney's office she was frightened, confused, and depressed over the upheaval in her life. A friend had referred her to the attorney and she didn't know what to expect. She wanted someone to take charge and her attorney, Sheldon, did exactly that.

Sheldon directed June to go home and take pictures of their possessions, get their financial information without telling her husband, and document anything inappropriate her husband did or said to her or the children. Walt came home from work while June was still taking photographs, and they had their first fight. After the fight, June documented his inappropriate behavior during the argument for her attorney. The divorce quickly became ugly, despite the fact that Walt and June were sensible, bright, and well-intentioned people.

❖ ❖ ❖ ❖ ❖

This is a scenario where a client goes to an attorney looking for guidance and believing that the expert knows the best way to proceed. A passive individual may put little thought into what kind of attorney she would like and may not even be aware of how different attorneys approach divorce. An aggressive, take-charge attorney can set the stage for a long court battle. Sheldon sent June home to behave as though her husband was untrustworthy and told her to look for inappropriate behavior. As often happens, what we look for is what we'll find. If June had been encouraged to be reasonable and fair and sit down with her husband in an effort to work things out, it's possible there would have been less conflict and less money spent on lawyers, leaving greater harmony and more resources for the family.

Can Lawyers Help to Reduce Conflict?

Many experts in the legal system agree that lawyers can take a proactive role in reducing conflict between disputing parents (Wingspread Conference Report, 2001). In order to minimize the conflict in divorces, attorneys can use their counseling function in assisting clients of divorce to avoid inappropriate conflict, particularly related to custody issues.

❖❖❖❖❖

When Jolene had her first appointment with an attorney, she was angry and admittedly was looking for ways to hurt her husband. The attorney, however, discussed with her the negative consequences of a custody dispute on their three children. He strongly advised her to work at settling their conflicts in the least damaging ways in order to protect their children.

❖❖❖❖❖

Lawyers can, as early as the first appointment, discuss the alternatives to litigation, such as mediation, counseling, divorce classes, or collaborative law. Instead of promoting conflict, attorneys can be well versed in ways to avoid conflict and can communicate this knowledge to their clients. They can also make every effort to identify those couples who are likely to become entrenched in high conflict and encourage these individuals to avail themselves of the resources for settling disputes outside of the courtroom and the legal process.

In some states and jurisdictions, an alternative process for resolving co-parent conflicts has been gaining support since the mid-1990s. Called *collaborative law*, the goal is to eliminate litigation in family matters. The co-parenting couple, as well as their attorneys (who must be trained in this alternative approach), commit to the process and agree they will not litigate to solve their issues. They enter a contract that establishes the most unique aspect of collaborative law: if the collaborative process terminates, the same attorneys can no longer represent their clients. If the collaborative law process breaks down, the couple can try to resolve their problems by litigating — if they choose. If they do, however, new attorneys must be hired to file motions or appear with the co-parent in court. Like mediation, the information learned in collaborative law is deemed to be confidential and cannot be used in any future litigation. The withdrawal option is rarely used because the disqualification of attorneys and information is a significant disincentive.

In collaborative law, the majority of negotiations take place among the couple and their attorneys at four-way meetings. The attorneys utilize many approaches to resolving conflict, including interdisciplinary teams that include therapists, child specialists, and financial advisors, who act as advisors, neutrals, and specialists in resolving issues (Lande, 2003).

You can provide a service to your client by helping her select a qualified and reasonable divorce attorney. You can advise your client to seek an attorney who is trained in child development, child abuse and neglect, domestic violence, family dynamics, and one or more forms of alternative conflict resolution. A well-qualified divorce attorney should be familiar with high-conflict divorces and how best to minimize conflict between co-parents following a divorce.

What kind of attorney to hire

❖ The Court and Judges

Like attorneys, judges have a role to play in either promoting conflict or reducing conflict during a divorce. For better or worse, judges are part of the adversarial system. This system, as some legal experts have pointed out (Elrod, 2004), is not suited to deal well with the complexities of interpersonal relations when divorcing couples with children are involved.

Judges who are untrained in the dynamics of divorce or child development may make assumptions that have no basis in fact. For instance, judges faced with a high-conflict divorce couple may assume that either or both co-parents are unduly adversarial and fail to make decisions that protect the present or future adjustment of the children. A family court judge may simply tell a couple to settle their differences before coming into her courtroom in the future. However, a judge who sees protecting the children as a high priority may order a couple to seek guidance from a counselor or a program designed to help ensure that the issues over which they have been squabbling are indeed settled before a return to court.

Furthermore, judges may assume that allegations made about the other co-parent are true and may issue tough protective orders that end up damaging relationships between parents and children (Weinstein, 1997).

❖ ❖ ❖ ❖ ❖

Rosanna filed a motion for a restraining order to have Ralph removed from the house because he was threatening her with physical assault unless she dropped her plans to pursue a divorce. The judge scheduled an evidentiary hearing, at which Rosanna and Ralph were given opportunities to bring witnesses or other evidence to help the judge determine whether Ralph should be required to leave the home. During the course of a three-hour hearing, there were no questions or testimony about the impact on the children if Ralph were ordered to live elsewhere.

❖❖❖❖❖

The legal divorce process, as Weinstein (1997) pointed out, can be demeaning for many parents. Divorce hearings are open to the public, and when the process is carried out in court based on a win-lose perspective, co-parents will try to exaggerate each other's flaws. This public display of what is wrong with each other can be embarrassing, and participants — used to dealing with family matters in more private settings — can feel demeaned.

The adversarial system also forces co-parents to put their fate in the hands of judges, many of whom will be undertrained and may well be (as attorneys) overly zealous about protecting the rights of one parent. Instead of having complete control over how a case is settled, parents give up the control. Yet judges are unlikely to know what is best for a family.

On the other hand, often judges and others in the system believe they can do nothing to affect the way some scofflaw parents behave. Instead of imposing sanctions, they may try to ignore such parents or angrily threaten them. However, the power and authority of judges can go a long way in reversing the behavior of parents who push the limits with the court.

❖❖❖❖❖

Raynold failed to attend a court-ordered conflict resolution program, although his co-parent, Beverly, did begin attending the program. When Raynold's absence was brought to the court's attention, the family court judge scheduled a show-cause hearing. Raynold came to the hearing offering transparently flimsy excuses as to why he couldn't attend the conflict resolution program.

"I'm ordering you to spend thirty days in the county jail," the judge announced. "This sentence can be suspended when you decide you will attend this program, which I strongly believe will help you and Beverly resolve some differences."

After serving twenty-four hours, Raynold told his attorney that he would attend the class. "I'll do anything," Raynold said, "just get me out of here."

Raynold did attend the program with Beverly, and they made considerable progress over the next several weeks. "I knew the judge was serious," Raynold later explained. "So I decided to attend and make the most of it. I didn't want to go back to jail."

❖❖❖❖❖

There are a variety of co-parents, like Raynold, who have a sense that they can get away with whatever they want to. They will continue to believe this and act as if their belief is true unless there is a very concrete response from the court. Each time a co-parent is able to manipulate the court, that parent is inclined to take greater liberties in interfering with the other co-parent and the lives of their children.

❖❖❖❖❖

Beth and Rich had been divorced for eight years. Rich and his new wife had custody of Aidan, age 13, and Olivia, age 10. In recent years, Rich had become more angry in his relationship with Beth and he wouldn't allow Beth to call his home. He also didn't allow her to pick the children up at his house, and he frequently made plans that interfered with Beth's parenting time. Despite the fact that the court had ordered phone calls and parenting time, Rich violated the court order for a year. Beth stopped contacting the family court counselors because she felt it did no good.

When the case was assigned to a new family court judge who understood the damage to the children, the judge ordered that Beth be given make-up visits and the right to call whenever she wished. Rich was told in no uncertain terms by the judge that the court would remove custody from him and place the children full time with Beth unless he complied with the court's orders. Consequently, Rich changed his behavior and became grudgingly more cooperative.

❖❖❖❖❖

❖ Timely Identification of High-Conflict Cases

Judges are, of course, part of a court system. And it is that court system that often fails to help parents in custody and parenting disputes. For one thing, few court systems make timely identification of cases that will become high-conflict divorces. If identified early, such cases can be earmarked for high-priority consideration, which might include pretrial conferences or early intervention conferences (Wingspread Conference Report, 2000).

Courts, having identified potentially high-conflict cases, can assign them to family court judges who have demonstrated effectiveness in controlling and providing services to these families. The best services from the most proficient judges focus on the needs of the children as the top priority. These judges will have had specialized education and training in the dynamics of high-conflict divorce and the most effective ways of managing conflict between divorcing couples.

In and out of the courtroom, judges can assist lawyers in maintaining a focus on the best interests of the children and in reducing conflict. Furthermore, judges may reduce conflict by utilizing appropriate sanctions for lawyers who file frivolous or bad faith motions (American Bar Association, 2006). In many high-conflict cases, judges may appoint a *guardian ad litem* for the children, to help ensure that the true best interests of the child are really considered.

As a mental health clinician with experience in working with couples experiencing high conflict, you can be a positive influence in the family court by providing your expertise both in and out of the courtroom. By working on family law tasks forces or meeting with judges, you can advocate for the justice system to coordinate services and use alternative dispute resolution programs. Based on your knowledge of the research on high-conflict divorces and the more effective ways that conflict between divorced couples can be reduced or resolved, you can help the court find the most efficient and effective ways of minimizing post-divorce disputes.

❖ *Psychological Evaluations*

When judges and courts need help in deciding cases, they often turn to the mental health professions for psychological evaluations or therapy. Psychological evaluations and assessments of co-parents can be extremely valuable in helping judges and referees make decisions for families. Sometimes, however, requests for psychological evaluations are simply stall tactics intended to delay a decision. The delay caused by carrying out an order for a psychological evaluation could make things worse because it gives hope and power to the child or to the violating parent. The interference with parenting time also creates a cycle that is difficult to break. Judges who have the training in child development and family dynamics can frequently make quick and powerful decisions without waiting for a psychological assessment and, therefore, substantially reduce conflict and avoid damage to children.

Judges can send the message that the court will not tolerate interference with parent-child relationships and will promptly respond to such interference. Attorneys can reinforce court orders by strongly encouraging their clients to support the parent-child relationship and to obey the court's decisions. Some skilled attorneys we know have told parents that their children need to be spared from any further conflict. These model attorneys refuse to file frivolous motions and recommend that co-parents work out their differences with a therapist or in a dispute resolution program or simply work with each other in appropriate ways to solve problems.

In general, therapists need to avoid being drawn into the adversarial nature that the justice system promotes. As a therapist, you can be a positive influence on judges and courts. You can, when possible, help to educate attorneys and judges. And when you find capable attorneys and judges who are experts in dealing with high-conflict divorce couples, rejoice in working with these competent professionals.

In this chapter, we have been addressing attorneys and judges as much as therapists. However, we think that you can be a positive force in the legal system by setting high standards, educating lawyers and judges — when necessary and appropriate — and by being active in organizations seeking to improve alternative dispute resolution.

In the next chapter, discussion will show how mental health professionals sometimes feed into the system that promotes high conflict when child custody evaluations or psychological assessments are requested.

10

Dysfunction in the Mental Health System: Psychological Assessments

I n the previous chapter, we wrote that the adversarial justice system itself often contributes to the conflict in high-conflict divorces. Unfortunately, the adversarial nature of the legal system has spilled over into the realm of mental health and frequently influences how psychologists, social workers, family therapists, psychiatrists, and other professionals think about conflicted divorces.

This can happen in two primary ways. First, courts frequently refer families for assessments to help the court make informed decisions about what is best for the children. Second, courts may refer individuals or families for counseling or therapy to reduce conflict. In this chapter, we discuss psychological assessment, and in the next chapter we examine families who are referred for mental health treatment.

❖ Who Decides What's Best for the Family?

High-conflict divorces create special and significant problems for decision makers in the judicial system. Who's telling the truth? Who has a mental disorder? Who should have custody of the children? What is a fair and equitable way of resolving this case?

Since the co-parents in a high-conflict divorce can't reach decisions on their own, they turn to others: family court counselors, attorneys, and, ultimately, judges. When these professionals don't have the answer, they look to additional specialists for guidance. The specialists they most often turn to are behavioral health specialists, most frequently psychologists, and the most common referrals are those for comprehensive child custody evaluations (Markan and Weinstock, 2005). Child custody evaluations typically involve assessments of family members to assist the judge in making child custody and parenting time decisions.

While any of a variety of mental health professionals may contribute to the court's evaluation and decisions regarding what's best for the children in a divorce conflict, it is psychologists who are most often called upon for formal psychological evaluations that include testing. Indeed, the late California family court Judge James Stewart, in *The Child Custody Book*, noted that, "In the jurisdictions of which I am aware, only psychologists — Ph.D., Ed.D., or Psy.D. — are recognized by the court as qualified to administer tests" (Stewart, 2000, p. 80). While family therapists, social workers or other professionals may be appointed by the court as custody evaluators, if testing or other formal psychological evaluation is ordered, it is likely that a psychologist will be selected to perform that function. This discussion reflects reality.

❖ *Psychological Assessment: Looking for Magical Answers*

A psychological assessment or evaluation will, it is reasoned, be able to delve into the minds, the thinking, the attitudes, and the behavior of the co-parents and the children. The psychologist and her assessment report, the overwhelming majority of judges and attorneys believe, will provide the impartial information that the court is looking for and will directly address the ultimate issue before the court (Bow and Quinnell, 2004; Tippins and Wittmann, 2005).

While most experienced psychologists have considerable expertise in evaluating people, they don't have the magic that attorneys, counselors, judges, and often the co-parents themselves are looking for to give satisfactory, impartial, definitive — and wise — recommendations that are certain to be accepted by everyone. The reason for this lack of omnipotence is simple. Psychological assessments are invested with more promise than reality can deliver, and these assessments are frequently misused — both by the psychologists themselves and by everyone else involved in the high-conflict divorce.

Psychological testing is usually performed by clinical psychologists trained in diagnosing and treating mental illness and in assessing individuals regarding their mental status, their emotional and intellectual functioning, and their personality characteristics. Psychologists who are specially trained can use psychological tests to provide information regarding these aspects of a person's life. Information gathered during a psychological assessment — which can take anywhere from a couple of hours to several days — is used to make decisions regarding the individual's ability to have custody of or to parent the children.

It's important to realize that not all psychologists are equally trained or qualified to perform custody or parenting time evaluations. In fact, not all psychologists are trained to conduct psychological evaluations. Only a clinical psychologist who has been trained to conduct and interpret various psychological tests, including supervised experience in the administration of such tests, is qualified to give the tests and write an assessment report. While the training of some psychologists prepares them to evaluate individuals in a clinical setting (such as a psychiatric hospital or an outpatient mental health clinic) or in a school setting (for instance, to determine if a child has a learning disability), it's rare that a psychologist has been trained to work in a judicial setting.

The average psychologist is unfamiliar with the adversarial process and has rarely testified in a court hearing of any kind, let alone a custody or parenting-time hearing. Many, if not most, psychologists are unfamiliar and uncomfortable with the idea of giving testimony and dealing with the peculiarities of being an expert witness.

Finally, psychologists trained in testing are capable of administering tests and providing a diagnosis and a treatment plan. As part of this, they can describe the personality of an individual to whom they have given a few tests. However, most psychologists trained in psychological testing are not trained to give a professional opinion about an individual — particularly when such an opinion favors one person over another as in custody evaluations, where a "compare and contrast" effort takes place. While psychologists are often good at finding diagnosable disorders, they have difficulty giving opinions about the future behavior of individuals who have no diagnosable mental illness or significant personality defects (Tippins and Wittmann, 2005).

❖ *What Psychological Testing Can't Do*

When appropriately used, a well-done clinical evaluation can be an effective tool in helping a couple move through the divorce process and come to a resolution about their conflict. It can assist the court in entering custody or parenting time orders by providing unbiased information that outlines what is in the best interests of the children. Such evaluations are complex and must be done by a clinician skilled in the nuances of the adversarial process. Although there are several things a psychological assessment can accomplish, let's consider a significant number of things it cannot do well.

A psychological evaluation can't determine who is telling the truth
Often, attorneys, judges, and either one or both of the co-parents want to find out who is telling the truth.

❖❖❖❖❖

Nick, the divorced father of 7-year-old Matthew, was accused by his co-parent, Vanessa, of inappropriately touching Matthew. Both Nick and Vanessa requested a psychological evaluation — Vanessa to "prove" that Nick was lying when he denied any inappropriate touching of their son and Nick to show that he was telling the truth when he made his denial. In addition, Nick felt that if Vanessa were evaluated, the testing would establish that she "made up" the accusation against him to reduce or eliminate his parenting time with Matthew.

The psychologist assigned to the case explained to Nick and Vanessa and the attorneys involved that a psychological assessment, while perhaps useful in determining the mental stability of the co-parents, couldn't ascertain the truth or veracity of either Vanessa's claims or Nick's denials.

❖❖❖❖❖

A psychological assessment cannot figure out what happened in the past

❖❖❖❖❖

Tami, the mother of 12-year-old Tracey, believed a psychological evaluation would show that Robert, her co-parent, had said things in the past to Tracey that were calculated to turn Tracey against her mother. The judge in the case wanted to know what happened in the past and turned to a court-appointed psychologist to discover what led to Tracey having negative feelings toward her mother.

A psychological evaluation interview can offer clues about whether a child's feelings and attitudes have been influenced by one parent against the other. For instance, if a child uses language that mimics that of a parent or is too adult-like for his age, this information supports but doesn't substantiate alleged alienation attempts. However, you should note that any skilled interviewer with experience in high-conflict cases is capable of drawing the same conclusions with the same degree of accuracy. The testing itself offers no such information.

A psychological assessment alone can't determine if a child has been sexually abused

Frequently, when there have been allegations of sexual assault, sexual abuse, or inappropriate touching, it's thought that a psychological evaluation of the co-parents and the child will reveal whether a parent has sexually abused the child. Unfortunately, this isn't likely to be determined through a psychological testing report. An assessment report may help to shed light on the psychological functioning of family members, but to determine whether a parent has sexually abused his child a team approach is necessary. A team approach involves the police, protective service caseworkers, social service professionals skilled in interviewing sexual abuse victims, and a physician.

A psychological assessment can't say why a co-parenting couple has high conflict

Often, couples engaged in high conflict long after their divorce has ended don't have diagnosable mental disorders. They may be fairly high functioning individuals who go to work every day, get along well with other people, are quite capable of caring for their children, and have never had any criminal behavior. The fact that they are in a high-conflict postdivorce situation doesn't mean they have a disorder that's found in DSM-IV (the American Psychiatric Association's *Diagnostic and Statistical Manual*). They may be angry and embittered, but they aren't necessarily mentally ill, nor do they necessarily have a severe personality disorder. A psychological assessment is a useful tool for determining the presence of symptoms of emotional and psychological disorders. It won't, however, tell why a particular couple continues to do battle after their marriage is over.

A psychological evaluation usually can't say which parent is better suited to have custody of a child

Unless they have received specialized advanced training, psychologists cannot reliably evaluate parenting styles, discipline skills, or the ability of a particular parent to meet a particular child's temperamental and personality needs. It may be easy for any psychologist to make a judgment about a parent's suitability to effectively parent a child if that parent is rigid and inflexible and the child is hyperactive and impulsive. That judgment isn't so easy when there are subtler shades and gradations in the styles and the temperaments of both the parent and the child. Significant advanced training and experience is crucial to sift through these nuances.

❖❖❖❖❖

In the case of R.J. and Anya, it wasn't easy to assess the needs of the children: they made conflicting claims about their suitability to have custody of their children. When they divorced, their two boys were 3 and 5. Anya asked for full custody, and because R.J. was more interested in pursuing his career in the construction business, he agreed. Anya raised the boys and R.J. admitted that he was a part-time weekend and summer father. Ten years later, however, R.J. was a successful contractor who was remarried in a stable relationship. The boys enjoyed their father and he wanted more time with them. He argued that he had enough money to care for them well.

R.J. filed for a change of custody and Anya was angry that he wanted to "waltz back into our kids' lives after I've done all the hard parenting." She was determined that he not have custody of the boys now. She told the court that a change of custody was unfair to her. The court referred the whole family for psychological assessments to help the judge reach a decision. In the report, the psychologist, disregarding the rhetoric on both sides, concluded that the boys and R.J. had a great deal in common. In addition, they wanted to attend a school that would give them the opportunity to be on teams that would enhance their interests and abilities. R.J. lived near a private school that seemed perfect for the boys — and he could afford to send them to the school. Furthermore, the boys had a more easygoing relationship with their father that would allow more opportunities to talk about important issues in their lives. The psychologist recommended that their father be given custody during the school year, given the wide range of subtle variables involved.

❖❖❖❖❖

A further reason psychological assessments may not be appropriate for recommendations regarding the ultimate legal issue (most often: which parent should have custody) is that those kinds of opinions are often based on "best interests of the child" standards. As indicated by Tippins and Wittmann (2005) in the *Family Court Review*, "The best interests standard is a legal and socio-moral construct, not a psychological construct" (p. 215).

As various experts have pointed out, there has been remarkably little research meeting minimal standards of methodological rigor about the effects of various custody arrangements on children and families of different characteristics (Melton et al., 1997; Kraus and Sales, 1999). O'Donohue and Bradley (1999) went even further by calling for a moratorium on all child custody evaluations by psychologists, asserting that mental health professionals may not ethically conduct these evaluations.

What Psychological Testing Can Do

On the other hand, psychological assessment does have an important place in high-conflict divorces.

A psychological assessment can determine if there is a mental disorder with a DSM-IV diagnosis

By using standard psychological assessment tools to complement a thorough clinical interview, a psychologist can determine if someone has a mental disorder. The standard psychological testing instruments most often used include the Wechsler Adult Intelligence Scale-III, the Minnesota Multiphasic Personality Inventory-2, the Millon Clinical Multiaxial Inventory-III, and the Rorschach; other recognized instruments may be used to fit unique requirements. By administering these tests, the psychologist is able to determine if there is a mental disorder that can be diagnosed using the DSM-IV diagnostic categories. (It's worth noting here that experienced and knowledgeable attorneys have been known to attack projective test interpretations during cross-examination in highly contested divorce trials.)

Even if the individual doesn't have a psychiatric diagnosis, a psychologist may be able to ferret out personality characteristics and traits that influence her behavior. Traits that are found to significantly affect behavior in general are likely to have consequences for parenting behavior as well.

A psychological assessment can present unbiased, neutral assessments of both parents

Attorneys in divorce and in high-conflict situations only work for one of the two parents; their job is to present their client in the best possible light. A psychologist asked to evaluate one or more members of the same family should be objective, neutral, and unbiased. By careful administration of the tests and through skillful scoring and interpretation of the results, the psychologist's report and testimony should give the court an objective view of each of the parents and children in a high-conflict family.

A psychological assessment can shed light on the needs of a child

Many times in conflicted postdivorce relationships that feature parents battling over issues that affect the children, the best interests of the children are left out of the process. Attorneys and courts may believe they have the children in mind as they try to reach settlements, yet the children are rarely brought into the courtroom and they seldom have a chance to have their voices heard. That's where a psychological assessment can be helpful.

When conducting a family assessment, the psychologist will often interview the children and report on their statements. Furthermore, by administering appropriate personality tests to the children, the effect of the conflict may be seen in test responses. A comprehensive written report will provide a document for the court on how the children feel and how the discord in the family affects them.

A psychological assessment can determine if there are other significant impairments in either parent

Aside from mental disorders or psychiatric illnesses, parents may have other impairments that would interfere with their ability to parent. We discussed substance abuse in chapter five. However, it is also important to point out that impairments can include intellectual or cognitive limitations as well as brain damage.

Careful administration and interpretation of the Wechsler Adult Intelligence Scale-III, can reveal a parent's intellectual abilities. In some cases, a low IQ or a significant deficit in one or more areas of intellectual functioning may not only have a serious impact on the individual's ability to be a good parent, it may also interfere with the person's ability to understand and cooperate with the other parent and/or to carry out a court-approved co-parenting agreement.

A psychological assessment can serve as a tool
to promote compromise
A competent psychological assessment can become a tool to help co-parents resolve their conflicts. An attorney wishes to represent the desires of her client. However, by pointing to the recommendations and advice that come from a psychologist's report, the attorney may in effect say to her client, "This recommendation is not coming from me; it's coming from an expert and the court is likely to listen to it. I think we have to find a compromise."

The Overuses and Misuses of Psychological Assessments

There are a number of factors that promote both the overuse and the misuse of psychological assessments. For one thing, both judges and attorneys tend to believe that psychological testing uncovers aspects of individuals and situations that can't be determined in other ways. The myth is that psychological testing allows psychologists to look into the minds of people and discover hidden truths about them. Many people believe that psychological testing allows a psychologist to "read an individual's mind."

Psychological testing reports are misused when they are biased and one-sided. Although many assessments will favor one side of a dispute, the truly useful psychological testing report is one that provides recommendations that are neither unfair nor subjective. Useful recommendations always guide the court toward ways of helping parents improve themselves by emphasizing their strengths. When provided with an assessment showing the strengths and assets of each parent, the court is in a better position to help families reunify and balance parenting time.

Psychological evaluations are also misused when parents and attorneys go "psychologist shopping." An attorney or co-parent, unhappy with a previous psychological assessment, may shop around until he finds a psychologist who will write a report favorable to his side. The new psychological assessment is then presented to the court as "scientific proof" that his side is the right one.

Psychological assessments can be overused when they "break the bank." It's expensive to litigate and continually file new motions in court. Likewise, it's expensive to have psychologists evaluate a whole family. It may take many hours to assess each individual in the family, and at a cost of up to two hundred dollars an hour for an assessment (plus additional costs if the psychologist is brought into court as an expert witness), many families will be overburdened.

One parent with greater financial means may also use requests for psychological testing as a way of forcing the other parent to capitulate and grant his wishes because the other parent can't afford to pay for more extensive testing. Given the limitations of psychological testing in high-conflict divorce cases, these burdensome costs may be unjustifiable and courts must be careful before granting requests for psychological evaluations. Mental health professionals should advise the court accordingly.

Although as indicated earlier in this chapter, psychological tools can shed light on people's intellectual abilities and personality characteristics, they can't help as much as many people expect them to in custody or parenting situations. Using "scientifically based" psychological tests doesn't mean that the court will necessarily have a clearer picture of which parent is the most loving, has the greater parenting ability, should have physical custody, or should have more (or less) parenting time.

Psychological assessments may also be misused if the psychologist doesn't follow the guidelines set forth in the *Ethical Guidelines of the American Psychological Association* (APA, 2002). These extensive ethical guidelines state (among other things) that a psychologist shouldn't be used to determine court outcomes if she has a prior relationship with a client. For instance, if the psychologist has been a therapist to one co-parent, it is unethical — except in the most unusual circumstances, such as in remote areas without alternative resources — for that psychologist to undertake the psychological evaluation of the whole family (or of one co-parent) to make custody, visitation, or parenting time recommendations.

(It should be noted that ethical standards of the American Association for Marriage and Family Therapy — AAMFT — the National Association of Social Workers — NASW — and the American Counseling Association — ACA — contain similar provisions.)

The APA's ethical guidelines and the APA's "Guidelines for Child Custody Evaluations in Divorce Proceedings" (APA, 1994) also state that a psychologist performing an evaluation cannot make judgments of people he has not personally assessed. For example, if a psychologist is evaluating the suitability of a mother to be a competent parent, the report can't include "hearsay" comments on the children's father (for example, on his abusive nature), or the mental status of the grandparents, unless the psychologist has personally evaluated everyone involved.

Psychological assessments may be used appropriately to assist in compromises or agreements. An assessment by an experienced psychologist can be used as an objective document that can lead to a new agreement. The competent assessment is a neutral, objective report that offers the recommendations of a qualified third party. In addition, once a report has been issued by the psychologist, both parents are to know what the report will recommend to the court. This information may convince someone who has been unwilling to compromise to negotiate, in view of the fact that the report doesn't recommend that she get what she has asked for.

❖❖❖❖❖

When Jessica asked the court for a change of custody, she claimed horrible wrongdoings on Ira's part. Her request for custody was based completely on her claim that he was mentally ill. When psychological evaluations were completed, the psychologist didn't find that Ira had a diagnosable mental illness or serious personality disturbance that warranted a change of custody. The parenting coordinator who was working with the case was able to use this report to convince Jessica that she was unlikely to obtain a custody change and to instead negotiate for an increase in her parenting time. In order to avoid further expense and conflict,

Ira was amenable to considering an increase in Jessica's parenting time.

❖❖❖❖❖

In summary, there are several things a psychological assessment can provide, as well as several things it can't. Psychological assessments can be misused and overused, causing harm to parents or children involved in high-conflict divorces. In the hands of a competent, experienced, and ethical psychologist, a psychological assessment can be a powerful tool in helping to resolve conflict and reduce arguments between co-parents.

11

The Role of Therapists in High-Conflict Divorces

❖❖❖❖❖

When 6-year-old Sheri was brought to a family therapist by her mother for treatment, the presenting problems were nightmares and anxiety, possibly related to her parents' recent divorce. The therapist, Mary Lynn, frequently treated children with adjustment problems. One of the qualities that made Mary Lynn a successful therapist was her highly sensitive empathy for children. She could immediately see that Sheri had anxieties and fears about abandonment by her parents, whose frequent violent arguments had continued after the divorce. Mary Lynn wanted to protect Sheri from the intensity of her parents' ongoing battle, so she found merit in Sheri's mother's suggestion that limiting Sheri's father's parenting time would help resolve the child's anxieties. After one session with Sheri's father, Mary Lynn wrote a letter to the court recommending that the father's time with Sheri be restricted to one day a weekend with no overnight visits.

❖❖❖❖❖

Mary Lynn's involvement in this high-conflict divorce is not at all unusual. Many therapists are willing to get involved in even the most contentious divorce case if they believe they can be helpful in protecting a vulnerable child. When therapists take this stance, they believe one of their primary roles is as protector of the child. Once a therapist has adopted this position, however, it is difficult for the therapist to see how the child's symptoms play a role in the family conflict.

When a therapist takes sides, as Mary Lynn did, she can become part of the adversarial process, and this may contribute to the conflict between co-parents. When one co-parent — in this example, Sheri's father — is not part of the therapeutic process, that parent is likely to blame the co-parent *and the therapist* for not getting what he feels is right. Rather than being an agent of change for the benefit of everyone involved, the therapist is an advocate for one side over the other.

Sheri's father can, in turn, find a therapist to take his side. This sets the stage for ongoing conflict that could last for several years.

❖ Why Therapists Get Involved in High-Conflict Divorces

Mental health clinicians are said to belong to the "helping professions." Psychologists, social workers, family therapists, counselors, psychiatrists, and other professionals in the field have an ethical responsibility not only to help their clients but also to avoid undue harm to clients and others. But helping professionals, in an effort to provide therapeutic services (or simply to earn a living), take on many difficult cases — including high-conflict divorces and postdivorce families. And when they have such cases, they are likely to become embroiled in the conflict.

❖❖❖❖❖

Jerrod entered treatment because a domestic court judge told him that he needed to get help to deal with his anger. Rather than risk going to jail, Jerrod opted to see a therapist.

Jerrod and Audrey continued to have serious communication problems after they were divorced. Jerrod was frequently late in picking up their 8-year-old son, Jacob. Jerrod blamed everyone but himself for his tardiness, and he always told Audrey it would never happen again — but it always did.

"It's bad enough that you ruin *my* plans when you're late," Audrey told him more than once, "but you don't know the effect it has on Jacob." She described to Jerrod how Jacob would look out the window for him when he was late.

"He gets so anxious, I can't calm him down," Audrey said.

"It's *not* that bad," Jerrod protested. "I usually call you and tell you I'm running late."

"Yes," Audrey agreed, "but then I still have to deal with Jacob's nervousness and his fear that you're not going to show up."

Sometimes these discussions between Jerrod and Audrey got heated, and Jerrod frequently lost his temper. He got so mad once, he slapped Audrey. Another time he pushed her down in front of Jacob. Audrey filed assault charges against Jerrod and, in a pretrial conference, the judge told him he had an anger management problem. The judge threatened him with jail time if he assaulted Audrey again and gave him a choice of a heavy fine or anger management treatment. Jerrod agreed to go to counseling to avoid the fine and possibly jail time in the future.

In treatment, the therapist taught Jerrod various anger management methods. When it was time to return to court to report on his progress, Jerrod asked the therapist to write a letter on his behalf. The therapist wrote that Jerrod seemed to benefit from the skills he was taught. He further wrote that Jerrod should resume regular visits with Jacob by picking him up at Audrey's and keeping him for overnight visits and that he didn't expect that Jerrod would be a threat to Audrey in the future.

Two weeks later, another argument occurred between Jerrod and Audrey and he hit her. Jerrod immediately returned to the therapist trying to explain how Audrey provoked him and asking for help "so I don't lose my parenting time." The therapist wanted to help him and said he could return to treatment.

❖ ❖ ❖ ❖ ❖

Clients like Jerrod who are involved in what Joan Kelly (2003) calls "enduring disputes" present particular challenges for the treating professional. One such challenge is the hostility and aggression some clients manifest. They have difficulty controlling their anger and this causes, or is at least related to, the ongoing disputes.

Another kind of challenge is that a high-conflict divorce may be viewed as one in which there is continual litigation and contacts with the court over unending disputes (Kelly, 2003). When you get involved in these disputes as a mental health professional (whether as child custody evaluator, parenting evaluator, or clinician offering treatment), you are potentially entering a legal realm. You are likely to be drawn into court hearings and legal decisions, and asked to offer evidence as to the stability of a client, his or her relative risk to others, or the change that has come about because of treatment. You may be asked to write letters or to testify as an expert witness to help your client.

A third challenge is that these cases are much more complex than they appear on the surface. When divorce cases, especially those with continual disputes, are processed in the family court, there is an appearance that these cases are simple and can be decided by a judge with the input of experts, such as those in the mental health professions. But cases in which there are ongoing conflicts and battles are more complex psychologically and socially than other types of cases you might treat. And no matter how well you treat an individual or family, resolution of the legal case often does little to improve or resolve the underlying family dynamics (Firestone and Weinstein, 2004).

As a therapist or counselor, you may well find yourself in an ethical bind. Do you provide treatment when you are relatively sure you can help relieve the emotional distress of a child, parent, or family? Or do you refuse to get involved in such difficult cases, recognizing that you may well be asked — or required by the court — to provide expert testimony that could compromise your obligations to your client or to your profession?

❖ *Professional Ethics for Therapists*

The ethical guidelines of the American Psychological Association, the American Association for Marriage and Family Therapy, the National Association of Social Workers, and the American Counseling Association are straightforward about a clinician's ethical stance (AAMFT Code of Ethics, 2001; NASW Code of Ethics, 1999; ACA Code of Ethics, 2005). For instance, Principle A of the APA document includes the following statement: "Psychologists strive to benefit those with whom they work and take care to do no harm" (APA, 2002, p. 4).

Given this ethical principle, when treating an individual involved in a high-conflict divorce it is necessary to be very clear about what you can and can't do. For example, you cannot undertake treatment in order to later testify for or against that person. But what if your client is a child, brought to treatment by a legitimately worried or concerned parent who later asks you to testify in a hearing to restrict the parenting time of the other parent?

It is almost certain that if you are conducting a custody evaluation or a parenting competency assessment, you are going to be pressured by someone — co-parents or their attorneys or the courts — to make a recommendation for or against one or another of the parents. You may, as we discussed in chapter ten, make every effort to maintain your neutrality and objectivity, yet this is very difficult to do. This will be especially true if your client is a child in a high-conflict divorce or if you are a therapist who isn't experienced with high-conflict divorces and how parents (and attorneys) in these struggles interact.

It becomes very easy to be sympathetic to a loving parent's concerns about his child's nightmares, anxieties, or inappropriate behaviors. Rather than trying to resolve problems with the other parent or understand the behavior in its context, you may become an advocate for limiting the child's involvement with the other parent until the child "works through her feelings."

❖ ❖ ❖ ❖ ❖

For instance, in the matter of 6-year-old Sheri, Mary Lynn was drawn into the situation by acceding to the mother's request to limit Sheri's father's parenting time. Mary Lynn wanted to advocate for her client but violated the code of ethics of marriage and family therapists by, in effect, conducting a forensic evaluation of the father without his knowledge or consent. After interviewing him, she wrote a letter to the court advising that the father's parenting time be restricted. This violated ethical principle 3.14 (AAMFT Code of Ethics, 2001).

❖ ❖ ❖ ❖ ❖

❖ *Therapist for Hire*

With the number of divorce cases, and with so many of them involving children, it's easy for a therapist to become a "hired gun." That is, if you present well and do well on the witness stand as an expert witness, you could become the therapist who is always available to find "psychological evidence" to support the side that hires you.

However, professional ethical standards prohibit you from doing this. For instance, the ethical principles of psychologists calls for psychologists to establish relationships of trust with those with whom they work. Furthermore, the APA principles declare that psychologists are to be aware of the professional and scientific responsibilities to society (APA, 2002, Principle B). Yet, we know that there are many mental health professionals, including psychologists, who make a comfortable living by testifying for whoever pays them. Although you are certainly entitled to testify on behalf of a client, you also have an obligation to do your job with responsibility and integrity.

❖❖❖❖❖

Marvin, a Midwestern psychologist, was deemed an expert in certain psychological assessment instruments, such as the MMPI-2. Marvin was frequently hired throughout the Midwest to evaluate a child or parent and testify as an expert witness for that side in court. For his time as an evaluator and expert witness, parents paid as much as ten thousand dollars.

❖❖❖❖❖

On the other hand, ethical therapists who are not for hire to support one side against the other view themselves as professionals who are trying to meet the needs of families and supporting responsible co-parenting.

❖❖❖❖❖

Raquel was such a therapist. She treated Sarah, an adorable 10-year-old girl whose parents had recently divorced. During the divorce, there had been an argument in which her father shoved her mother who fell and was hurt. Sarah hadn't witnessed the incident but had been told about it in detail and had been taken to a local abuse facility for intervention. At the time she came to treatment with Raquel, Sarah refused to stay overnight with her father, cried before visits with him, and called her mother constantly during those visits. Sarah was angry with her father for hurting her mother, complained of him yelling at her and leaving her alone when she was spending time at his apartment, and stated that she was afraid of him.

Sarah's mother hated her former husband and believed it was in Sarah's best interest that she not have any contact with him. Although this mother didn't regularly say bad things about him to Sarah, her feelings of disgust were hard to mask. Sarah's father wasn't sensitive to his daughter's feelings and needs and was rather gruff at times. However, he truly loved his daughter and felt bad about the physical incident with his ex-wife.

Raquel brought both Sarah's mother and father into treatment and frequently saw Sarah and her father together. Raquel observed that Sarah never seemed afraid of her father in therapy sessions. In fact, she was quite rude and confrontational at times. Her father apologized numerous times and repeatedly asked what he could do differently. In one session, Sarah got so worked up about going with her dad after therapy that she threw up in the wastebasket.

By going to a family therapist who was concerned about the whole family, the focus with Sarah was on healing rather than choosing sides. Raquel didn't ignore the father's abusive action but dealt with it as one incident in a volatile divorce rather than labeling him as an abuser. The father apologized to Sarah's mother, and he was taught to be more sensitive to Sarah's needs. In fact, both parents had to be taught how to stop reacting to each other and to Sarah. As Sarah's mother became resigned to Sarah spending time with her father, she became less angry. Sarah, in turn, ended up being able to spend the night with her father without problems.

❖ ❖ ❖ ❖ ❖

This treatment was successful because Raquel involved both parents along with the child. It's very important to involve both parents in therapy to minimize the risk of the therapist becoming part of an unhealthy adversarial system. As a professional working with families where there is high conflict, you have an obligation to get to know both parents before determining how to proceed with treatment. Knowing the other parent is even more critical when making recommendations to the court in regard to matters concerning the co-parent who is not your client.

Therapist Shopping

Therapists run the risk of being "fired" when clients engage in what might be called "therapist shopping." The co-parents in a high-conflict divorce each may go from one therapist to another to find one who supports their point of view. You can avoid this if you make it clear at the beginning of treatment how you deal with families when there are ongoing and intense disputes.

❖ ❖ ❖ ❖ ❖

Dina was a 12-year-old girl whose parents were in a hotly contested divorce for three years. During that time Dina decided that she no longer wanted to see her mother at all. The court ordered her to be taken to treatment by her father, Herb.

In the initial interviews with the therapist, Dina was quite pleasant and charming. She was a good student, had many friends, and was involved in sports and extracurricular activities. However, Dina had a long list of complaints about her mother, who had been sick for the past year, and Dina showed no empathy for her mother's illness. When her mother, Vivian, came in for an appointment, she acknowledged some conflicts but had a very different picture of their relationship. Vivian remembered baking cookies together, going on outings, helping out with Girl Scouts, and volunteering in her classroom at school. Dina remembered none of those things.

In his first interview, Herb stated that he was just trying to support his daughter in what she felt she needed. Herb was careful to say all the right things about children needing their parents, while at the same time relating his belief that Vivian was a liar and was unable to put Dina's needs before her own.

When Dina was told that therapy would focus on improving her relationship with her mother, Dina became angry. A few sessions later, Herb called to say Dina no longer wanted to come to therapy. It was clear to the therapist that both Dina and her father were seeking a therapist to support their point of view. When the therapist challenged their thinking, they refused to come back.

❖ ❖ ❖ ❖ ❖

Perhaps no therapist could have avoided this abrupt termination of treatment. However, by making the intent of therapy crystal clear from the beginning, in front of the whole family, it might make it easier for everyone to accept therapy.

❖ Be Aware of Your Opinions and Personal Judgments

As we pointed out in the last chapter, there are potentially significant problems associated with using clinical interviews and psychological tests to assess children and their parents in child custody and parenting fitness or competency evaluations (Tippins and Wittmann, 2005). Similarly, there is scant empirical literature that will provide the scientific basis for therapists to appear in court as expert witnesses or write reports to courts making recommendations in the areas of custody, parenting time, or parental adequacy (O'Donohue and Bradley, 1999; Tippins and Wittmann, 2005). No matter how long you've been treating a child or one or both parents, you cannot make any such pronouncements with the backing of good psychological evidence. In effect, if you do that, you are violating your professional ethical guidelines (note APA ethical principle 9.01) and you are going well beyond what you can say with scientific certainty.

You can give your opinions and your personal judgments and, if allowed, discuss your values and morals. If you are allowed to talk about your personal opinions, you have to be sensitive to how your own values influence the recommendations you are making. Any opinions you give should be based on sound clinical judgment and on the facts of the case as well as on any scientific evidence — if it exists.

As you consider what you should do in treating individuals or families involved in high-conflict divorce, here are several points to remember:

❖ One of the recommendations of the Wingspread Conference (Wingspread, 2000) is that mental health professionals *make every effort to obtain permission from both parents* to treat a child in a high-conflict divorce. If you can't obtain such permission, you should only agree to treat that child if there is a court order mandating such treatment. (The Wingspread Conference was sponsored by the American Bar Association and held in Racine, Wisconsin in 2000. The goal of this interdisciplinary, international conference was to develop recommendations for changes in the legal and mental health systems to reduce the impact of high-conflict custody cases on children.)

❖ Always, when a child is brought to you, *try to determine if there is a custody dispute* or ongoing conflict between co-parents. That way you will be able to request permissions and discuss what your ethical guidelines will or will not allow.

❖ *Privileged information, even about a child, should not be shared with attorneys.* If there is a therapeutic reason to share information with attorneys or the court, there should be releases of information signed by both parents and the child should be aware of whom you are talking with and why.

❖ *Always be aware of the possible negative impact of your testimony* in court on your client and other family members

(Wingspread, 2000). In any testimony, be clear about your ethical responsibilities and be clear to yourself and the court as to the lack of knowledge or information that prohibits you from giving specific custody or parenting time recommendations.

❖ *Avoid comparing the parents, do not make pronouncements about a parent you have not met, and stay clear of stating how a child will react* to custody or parenting time arrangements. Remember, there is little or no research to back up these kinds of recommendations.

It's rare to find a situation where either person is blameless. Blaming usually results in the conflict between parents getting worse rather than better. Looking at the entire system and its interactions, we can intervene to change the pattern without assigning blame. Each parent only has control over his own behavior and his own responses to his co-parent. We can make a positive difference in the resolution of the conflict by encouraging each parent to respond differently, no matter how the other parent behaves.

Part IV

Making Changes in High-Conflict Divorces

Which Interventions Work and Which Don't?

W hen you confront the most difficult and intractable cases of co-parent fighting and hostility, you'll have the same nagging questions and concerns as many professionals who work with this tough population:

- ❖ Are high-conflict divorces a new epidemic in American culture?
- ❖ How should you treat families in high-conflict divorces?
- ❖ Does anything really work with high-conflict divorce couples?
- ❖ Is it even worth trying to treat couples in high-conflict divorces?

We believe the number of high-conflict divorces in the United States *is* growing, and it is of the utmost importance that we try to help these couples because of the profound negative impact their conflict has on their children. What can we, as therapists and counselors, do?

❖ High-Conflict Treatment Services

At one time it seemed that any literature review of treatment options would have to conclude that the options were simply a fractured grouping of services designed for treating almost everything *except* high-conflict divorce. For instance, it was relatively easy to locate treatment services for such conditions as mental illness, criminal behavior, poor parenting, alcohol and drug problems, and children's fears and symptoms. There have been excellent clinics that specialized in treating children with Attention

155

Deficit Hyperactivity Disorder, therapists who specialized in working with gays and the problems they face, and counselors who were experts in diagnosing and treating postpartum depression. But you would look in vain for the clinics and specialists who boldly advertised themselves as experts in treating couples who were in a high-conflict postdivorce relationship.

Yet the need for such services became evident as early as the 1980s. During the late 1980s and into the 1990s courts began to develop programs to meet the needs of frustrated judges, court counselors, and co-parenting couples.

Part IV of this book is about the variety of programs and treatment services that have developed over the past two decades to treat high-conflict divorce couples. In this last section of the book, we give you an overview of the various types of intervention programs and approaches you can find these days (chapter twelve). Then, we describe three approaches in much more detail. In chapter thirteen, we describe mediation. In chapter fourteen, parent coordination as an intervention for high-conflict divorces is discussed. Chapter fifteen describes in considerable detail a court-based psychoeducational program that presents an excellent example of a successful high-conflict group treatment approach. Finally, in chapter sixteen, we talk about the treatment team approach, an intervention developed in a Michigan clinic.

Court Programs to Treat and Prevent High-Conflict Divorce

Courts don't typically have one, standard approach to dealing with high-conflict divorces. Instead, family courts throughout the United States have instituted counseling and therapeutic programs, parent education classes, and mediation programs to help reduce the conflict in ongoing postdivorce disputes. The different kinds of interventions that have developed in this country have arisen out of the needs of courts, judges, and attorneys as well as the experience and clinical expertise of therapists and counselors. Both mediation and parent education programs seem to predominate in court systems. Divorce mediation has been viewed since the 1980s as a promising alternative to the more traditional courtroom method of resolving issues between two co-parents engaged in hostile conflict. However, with concern about the increasing number of high-conflict divorces, courts have turned to interventions that range from divorce education plans to intensive co-parent counseling, therapeutic programs, and binding arbitration.

There are, however, five types of interventions for divorced families and high-conflict postdivorce couples that have been most commonly used:

1. Parenting Education Programs
2. Mediation and Counseling Programs
3. Skill-Building and Psychological Treatment Programs
4. Parent Coordination and Arbitration
5. Supervised Visitation and Monitored Exchange Programs

Parenting education programs have sprung up around the country in response to the growing number of divorce cases seen in family and juvenile courts. One study in 1996 found that there were over 500 parent education programs in forty-four states (Ellis, 2000). Some of these programs were court mandated, while others were voluntary. The majority of these parenting education programs are one session in length and generally last no more than four hours.

A typical educational program features speakers, specialty videos, and literature handouts. All aspects of such programs, including speakers, videos, and handouts, usually are aimed at getting across one important message: That it's important for co-parents to work together for the sake of the children. To date, there has been only limited research on the effectiveness of such short-term educational programs (Ellis, 2000). However, it appears that educational programs do influence those co-parents who are inclined to be cooperative after divorce.

❖❖❖❖❖

Kim and Ron had just divorced after an eight-year marriage and three children. They got caught up in the adversarial nature of the divorce proceedings and they argued bitterly over custody, parenting time, and financial support. They were able to finally come to an agreement on their major issues, and they appeared in court where the judge signed a divorce decree.

Within two weeks following the settlement of their divorce, they received letters in the mail from the family court directing them to attend a divorce education program. Before the evening when they were scheduled to attend, they checked with each other to see if both were planning to attend. Kim said she was planning to attend. "It's inconvenient, because it's on the night I have parenting time," Ron told her, "but I'll get a baby-sitter and come."

In the two-hour program they attended, a family court judge spoke about the importance of parents working together and a video was shown depicting the devastating effect on children when divorced parents couldn't get along. Following the video, a social worker reinforced the message that parents need to get along to protect the mental health of their children.

After a question and answer session, Ron and Kim saw each other at a table in the back of the auditorium where they both picked up literature on parenting after divorce.

"Let's walk out together," Kim suggested to him.

As they walked to the parking lot, Kim said the program helped her realize how important their working together as parents would be for the future of their children.

"I know," Ron said. "I get pretty angry with you sometimes, but we shouldn't let that stop us from being good parents."

"You're right," Kim said. "Our kids are too important to both of us to mess them up over our problems with each other."

"I guess when you think about their happiness and their lives," Ron said, "nothing we have to argue about is really that important."

"No, not really" Kim said. "I'll really try if you will."

Ron and Kim were able to put aside their emotions and their differences for the sake of their children. The educational program they attended had opened their eyes to how much damage their arguing could cause to their children. Although there's no way to know, Ron and Kim might have come to an amiable reconciliation of their differences anyway. A short-term educational program would have been less likely to have any significant effect on Ron and Kim if they had been co-parents who were experiencing high levels of conflict.

❖ ❖ ❖ ❖ ❖

Many courts offer some type of parent education class for divorcing parents. The intent is to educate parents about the dangers of conflict following divorce and the specific harm to children of high conflict. Critics of short-term parent education programs contend that they aren't educational because they don't help divorcing parents learn new skills or practice any skills that will help them to deal with each other in more cooperative ways.

However, for some parents, hearing professionals talk about the dangers of ongoing conflict is sufficient to bring about a more cooperative relationship.

❖ Mediation and Counseling Programs

Mediation is such a key resource in dealing with high-conflict situations that we have given it a chapter of its own: chapter 13.

Community-based programs for high-conflict divorces are almost exclusively counseling and therapy sessions offered by a range of mental health professionals, including family therapists, social workers, psychologists, psychiatrists, and counselors. Such programs are offered on an individual or family basis. Since there has been little or no research on therapy with co-parents involved in a high-conflict divorce, there is no generally agreed upon approach to treating them.

Articles reporting on counseling and therapy models most often focus on clinical issues related to grief, hostility, divorce, and child adjustment. Doing therapy with high-conflict couples with children requires clinicians with sophisticated skills and experience, and it's difficult to find models for treating high-conflict divorces that can be used by a variety of clinicians effectively. In chapters fourteen, fifteen, and sixteen we offer specific programs, techniques, and interventions that we've found effective in helping high-conflict postdivorce relationships.

❖ Skill-Building and Psychological Programs

More specialized educational programs are often used to teach co-parents about the psychological effects of conflicts on children and to help them learn better communication skills. These skill-building classes may use exercises and role-playing to teach effective communication and problem-solving techniques.

While short-term programs don't tend to show as many positive effects as do longer-term programs, brief interventions often lead to indirect results because of referrals and links to other community resources. Family counseling programs using trained facilitators and therapists seem, however, to show better outcomes for couples experiencing problems related to divorce. Wallerstein and her colleagues (1985), as early as 1985, tested a number of counseling and therapy programs and concluded that many were useful for children. Unfortunately, there have been few attempts in the psychological literature to identify the level of conflict in families and determine how various therapeutic programs help parents to resolve conflict. While there is little or no reliable information about the number of courts that utilize referrals to family counselors or to private groups, researchers believe that programs that invite parents to participate through role play, interactive discussion, and skill-building activities have an enhanced opportunity to reduce conflict (Kramer et al., 1998).

Other psychological or therapeutic programs deal directly with the psychological factors that lock co-parents into ongoing conflicts and disputes. *Impasse-directed mediation* is among these types of programs. This approach, reported by Johnson and Roseby (1997), differs from regular mediation in three significant ways. First, this approach brings together therapy and mediation. The idea is to deal with some of the underlying emotional factors that have led to the bitter conflict and to resolve this conflict so co-parents can work more effectively together. Second, because co-parents involved in serious and prolonged dispute often fail to protect their children from the conflict, the approach is directed at helping co-parents better understand children's needs and then to teach them to be more protective and helpful to their children. Third, this approach doesn't concentrate on developing a specific plan to solve the problems. Rather, it focuses on helping to build a structure and a way of working together that will allow the family to move forward in dealing with the postdivorce transition.

In chapters fifteen and sixteen, we consider related approaches that involve longer programs designed to change communication patterns and skill building.

❖ *Parent Coordination and Arbitration*

When co-parents are so entrenched in their conflicts that all other attempts to intervene have failed, the court may have no choice but to refer them to a parent coordinator or an arbitration program. Parents who are in high-conflict postdivorce situations have often attended educational programs without effect, been unsuccessful in counseling or therapy, or refused to engage in meaningful mediation sessions. The court will often then appoint a person, sometimes called a *special master, parenting coordinator, family court advisor,* or *custody commissioner,* whose job it is to manage the conflicts and disputes. These specialists may use their authority to make recommendations both to the family and to the court. Because of the role parent coordinators play, they are often referred to as *co-parent arbitrators.* However, the title of parent coordinator has taken on a life of its own and has come to describe a discrete area of clinical practice regardless of whether a court has appointed a therapist to this role. When parent coordination is conducted privately, the professional chooses whether to accept binding authority from the court or maintain his neutrality in a purely therapeutic fashion. In chapter fourteen, we discuss parent coordination as a therapeutic practice approach.

There are two models of parent coordinator or co-parent arbitrator commonly used. In one model, the co-parent arbitrator is called on to play a role only when parents can't solve a specific problem or conflict. In the second model, the coordinator or arbitrator acts as a counselor, mediator, or family therapist. However, both models include the function of helping co-parents to carry out a parenting plan or solve conflicts related to parenting.

In some states, including Michigan, Friend of the Court offices have been created by state statute. Friend of the Court counselors, who are employed by each county throughout the state to work with family courts, have the authority to ensure compliance with court orders related to parenting time, child support, and custody. The Friend of the Court counselors act as mediators, parent coordinators, and family therapists. Because of their high caseloads, if Friend of the Court counselors are unable to bring about agreement in a relatively short time, they commonly refer the feuding co-parents to a private practitioner or community agency for the ongoing provision of parent coordination or family therapy. If co-parents don't follow court orders, the Friend of the Court counselor can begin civil hearings in which one or both co-parents could be found in contempt of the court.

❖ *Supervised Visitation and Monitored Exchange Programs*

When there has been ongoing high conflict as well as threatened violence, domestic violence, or abuse, the court can order supervised visitation for one or both parents. The visitation and parenting time can be supervised in a therapist's office, at an agency providing this service, or in the presence of a guardian ad litem who is appointed to represent the interests of the child. Often, too, when there is domestic violence and assault, the exchange of children for parenting time may take place at a police department or in a situation where both co-parents feel safe.

❖❖❖❖❖

Curtis and Vanna had such a stormy and violent relationship with each other that the court ordered that they exchange the children for parenting time in the parking lot of the local police department. The police department was aware of this arrangement and made sure an on-duty police officer was monitoring the exchange of children. This supervision reduced the threat of domestic violence accusations between them.

❖❖❖❖❖

Supervised parenting time exchanges and supervised visitation may be appropriate when there is ongoing high conflict and domestic violence. It is also appropriate when there is parental substance abuse, fears about child abduction, and concerns about the safety of either co-parent or the children.

In examining the variety of high-conflict divorce programs and treatment services that have developed in recent years, we've presented only an overview in this chapter. In the following three chapters, we describe three important approaches in much more detail. Our focus in the next chapter will be on the popular and often effective process of *mediation*.

Mediation

Mediation was first used in the early 1980s in California (AFCC, 2006). Since then, attempts to settle disputes outside of the courts have grown throughout the United States. In mediation, a third party, usually an attorney or therapist trained in mediation work, attempts to help co-parents reduce conflict and increase cooperation. Although having similarities to family counseling, mediation usually lasts from one to five sessions and attempts to resolve issues through compromise. A mediator has no authority to force an agreement or resolution; however, the process — in the hands of a skilled and experienced mediator — can be useful in helping parents resolve some tough issues and come to lasting agreements (Emery, Sbarra, and Grover, 2005). Depending on the co-parenting couple and their particular issues, mediation is likely to focus on the following topics:

❖ Custody and visitation of children
❖ Division of property or assets
❖ Spousal maintenance or alimony
❖ Child support

Studies have found that success rates for co-parents who accept mediation is between fifty and eighty percent, especially when the parents have custody or parenting time issues (Kelly, 1996; Johnston and Roseby, 1997; Emery, Sbarra, and Grover, 2005). Mediators usually focus on the needs of the children while promoting communication and compromise between the co-parents.

❖ How Mediation Works

❖❖❖❖❖

Elaine and Ruben couldn't work out a parenting time arrangement that they could both agree on. Elaine thought that since she had been the primary caregiver during the eleven years of their marriage, she should have full physical custody and Ruben should be limited to spending time with their two children only every other weekend.

Ruben disagreed. He contended that he had been a hard-working husband and father who spent less time with the children only because Elaine was a stay-at-home mother. Following their divorce, Ruben wanted equal time with the children. Elaine said that a fifty-fifty custody arrangement would be unfair to her and would be disruptive to the children.

After their attorneys and the special family counselors for the court tried unsuccessfully to help Ruben and Elaine reach a settlement on the issue of custody and parenting time, the judge ordered them to attend mediation. In consultation with their attorneys, Ruben and Elaine were able to agree on a private mediator. Abe was both an attorney and a psychologist who had been trained and certified as a mediator.

In the beginning of the mediation session, Abe explained that he had no authority to make a decision or to recommend to the judge what should happen. His job, he explained, was to help Elaine and Ruben find their own solution to their dispute.

"I'm prepared to stay here all day and help you work out this problem," Abe said, "so we are under no time pressure. As long as our efforts are productive, we'll stay here until we have an acceptable agreement." Abe then said they would begin by having Ruben and Elaine each give an opening statement that reflected their individual points of view. He then set some ground rules.

"While one of you is talking, the other will be respectful and listen without interrupting," Abe said. "Is that understood?" Elaine and Ruben both indicated they understood. "After you both have a chance to present your positions," Abe said, "we will begin discussion. You can say anything you like to counter what the other person said, to present evidence on your own behalf, or to dispute a position. But one thing I won't allow is for you to swear or be disrespectful to each other. Understood?" Again, both Ruben and Elaine nodded in agreement.

Ruben allowed Elaine to talk first and she presented her position, telling how she had loved and cared for their children and how Ruben was an "absentee" father. She said that her devotion to her children entitled her to have full-time, exclusive custody and that Ruben should have limited parenting time. When Elaine finished, Abe asked her a few questions to clarify a couple of points. Then Abe indicated that Ruben could present his side. He told about his own love for the children and how he thought that working hard and providing a good living was what a father should do. He said that he wanted a fifty-fifty custody arrangement that would give him time to be a better father than perhaps he had been in the past. Again, Abe asked a few questions to understand Ruben's position better.

When both were finished with their opening statements, Abe summarized their positions and the issue as he saw it. Elaine and Ruben agreed that it was a narrow issue: should the custody arrangement be equal or should Elaine be given more time with the children?

Abe then asked them to consider all their options. He requested that they make a list of all the custody options they could think of. Together, Elaine, Ruben, and Abe made a comprehensive list of all the options they had ever heard of or considered. When they were finished, Abe asked them to go over each option, one by one, talking about the pros and cons of each.

When they had thoroughly discussed the pros and cons of each option, Abe summarized what he heard them saying. He helped them eliminate some obvious options that both saw as having too many disadvantages. When they'd narrowed down the options, he directed them both to talk about their feelings about the remaining options. After each emotional statement, he requested the other to reflect back what he or she heard the co-parent say. When this had been accomplished, Elaine and Ruben seemed to have an understanding of what each thought and felt about the possible custody arrangements. Abe then talked about negotiation and compromise.

"I hate to be the bearer of bad news," Abe said, "But neither of you can get everything you want in this negotiation. You are both going to have to compromise. However, keep in mind that this is for the welfare of your children. When you negotiate here and each of you gives up some part of what you came here today expecting to get, think about how giving a little will help to benefit your children in the long run."

Abe then asked them to each suggest a compromise solution that would be best for their children. "I know Elaine is a really good mother," Ruben said, "and I know the children love her. I would suggest that maybe she should have a little more time with the kids than me."

"I have to admit," Elaine said, "that I never doubted that Ruben loved the children. I see the way he wants them to be happy and successful. The children enjoy being around him because he likes to keep them busy. I think they deserve to spend time with him. Maybe more than I was willing to allow before."

As they each proposed compromise solutions, Abe pressed them for more details about a custody plan. When each had compromised as much as they felt they could, Abe said that he thought they were very close to an agreement in principle. He said he would prepare a draft of their basic agreement and meet with them in a week to go over the details and to deal with any aspects of it that were left unsettled.

A week later, Ruben and Elaine met with Abe and finalized a custody agreement that divided parenting time such that Elaine would have about three-quarters and Ruben one-quarter of the children's week. Both signed the final agreement, and Abe sent it to the court. Elaine and Ruben were able to maintain the agreement with minimal problems.

❖ ❖ ❖ ❖ ❖

In contrast to the adversarial approach, where co-parents view themselves as winners or losers, in mediation both parents are more likely to report themselves as "winners" (Emery, Matthews, and Kitzman, 1994; Kelly, 1996). Research has shown that co-parents settled their disputes in about half the time when assigned to mediation versus the traditional adversary settlement (Emery, Sbarra, and Grover, 2005).

❖ *Mediation Is Not for Every High-Conflict Case*

Often mediators refuse high-conflict cases because of the seriousness of the claims each is making against the other (e.g., violence, substance abuse, sexual abuse, etc.). Those co-parents who have been locked in a heated battle who do attempt mediation often withdraw early or fail to reach agreements in mediation and relitigate following mediation.

❖ ❖ ❖ ❖ ❖

Warren and Wanda met with a mediator over medical bills. Wanda accused Warren of never helping with medical bills as he was court-ordered in their divorce decree. Warren flatly denied this. However, he contended that what Wanda saw as medical bills — like a large orthodontia bill for their daughter — were "frivolous" expenses that Wanda had never discussed with Warren ahead of time.

In mediation, the rancor and hostility was so prevalent that carrying on a rational discussion was nearly impossible. Wanda angrily accused Warren of "lying through his teeth." He said that she was such a vindictive "witch" that he couldn't stand being in the same room with her. After two sessions in which the arguing continued unabated, the skilled mediator (similar to Abe) said that he didn't see how they were going to be able to reach an agreement. He sent a report to the court stating that mediation did not seem appropriate "at this time."

❖ ❖ ❖ ❖ ❖

Successful mediation requires that both parents be able to participate effectively. If either individual is so impaired psychologically or emotionally that she or he is unable to discuss the divorce rationally, mediation is likely to be ineffective.

❖ ❖ ❖ ❖ ❖

Scott and Michelle were both angry, and while Scott could control himself at times, Michelle said provocative things that incited Scott's anger and set the tone for both of them to hurl recriminations at each other.

❖ ❖ ❖ ❖ ❖

On the other hand, co-parents don't have to like each other or talk to each other outside of the mediation sessions. Parents who have successfully mediated their disputes are often still dissatisfied with each other — they have simply found solutions to difficult problems. When disagreements are mediated, an agreement is written up by the mediator, approved and signed by the co-parents, and submitted to the court. Attorneys may or may not be involved in this process.

❖ *Court-Sponsored and Private Mediation*

There are two basic and very different types of divorce mediation offered throughout the country today: court-sponsored mediation and private mediation (Lovenheim, 1996). Court-sponsored mediation is offered in a majority of states where courts can require co-parents to mediate issues related to divorce or care and custody of the children. Most court-sponsored mediation is of short duration, lasting just one or two sessions. When mediation is court sponsored, it's either free or provided at minimal cost. Mediators might be court employees or attorneys appointed by the courts as mediators.

In private mediation, co-parenting couples retain the services of a mediator of their own choosing. The couple can also choose whether they wish to mediate all of the issues that divide them or whether they prefer to deal with just a few issues. A half dozen or more lengthy sessions may be required, depending on the number and complexity of the issues being addressed. Fees for private mediation vary widely, but they can range from fifty dollars an hour to well over three hundred dollars an hour, as this is written. Private mediators may be attorneys, mental health professionals, or a co-mediation team of an attorney and a mental health professional.

❖ *Family Adjustment Following Mediation*

Research has demonstrated that reduced parental conflict following mediation is associated with children's improved psychological adjustment more than a year following the settlement of disputes (Kitzman and Emery, 1994).

Some advocates of mediation (such as Emery, Sbarra, and Grover, 2005) believe that even a short experience with mediation helps high-conflict families take the long view of their families. That is, parents engaged in high conflict who are exposed to mediation are able to see that if they learn to cooperate with each other, in the long run their children will be much better off.

Parent Coordination for High-Conflict Divorces

When two people have dissolved their marriage but continue to fight, thus exposing their children to ongoing conflict, they need help in managing their co-parenting relationship. That's where a parenting coordinator can be helpful.

Parent coordinators are specially trained and experienced professionals who provide a specific type of dispute resolution service to parents who have been unsuccessful in reducing their conflict.

❖ ❖ ❖ ❖ ❖

For example, Marta and Gregor had been divorced for three years, which is generally sufficient time for couples to settle into a pattern of co-parenting in which they avoid hostile confrontations and no longer have acrimonious arguments. However, that wasn't possible for Marta and Gregor, the parents of four children.

Marta was angry that Gregor filed for the divorce, even though she agreed that they had a destructive relationship. She was determined to make him suffer for abandoning her with the children. Marta vowed that she would make it difficult for him to have a relationship with his children. She first tried to undermine every attempt at reaching an agreement on parenting time. When the court stepped in and ordered a parenting time schedule, Marta failed to abide by it — often scheduling the children for activities during Gregor's parenting time, so that when Gregor arrived to pick them up the children would be gone.

Gregor, in turn, was angry at Marta. Not just because she interfered with his efforts to be an involved father, but because he saw her as the reason he had to file for a divorce in the first place. He said she was impossible to live with and her anger and moodiness were the reasons for the divorce. He said he feared for the safety and well-being of the children if they remained with her. He accused her of trying to turn the children against him. And he wrote letters to the court stating that she had men staying overnight in the home and that the children were exposed to inappropriate sexual situations.

During the divorce, the court ordered Gregor and Marta to go to mediation to settle their disputes. After two lengthy mediation sessions, the mediator reported to the court that the couple could not reach any agreements. They were then sent for psychological evaluations and then to another psychologist for therapy. Despite the efforts of the therapist, Marta and Gregor's volatile relationship, their accusations toward each other, and the extreme bitterness they manifested in therapy sessions led the therapist to conclude that change was unlikely.

The court's next step was to mandate that this difficult high-conflict couple go to a parenting coordinator, an experienced professional who worked with co-parents with high-conflict postdivorce relationships.

❖❖❖❖❖

What Is Parent Coordination?

Parent coordination is a form of dispute resolution that goes beyond mediation, psychotherapy, and other forms of resolving conflicts between co-parents (Boylan and Termini, 2005). It's often referred to as a child-focused alternative conflict resolution process that's centered around the formulation and implementation of a parenting plan (AFCC Task Force on Parenting Coordination, 2006).

Johnston and Roseby (1997) described parent coordination as an approach that provides highly conflicted families with an appointed co-parenting coordinator to help them make ongoing decisions. One of the distinguishing features of parent coordination, according to Johnston and Roseby, is that the parenting coordinator is given some kind of arbitration power by the court.

The History of Parent Coordination

The first book on parent coordination didn't appear until 1994, when Carla Garrity and Mitch Baris wrote *Caught in the Middle: Protecting the Children of High-Conflict Divorce*. However, as far back as the early part of the twentieth century, the first model of parent coordination was designed in California (Boylan and Termini, 2005). As an outgrowth of this, professionals in California were able to develop a detailed order outlining the appointment of a parent coordinator. However, it wasn't until the early 1990s that parent coordination truly began to develop, when mental health professionals and family lawyers began talking seriously about the role of the parent coordinator.

In their book, Garrity and Baris (1994) described a parent coordinator as a person with a background in both family law and psychotherapy. They proposed that the parent coordinator have such functions as helping parents develop a parenting plan, monitoring co-parents' compliance with a parenting agreement, mediating disputes, and teaching co-parents how to minimize disputes.

A few years later, Johnston and Roseby (1997) wrote about a "co-parenting arbitrator." This was a trained professional who would help highly conflicted parents resolve their impasses and learn to make important decisions related to their children. Since then, the Association of Family and Conciliation Courts has become active in further defining the role and the duties of the parent coordinator. Having appointed a task force, the AFCC put out guidelines for parenting coordination in 2006 (AFCC Task Force on Parenting Coordination, 2006).

The overall objective of parent coordination, according to the AFCC, is to help high-conflict parents implement their parenting plans, to resolve conflicts regarding their children and the parenting plan in a timely manner, and to protect and sustain safe, healthy, and meaningful parent-child relationships.

Furthermore, the AFCC specified that parent coordinators be trained in family mediation, be licensed mental health professionals or lawyers, and have extensive experience and training in working with co-parents with high-conflict relationships. In addition, the AFCC stated that parent coordinators should be granted authority by the court to make decisions for the co-parents when they cannot agree.

How Do Parent Coordinators Do Their Work?

In the last several years, much has been written about the duties and responsibilities of parent coordinators, and guidelines have recently been set forth explaining how parent coordinators should go about their jobs and the outcomes expected from their work (Boylan and Termini, 2005).

There are many practitioners providing parent coordination services, all with their own, unique approaches. Parent coordination tends to be a specialty niche for therapists in private practice that offers the advantage of the clients being court-ordered to attend and mandated to pay their fees.

As in the case of Marta and Gregor in the vignette that opens this chapter, the court often appoints a parent coordinator when a divorced couple continues to be unable to cooperate for the sake of their children despite repeated court contacts or hearings to resolve their issues. Most often, a parent coordinator is appointed after initial attempts to use mediation and psychotherapy. When the judge sees that these efforts at ameliorating the conflict have been futile, he may view the parents as two intractable people who won't give up their constant arguments, frequent accusations, and intense fighting. Then, the judge chooses to mandate parent coordination attendance for both parents.

Often, too, attorneys get involved by trying to convince their clients to voluntarily seek parent coordination. If the attorneys are both successful, a consent order can be signed by the court for parent coordination services.

❖ Skills Needed by Parent Coordinators

In general, a parent coordinator is a clinician trained in techniques for actively helping people resolve serious conflicts and reach tough decisions. This practice has elements of mediation in that the parent coordinator, when possible, helps divorced couples negotiate concrete agreements on specific issues concerning the children's welfare. It's also necessary for the parent coordinator to have excellent advanced relational therapy skills for helping couples in high conflict to transform their struggles into cooperation.

An approach to therapy is either relational or intrapsychic by definition. If the therapist believes that pathology resides within the individual, she is working from an individual, intrapsychic model. If she believes that emotional problems evolve as the result of problems in people's interactions with each other, then she is a relational therapist. Problems with couples, married or divorced, must be approached as relational problems.

When parent coordinators have a systems therapy orientation, it is never presumed that the behavior of the co-parents in a struggle is the result of pathology. Rather, it is assumed that the struggle itself is bringing out each person's worst qualities and potential. Then, if a relational problems orientation is used, the parent coordinator targets his or her intervention at the couple's interactions, not their psyches. Investigations into each parent's emotional stability are only pursued based on the guidelines we've presented in chapters seven and ten on psychological evaluations. For relational parent coordinators, the point at which they might pursue evaluations of each parent's mental health comes after serious attempts have been made in parent coordination.

❖ *How Does a Therapist Become a Parent Coordinator?*

As with many areas of specialization, few therapists set out to become parent coordinators. Those who are successful at it have typically been therapists for many years before the court starts referring cases. They've developed highly honed skills for resolving serious conflict in families and have usually developed a reputation for working with the most difficult cases. Typically, as we noted above, these therapists, either by training or by practice, have learned advanced techniques in relational therapies and focus on how to transform an interaction rather than changing a person's feelings.

A therapist who treats a large number of families in which high conflict is a feature is likely to have many clients who are involved in court struggles. Therefore, the therapist may write letters to the court, provide testimony, and, in general, demonstrate a willingness to seek out all of the pertinent family members when thoughtfully providing a recommendation to the court. As she interacts repeatedly with court family counselors, referees, and judges, the therapist gradually receives more referrals from the court for therapy of divorced couples in high conflict. Over time, it becomes clear that what the therapist does in therapy is almost identical to the services provided by a court-ordered parent coordinator. Once this connection becomes clear, either the court begins making formal appointments to the therapist to be the parent coordinator, or the therapist, wishing to clarify a growing niche for her practice, suggests that she could serve in this capacity. Thus a parent coordinator is born.

❖ ## The Steps in Parent Coordination

How does a parent coordinator carry out her job? What follows are important steps that indicate what series of actions a parent coordinator might take to engage a couple and begin the task of helping them reach agreement on their issues. These steps are based on our experiences with parent coordination.

The phone contact. When the two co-parents call for their intake appointments, it's important to have a personal discussion with each to clarify the ground rules and do some initial bonding. Advance planning and intervention of this sort is critical in high-conflict cases. You must be proactive by anticipating each type of resistance you're likely to encounter and should begin planning strategies for avoiding the struggles that exist between feuding co-parents.

In the initial phone contact, you should emphasize that you're not employed by the court and are offering a private, voluntary service. Many clients ordered by the court will emphasize at this point that they have no choice and must attend. It's recommended that you clarify that they don't have an obligation to see you in particular. Offer to clarify for the court, if one or both of them wish, that you aren't a suitable parent coordinator in this case and that you don't see people who do not wish to attend. This approach puts the responsibility for the treatment on the client, because he must now either say that he chooses to attend parent coordination services at your office or that he doesn't. Although we know that he is under court order, our insisting that the parent take responsibility for the decision to attend helps to clarify that we have no intention of participating in an adversarial process. Both people must come to see you of their own choosing rather than attend with an angry air of martyrdom. You may have to emphasize this "pseudovoluntary" atmosphere throughout the first session.

In this initial phone conversation you can clarify the cost per hour for services, methods of payment, and the need for an hour-and-a-half first session. It's also necessary to point out that fees will be split between the co-parents once they both attend together — this fact is a built-in reward for cooperating in sessions rather than continuing hostility that will require more individual sessions. It's wise to recommend to them that they make their own separate decisions about pursuing the first session, rather than making their compliance with the court order contingent on the other parent complying. Otherwise, both parents will wait for the other and neither will proceed with the parent coordination. You then invite the caller to schedule her first consultation session or wait and think about what you have shared with her. This offer to think about it is important because couples in high conflict are distrustful and usually want to blame the therapist for the pressure they feel to comply with the court order. Offering a delay shows them that you're not out to pressure them into giving you their money.

The first sessions (one with each parent). You must take charge in the very first session. Again, in an attempt to be proactive and avoid anticipated resistance, the parent coordinator should take immediate charge of the session by beginning to speak and setting the scene for how the session will proceed. You can carry this out with a speech that you use in most cases.

❖❖❖❖❖

Marta and Gregor's parent coordinator, Wes, told them this: "I call this a first consultation session because I want you to understand that this session is intended for me to learn about your situation and for you to decide whether or not you think I can be helpful. As I told you on the phone, if you decide that you don't want to proceed beyond today's session, I'll contact the court and let them know that they should refer you to another parent coordinator. In this process, I work for you, not the court."

❖❖❖❖❖

Having made a statement about not working for the court, the parent coordinator should immediately address the question of confidentiality. The legal guidelines for confidentiality are different in different states, but you can assure the parents that you will protect their privacy to the extent that the law allows you to.

We've found that most judges and attorneys, although not always happy about it, are willing to work within the ethical guidelines of the parent coordinator's professional association.

When you insist that proper releases of information be signed, most judges and attorneys will obtain them before getting information, despite the fact that a court order can override the need for releases.

You can urge the court and attorneys to cooperate in following your professional procedure for information release so, again, the parents can see that you are a separate service that operates by a code of ethics. We've had very few situations over the years in which a judge threatened contempt of court charges if we didn't abandon our usual protocol for information release. We've been threatened by many attorneys who believed we must respond to their subpoenas with immediate release of the information they're seeking, but almost all of them can be persuaded to understand the need for honoring our ethical policies and will seek the necessary releases or a court order that specifically overrides confidentiality.

Before giving the floor to the parent in the first session, it's essential to explain your role.

❖ ❖ ❖ ❖ ❖

Wes did this with Gregor and Marta. He emphasized that he did not intend to serve as a reporter for the court about which parent was right and which was wrong. Instead, he told them that as the parenting coordinator he would listen and understand each parent's position and his or her reasons for having that position. Wes also told Marta and Gregor that he wouldn't offer value judgments about rightness or wrongness but instead would use what each told him to make his own assessment of whether or not their situation was suitable for parent coordination.

❖ ❖ ❖ ❖ ❖

In the first session in which both parents are seen together, perhaps the third session overall, you can tell them whether you'll accept them as an ongoing case, and they'll each tell you whether they accept working with you toward the goal of better communication and greater cooperation.

However, in the first session with each parent alone, the parent coordinator is walking a tightrope. You must get each parent to like you and believe in your neutrality. Simultaneously, you must make small attempts at challenging their thinking in order to see how rigid each parent's view of the situation is.

❖ ❖ ❖ ❖ ❖

Gregor said that Marta's main goal was to keep him away from his children. Wes responded by saying, "You know, I've seen many situations in which a mother was having a lot of separation anxiety because of having to let go of her child at a young age. And it looked like a malicious attempt to interfere with the dad. I wonder if that might be going on with Marta."

Gregor's response to this was important information about whether he was willing to entertain, even to the smallest extent, a statement meant to create doubt within his usual certainty about Marta's reasons for denying him visits with his children.

❖ ❖ ❖ ❖ ❖

You should be aware that an initial high level of dogmatism and inflexibility in the first session isn't necessarily an accurate indicator of how flexible the parent might become in later sessions. A parent's rigidity guides you on what sorts of techniques you might need to use.

❖ ❖ ❖ ❖ ❖

Sandi wanted physical custody of her children; she stated that under no circumstances would she accept anything but a change of custody as the outcome of parent coordination. It was tempting for the parent coordinator to tell her that they would not be able to proceed and coordination should be cancelled. However, the parent coordinator in Sandi's case chose to utilize her resistance to help her change by sending her home with the following direction: "Despite any evidence that you might see to the contrary, during the next week you must not change your position. You must work this through gradually in your mind and shouldn't change your opinion too quickly."

❖ ❖ ❖ ❖ ❖

This method makes it harder for a parent to continue her resistance to change by creating a paradox in which the parent coordinator is encouraging her to remain unchanged at a time when she is resisting any direction from the coordinator. If the parent opposes his direction, she changes her views. If she doesn't change her views, she is cooperative because she has followed directions to the letter. In addition, the statement about working it through gradually in her mind and not changing "too quickly" sends her a covert message that says she will change her opinion — the question is just how long it's going to take.

Looking for the pattern in the first session. The first session with each parent is an investigative process. You're learning about each parent's views and each one's ability to be flexible and change. Simultaneously, you're looking for the pattern of interaction that the co-parents' struggles are caught up in. Simply stated, you need to locate the troubled interaction or set of beliefs and make a small change in that interaction to bring about larger change. The following steps will guide you through carrying out this investigation and the beginning of the intervention process:

1. Assess whether straightforward negotiation of issues will work. Before entering into any intricate assessment of interactional patterns, assess carefully if this couple may simply need to come to agreement and if they seem capable of doing so. Are they more caught up in their anger and hurt, or are they more interested in the issues themselves?

❖❖❖❖❖

Donte filed a motion for full custody of his two daughters. But what did Donte really want? As the parent coordinator quickly discovered, Donte was attempting to take full custody of his daughters only because he wanted more parenting time and easier telephone access to his children and his co-parent, Clarita, had been making both parenting time and access difficult.

In this case, the parenting coordinator found it was possible to convince Clarita to consider reassessing parenting time and making phone access easier. Donte and his co-parent agreed to renegotiate those particular issues and that helped them avoid the hatred and animosity caused by returning to court and criticizing one another in public.

❖❖❖❖❖

If straightforward negotiation seems impossible due to a high level of hurt, animosity, or other emotions, move to the next step.

2. Allow co-parents to describe the situation as they usually describe it.
As each parent describes the divorce or postdivorce situation, you're hearing a rehearsed litany that they have gone through

many times with many people. This story has taken on the quality of a saga. Allow the co-parent's more extreme statements, which ordinarily you might want to challenge or correct, to go unedited in order to understand the parent's belief system. Pivotal beliefs that maintain the problem can be identified by either exaggerated emotional outpourings when making the statements (e.g., sobbing while saying, "I don't know how he could leave me while my mother was dying") or a sense of drama and overstatement (e.g., "She's just a controlling, bipolar maniac who wants to control everyone and everything around her"). In most cases, you'll see the parents expressing an angry sense of martyrdom compounded by their attempts to "prove" to you that they're the wronged party — telling the same story they've told many times in court.

3. Describe both parents' pivotal beliefs and how those beliefs explain their interactions.

Pivotal beliefs describe pivotal interactions. What does Clarita do as a result of her anger at her co-parent for leaving her when her mother was dying? Which of his co-parent's behaviors does Donte consider controlling, and what does he do in response to those behaviors? You can ask these questions directly without anyone taking offense because both Clarita and Donte want to tell their story and will revel in an opportunity to elaborate at greater length about the other's wrongdoings and their own necessary responses.

❖❖❖❖❖

Donte and Clarita had been divorced for five years and had two children, ages 11 and 8. Donte was the parent saying that Clarita was controlling while Clarita was angry because Donte left her and the children when her mother was dying. When the parent coordinator asked Donte to be more specific about Clarita's controlling ways, he described her making it difficult for him to talk to the children on the phone. She would hand one of the kids the phone and then, in the background, he'd hear Clarita say, "Ice cream in two minutes, kids." When they exchanged the children for parenting time, Clarita often left the agreed-upon location five minutes after the exchange time. Clarita turned her cell phone off, making it impossible for Donte to let her know he'd be there in five more minutes.

The parenting coordinator asked Clarita what about Donte's current behavior bothered her and how that behavior was connected to her feelings about his having divorced her at a bad time in her life. Clarita stated that her anger was fueled by Donte's smug, nonchalant attitude that showed that he didn't care about her feelings and never had.

Donte explained that he refused to speak with her or make eye contact, because it would only cause a fight. He said that he got away from her as quickly as possible. These were pivotal beliefs that, once identified, were important indications to the parent coordinator of what could be changed to improve each co-parent's opinion of the other.

❖ ❖ ❖ ❖ ❖

Session two intervention. Once you've identified the pivotal beliefs and interactions, it's time to direct each co-parent to take a step toward change. It's best in many high-conflict cases that you not tell them that they're taking these steps to improve the relationship or to meet the needs of the co-parent, because this might discourage them from taking action. It is wiser to frame the directive in terms that describe the new behavior as a way of having less trouble with the co-parent and, thereby, getting more of what he or she wants.

You could instruct Donte, for instance, to ask himself: "How could Clarita change her behavior in a way I would notice and that would make it harder for me to keep my pivotal beliefs about her?" Likewise, have Clarita ask herself what might Donte do that would cause her to question her pivotal beliefs about him? You can now direct both to take a step, either in separate meetings or with both together, depending on which you think will work better.

❖ ❖ ❖ ❖ ❖

Clarita was still emotionally raw and angry because of Donte leaving her. What was most important to her was that she see that he cared about her welfare. Donte saw Clarita as controlling and wanting everything her way. What Donte needed to see was Clarita doing something to help facilitate his parenting time, particularly if she had to inconvenience herself to do it: a controlling person wouldn't be that helpful or thoughtful. Therefore, in separate talks at the same session, the parent coordinator asked Donte to make eye contact with Clarita at their next exchange, say hi to her, and ask her how her day was. Donte was taking their 9-year-old on a field trip on the coming Monday. The parenting coordinator asked Clarita, who had their daughter that morning, to not only make a lunch for their daughter, but also to make a nice lunch for Donte as well with food and snacks she knew he liked. If both did as they were asked, a significant seed of doubt would be sown as to the accuracy of their pivotal beliefs about each other.

❖❖❖❖❖

You should expect both parents to give little credence at first to the co-parent's new behavior. Tell both to keep up this new behavior for at least a month. It seems, from our experience, that people don't believe new behaviors are sincere until they've continued for at least that period of time. In some high-conflict cases it might even take longer than a month.

You can reinforce continued change by complimenting both on doing the right thing regardless of the co-parent's behaviors or reasons for those behaviors. Urge both, if they consider themselves nice, for example, to act nice rather than being reactive. If they see themselves as helpful, they should act in helpful ways. This understanding is a straightforward therapeutic technique common to many clinical schools of thought. It's wise to spend several sessions chipping away at the divorced couple's embedded beliefs and behaviors before concluding that intervening in the patterns of interaction alone isn't going to work.

Using persuasion when intervening in the patterns of interaction alone isn't working. Parent coordination offers greater latitude, as you can see, than mediation or arbitration as to the range of techniques a coordinator can use in treatment. Mediators are discouraged from imposing specific recommendations or persuading. When the styles of intervention offered above continue to fail in the face of high emotion and high conflict, it's time to become more persuasive.

The simplest form of persuasion is to utilize your expertise as a parent coordinator to push for outcomes that are necessary for the welfare of the children. Most clients come in touting the phrase, "the best interests of the child." As a parent coordinator, you can take a specific position on what is in the children's best interests. For instance, if you believe more parenting time for one parent is necessary for the welfare of the kids, this is the time to tell the other parent that this is your clinical assessment.

This is exactly what Wes did with Marta and Gregor as did Donte and Clarita's parenting coordinator. If you believe that changing parenting time, allowing one parent to have full physical custody, or asking for supervised parenting time for one co-parent would be harmful, use your professional status to persuade the other parent that this isn't a necessary step and that few coordinators would support such a move were they to take this issue to court.

You should persuade parents to cooperate and negotiate based upon the likely legal outcome of a motion that you're trying to help them settle. If you are not an attorney, you should typically obtain permissions from the co-parents and call or meet with the family court counselor who makes the recommendations to the referee or judge — or even directly with the judge. In other words, meet directly with the person who can best tell you what is likely to happen if this case were to come to court. Once you know the likely outcome of the case, you can use this information for balanced persuasion. If it's highly unlikely that the court would grant one co-parent's request for supervised parenting time for the other, you can use this information to discourage that parent's continued mission for supervised parenting time.

You may wish to replace the discussion about supervised parenting time with a discussion of what changes in the other's behavior would lead the distressed parent to feel okay about the situation.

❖❖❖❖❖

For instance, Geraldine was requesting that her co-parent, Gordon, have supervised parenting time because she believed that Gordon repeatedly said bad things to the children about her. The parenting coordinator changed the discussion to whether Gordon would be willing to commit to the coordinator to stop having discussions with the children about Geraldine or about other adult issues. If Geraldine was willing to suspend her court action pending an outcome in parent coordination, this could be a powerful motivator for Gordon to change his behavior.

❖❖❖❖❖

Sessions three and beyond. Although not mandatory, it works best to ask both parents to agree to not file any further motions in court during the period of parent coordination. Some parent coordinators require a contract that includes this agreement. The parent coordinator can also ask the court to include this stipulation in the order for parent coordination.

Each additional session should be spent celebrating improvement and refining changes. Again, it may take several weeks to see if a reliable change will continue. Therefore, you may need to spend time persuading each parent to continue with a current agreement despite the fact that neither may be entirely satisfied with the other parent's level of compliance. If a particular approach isn't working over a period of several weeks or seems in error in the short run, revise plans, change strategies, or move on to methods other than parent coordination.

When everything you've tried fails. If you act as both a therapist and a parent coordinator, you may find that your success rate in high-conflict divorce cases will be lower than you've come to expect in your non-high-conflict client population. These are tough, seriously conflicted families. At the point at which the parent coordination has continued to fail, a parent coordinator typically withdraws and refers the couple back to court for psychological evaluation, appointment of a guardian ad litem, or a more intense form of intervention.

The Future of Parent Coordination

Parent coordination is a relatively new and growing field of practice. Currently, only a few states, including Oklahoma, Idaho, and Oregon, have parent coordinator statutes (Fyfe, 2003). However, the parenting coordinator model has been implemented in many states as an important intervention for dealing with high-conflict families who appear regularly before the courts (AFCC Task Force on Parenting Coordination, 2003).

The use of a parent coordinator offers a nonadversarial method to help families either before or after high conflict develops. Parent coordination has a wider range of therapeutic treatment methods available to it than does mediation or family therapy alone. The parent coordinator's interaction with the court and the authority that goes along with having been appointed by the court may give greater weight to the parent coordinator's words than a therapist alone has.

We consider parent coordination to be an expansion of the practice of family therapy, and invite professionals with a particular interest in divorce work to consider preparation for this growing specialization.

15

ADEPT: A Court-Based Group Treatment Program for High-Conflict Divorces

W hen mediation, parent coordination, or psychotherapy has failed, interventions directed at breaking up the impasse between the co-parents are often attempted. Many such programs have been developed. Often they are longer than the typical parenting education or psychoeducational program (Geasler and Blaisure, 1999), usually lasting from four to twelve weeks (Goodman, Bonds, Sandler, and Braver, 2004).

❖❖❖❖❖

When Albert and Carrie got a divorce three years ago, they attended a one-evening program that had the intent of educating co-parents about the hazards of ongoing conflict between parents. As their charges and countercharges against each other continued over the months following their divorce and after they had returned to court to settle custody and child support issues, Albert and Carrie's judge ordered them to attend mediation. They paid for several mediation sessions, but they failed to agree on either custody or new parenting time conflicts that had begun to surface in the second year after their divorce. Next, they were assigned to a parenting coordinator. That intervention, too, failed to lead to an agreement. Finally, the judge mandated that they go to a program designed for co-parents who were deemed to have a high-conflict relationship.

❖❖❖❖❖

Reviews of psychoeducational programs targeted for high-conflict couples show that they generally include activities to reduce

185

interparental conflict (Goodman, Bonds, Sandler, and Braver, 2004). The ADEPT program (After Divorce — Effective Parenting Together) is one of the programs that has been developed to help reduce interparental conflict. It is similar to the Group Mediation Model Program of Family Court Services of Alameda County Superior Court, California, although they were developed independently (High-Conflict Separation and Divorce, 2004). The two programs both use a group model; however, the ADEPT program, described in this chapter, does not include children in the process and features a greater number of hours of class than the Alameda program.

❖ *ADEPT*

The ADEPT program was developed as a response to the amount of court time and litigation that a few divorced parents consumed in a county family court. ADEPT has a primary goal of improving communication and resolving conflicts in a brief period of time by working with groups of co-parents who have continually engaged in conflict long after their divorces have ended.

An eight-week, sixteen-hour program, ADEPT is based on a communication model that emphasizes the psychological and emotional damage to children that occurs when co-parents engage in ongoing conflict and continually take each other back to court. Through role-plays, skill training, peer coaching, and supervised practice, parents are taught appropriate communication techniques and conflict resolution skills.

Like many courts around the country, the Oakland County (Michigan) Circuit Court in 2000 found itself overwhelmed with the number of divorced couples who were continuing to fight and consume the court's time with their squabbles. As a result, in this county of one million people just north of Detroit, Michigan, family court judges gave an assignment to the family division's psychological clinic: *design a program to reduce the conflict between postdivorce couples raising children.*

Pledging cooperation, the six circuit court/family division judges began ordering couples who were entrenched in custody, parenting time, and child support conflicts to attend the new program in early 2001. Two court psychologists designed and ran the eight-week program. ADEPT was an immediate success with judges, referees, and Friend of the Court counselors, who have provided enough court-ordered referrals to keep the program busy since its inception.

At the writing of this book, more than 300 postdivorce couples have been through the program. Research shows that the number of new court contacts by co-parents who complete ADEPT are reduced by an average of over fifty percent. Many couples completely give up serious bickering and begin to talk to each other for the first time in years. Not only do a good many of these co-parenting couples begin talking to each other, but many are able to solve the kinds of conflicts that have stymied them for years.

This chapter provides a description of the innovative program that has won high praise not only from judges, attorneys, and counselors, but also from those who successfully complete it.

❖❖❖❖❖

The first session of ADEPT

Eight women are meeting with a male therapist in a room on the second floor of the Oakland County, Michigan, courthouse. The issues that compel these women and their co-parents to file new motions regularly can never be adequately resolved by the courts, but that doesn't stop them from trying. That's why these women are seated around a conference table with a psychologist at its head.

"I know you don't really want to be here," therapist Jay says during his introductory remarks to the group, "but the damage you're doing to your children by continuing to battle with your co-parent could be irreparable. In this program, over the next eight weeks, you will learn to communicate better with your co-parent. And although this may seem overly optimistic — if not impossible — in eight weeks, we can guarantee you that most or all of you will have resolved some of the conflicts that keep you and your co-parent coming back into court."

A woman at the other end of the table raises her hand. "If I never talk to my ex again that will be okay with me," she says. "He's said some horrible things to our son, particularly since I got remarried."

Another woman next to her spoke up. "I'm afraid to be here," she says. "It's taken a year of therapy to really get strong and not let him push my buttons. If we have to face each other in this program, I'm afraid I'll fall apart and be weak again, and I know that's the way he likes me to feel."

A red-haired woman with a tattoo on her right wrist quickly raises her hand. "I have a personal protection order against the father of my children," she says. "He could try to hurt me on the way in or out of this building."

"Yes," says Jay. "We understand the things you're saying and we share your concerns. If you feel stronger now, we don't want to contribute to you feeling weaker. Nor do we want you to be exposed to danger in this program. That's one of the reasons we're meeting together in this room."

Jay explains that the reason women and men meet in separate rooms at the beginning of the ADEPT program was originally to give women a chance to get to know each other and develop strategies for protecting themselves by walking in and out of the building together.

"We'll protect you, and if we need to have the police here," Jay adds, "we'll arrange that."

Several of the women nod and look both appreciative and relieved.

The therapist shifts the conversation to another hot topic. He knows from experience with hundreds of both men and women who have attended ADEPT in the last five years what's on their minds.

"We sent you a questionnaire and a participation agreement before you came tonight," he says. "Some of you filled those out and sent them back; some of you didn't. If you didn't, it's probably because you have questions about one of the clauses in the agreement. Clause number eight maybe?" He looks around the table and several women look anxious to speak.

Paula, a woman who has not spoken yet, says, "We're going back to court in a week over child support. You don't expect me to wait until this program is over to try to get some money, do you?"

"What about if he violates the personal protection order?" another woman asks angrily.

"Okay," Jay says, "let me to try to clear this up for you."

"The reason that clause number eight is in the agreement," he tells them, "is to prevent people in the program from thinking they can just go on with business as usual." He reads the clause aloud: "During the course of this ADEPT program, I will *not* initiate any legal action, I will *not* serve or cause to have served any legal notices, and I will *not* deliver any materials that may provoke conflict with my co-parent."

"You haven't gotten satisfaction from the court yet, otherwise you wouldn't keep going back into court to file new motions," Jay explains. "When we started this program, we agreed with the judges that we would require people to avoid starting any new legal proceedings. We want you to discuss and work out conflicts here — not try to do that in a courtroom. You already know the judges can't solve problems to your and your co-parent's satisfaction. We know that, too. So do the judges. So, we're asking you, unless it's an emergency, to refrain from starting any new actions."

After answering more questions, Jay reads the whole agreement, which is two pages long, and answers more questions. Then he goes through the notebook that has been provided to each member. He explains the learning objectives, the goals, the format, and the procedures for the eight weeks of the ADEPT program. He relates that in this program they don't refer to divorce families as broken families ("Families are redefined by divorce," he says, "not broken"), and they don't call previous spouses "exes" (the term is "co-parent").

When he finishes, Mary Anne, the woman who said she was afraid to be there, has a question. "Do we have to begin talking to our co-parent tonight?" she asks.

"No," Jay assures her. "We take things very gradually. You will be in the same room with him later tonight, but you won't have to speak to him. We want you to be prepared for that. And let me assure you that you'll never talk to your co-parent alone. There will always be a group of people present."

He then asks the women in the group to introduce themselves and tell everyone some things about their family and their children. The eight women all eagerly take a turn. The stories they tell are compelling, fascinating, and, in some instances, harrowing.

Mina, who was married for seven years, says she filed for a divorce the day her co-parent fell asleep while driving with their children in the car, nearly killing their sons. She tells the group that he had been high on a combination of drugs and alcohol. Women lean forward to listen to Mina's story.

Janelle, a woman in her fifties, says she was never married to her co-parent. "But at age 40 I found myself pregnant and I didn't think I needed or wanted a father for my child," she says. The other women laugh. "Now I can't get rid of him and his job seems to be to make my life miserable."

Each of the women in turn tells the story of her relationship with her co-parent.

At the same time, down the hall, eight men meet in a room with a female therapist, Renee. They too are telling their views of their marriages and divorces.

"I try to talk to her," a thin man with a goatee says, "but she gets so angry. She usually slams the phone down."

"She's the one who always gets mad?" Renee asks.

"Okay," the man, Bruce, says, "I have to admit I get pretty mad myself. I guess I've been a pretty angry guy."

Renee follows the same procedures as Jay does in the women's meeting. After everyone in both classes introduces themselves, they get an assignment. They're told to write down three ways they've been ineffective in trying to communicate with their co-parents. As most of the men and women, still in separate rooms, get busy writing, some look perplexed.

Mina looks up and says, "I think I've done everything I possibly could to get along better and communicate with him. I don't think I've done anything wrong."

And in the men's group, Randy, a tall man with glasses says, "I really have tried to talk with her. I don't know how I've been ineffective."

Both leaders ask others what they've written. This usually helps people to look at ways they've sabotaged communication.

Sharon speaks up and volunteers to read one of hers. "I've been ineffective in communicating with my co-parent by not listening to what he has to say."

And in the men's group, Chris volunteers one of his. "I've been ineffective in communicating with my co-parent by getting too mad and yelling at her on the phone."

"Thank you," Renee says. "That takes courage to say."

When everyone finishes, the women leave the relative security of the single-gender group and come into a larger conference room where the men also congregate. When everyone is settled, Renee and Jay lead the group and make some introductory comments. Even though everyone is court ordered to be there, the leaders thank these parents for attending.

Renee and Jay give a brief history of marriage and divorce in the United States. They note that most parents who get a divorce usually work out their problems in about one to two years and are able to communicate — at least moderately well — for the sake of the children. However, there are about fifteen to twenty percent of co-parents who continue to battle after the first two years have come and gone. "We call these high-conflict parents," the leaders say. "It isn't divorce that causes children to be upset. It's conflict during and following divorce that's so upsetting to children."

Jay and Renee tell the parents that the goal of ADEPT is to teach them how to communicate and how to resolve conflicts with their co-parents. As they ask the co-parents to do the first of two tasks, they note that these tasks will be difficult for them. First, the facilitators ask them to go around and tell one characteristic of at least one of their children that reminds them in a positive way of their co-parent. Parents comment about artistic ability, intelligence, personal attractiveness, and a sense of humor.

The second task is for them to say aloud in this group that now includes their co-parents, one way they've been ineffective in communicating with their co-parents. Although it proves tough for some people, everyone tells one way they have been ineffective. Adam talks about his anger. Mary Anne says she never confronts her co-parent because she doesn't want to cause any problems. When Russell uses the opportunity to make a verbal jab at his co-parent, the leaders quickly stop him, point out that they don't want anyone to criticize each other, and ask him to try again. He does better the second time.

"We ask you to do this exercise," Jay says, "because we've learned from our years of working with co-parents with conflicts that venting your anger or saying mean or sarcastic things about your co-parent won't solve your problems. All of you have been negative to one extent or another, and you've all been court ordered to attend this program. Obviously, your negativity hasn't made things better. We'd rather have you concentrate on what you can change. You can't change your co-parent; you can only change yourself. By expressing how you've been ineffective in communicating with your co-parent, you've taken a first step at accepting responsibility for your own actions. In doing this, you've shown us and your co-parent that you are willing to make some changes."

With that positive feedback, the leaders hand out a quiz and the first homework assignment. When everyone has finished the quiz and handed it in, they're free to leave.

❖ ❖ ❖ ❖ ❖

The second week of ADEPT

As during the first week of ADEPT, men and women meet in their respective rooms with a group leader. The men start talking about their homework assignment. One of the homework tasks required them to keep track of conflicts with their co-parents. Renee asks how they did in tracking their conflicts. Phil responds, "I have to say that we didn't have one conflict this week."

"Is that out of the ordinary?" Renee asks.

"Oh, yes!" Phil says. And that gets a laugh from the other men.

"So I guess you could say that ADEPT has really helped you so far?" Russell asks.

"You can say that again," Phil says.

Down the hall in the other room, the women are talking about the goals and dreams they have for their children. "I want my children to get along with each other," Julia says. "I have a boy and a girl and they fight all the time."

"I want my children to do well at school," says Paula.

"And I just want my kids to be happy and successful," Danielle adds. Most of the other women nod.

"But now I want you to say how you interfere with those goals and dreams," says Jay. "How does your behavior get in the way?"

"I can tell you straight out," offers Julia. "I said I want my kids to get along with each other, but how can I expect that when their father and I fight and argue all the time?"

"You're not a good role model for them," Wendy comments.

"I know," sighs Julia.

"I know how I interfere with my goal of wanting my sons to love and respect both of his parents," says Mary Anne. "We say negative things about each other to them. I know that's wrong, but we do it anyway."

Back in the men's group, Renee asks if everyone has done the last part of the homework assignment. "Did you write out three important conflicts you have with your co-parent?" she asks.

Several men nod their heads. "Can you share what you've written down?" she asks.

"We ask each other about things that have nothing to do with the kids," says Phil. "And that leads to arguments."

"I don't think my co-parent takes enough time to help our son with his homework," Rod volunteers. "So I bitch at her and then we get into fights — well, not fights — just arguments."

"I'd just say that communication is our biggest conflict," says Adam. "We can't really talk about anything."

In the other room, Wendy says her three conflicts with her co-parent are the bitter feelings they have for each other, not being able to talk in a civil manner to each other, and not being able to agree on a flexible schedule.

"Child support is my biggest conflict," adds Mary Anne. "He owes me more than fifteen thousand dollars." She also admits that they both make accusations against each other.

"Here's how we're going to use the three conflicts you've written down," explains Jay. "You're going to work with a coach to come to an agreement on three conflicts with your co-parent that will be the basis for all of our work throughout this program."

"You mean we have to start talking to our co-parents?" Mary Anne asks anxiously.

"No, I didn't say that. You'll be working with a coach. That coach will communicate with your co-parent's coach. You are directed not to talk to your co-parent."

"I don't get it," Danielle says.

"Here's how it works," Jay explains. "Each of you will have a coach and each of you will be a coach. Men coach men and women coach women. We'll divide the group in half and each of you will learn about your partner's conflicts and then you'll try to come to an agreement with your co-parents' coaches about the conflicts."

"We have to meet with angry men?" Mary Anne asks timidly.

"Co-parents may be angry toward each other, but when you are coaching and working with other coaches, you'll find that people are reasonable and rational," Jay says.

"How can we be coaches when we are here because we can't solve our own problems?" Sharon asks.

"Great question!" Jay encourages. "All of you are capable of seeing problems and using good communication skills with other people — except your co-parent."

"I think this is a violation of my confidentiality and I'm not going to do it," Mina declares.

"You might see it that way, but when you couldn't solve your problems in group therapy or in court hearings you gave up some rights."

"How long will I go to jail for if I don't do this?" Mina asks.

"If you have Judge Jensen," Julia chips in, "it might be quite a while."

"I still think it's a violation of my rights," Mina says again. "I don't want to discuss my business in front of others."

"I can understand that," Jay sympathizes, "but we've found that the program works well this way."

It is now time for the women to meet in the larger conference room with the men. When everyone is settled in the larger room, the leaders show some videos of co-parents in conflict. They also pass out a sheet listing the specific ways that children are hurt by conflict between parents. "Each of these videos shows one or more ways that children are hurt by being involved in or aware of their parents' conflicts," Jay explains. After each short scene, various co-parents indicate their understanding of how the children were hurt.

The next order of business is for the leaders to teach the co-parents a formalized method for discussing their differences. "It's critical that co-parents replace their usual ritual language of mutual animosity with a more kindly, business-like language. In our program, we've chosen 'I' messages and reflective listening as the new language they will use."

Renee then begins to explain "I" messages. "'I' messages," she says, "are useful communication skills because they show you how to raise issues with your co-parent without pointing fingers. It's one communication technique for defusing anger and the inevitable conflicts when you're trying to discuss serious issues related to the children."

She asks for a volunteer to give an example of an "I" message using the form they have in front of them.

"I feel angry when you come late to pick up our sons because I have plans," Danielle offers. "What I'd like is for you to be on time to pick them up."

"That's excellent," Renee says. "Good example."

Jay announces that it is time to do the first task that was explained in the single-gender groups. "I'm going to pick four couples at random. We'll assign you coaches, and you'll begin talking to your coach about the conflicts you wrote down in the homework. When both coaches have learned about the three conflicts from the co-parent they're representing, the coaches will get together and begin negotiating to settle on which three important conflicts to address."

Jay then picks four couples, and their coaches are assigned. The leaders go around to make sure co-parents and their coaches have the right forms and are following procedures. The co-parents and coaches meet together to discuss the co-parents' conflicts. This keeps everyone busy until it's time to hand out the quiz for the night and the homework assignment.

"We'll meet again and pick up from where we left off next week," Renee says. "Then those who were coaches will switch roles and work with their own coaches."

After everyone completes their quizzes, Session Two is officially over.

❖❖❖❖❖

The third week of ADEPT

The third session begins with both groups talking about their homework assignment. An important part of the homework assignment was to answer the following questions:

❖ What did you enjoy from your previous relationship with your co-parent?
❖ Give an example of any good times the two of you had while together.
❖ What would you have to hear from your co-parent to believe that better communication with him/her is possible?
❖ What would he/she have to do to make things right between the two of you?

"To tell you the truth," says Julia, "I can't really remember the good times because the bad times have overshadowed the good since then." Several women nod vigorously in agreement.

"His abuse was so bad," complains Mina, "I just wrote that that question wasn't applicable to me."

"I think one of the best things I can remember," offers Sharon courageously, "was that I got two beautiful children from the relationship."

"There were plenty of good times in our marriage," Mary Anne says. "I like to remember the Chris who was funny and just a lot of fun to be with."

"You know what I remember," adds Danielle, "was the time we went to Las Vegas and had so much fun in the casinos. Then there were the motorcycle trips we used to take together. We both enjoyed those."

"I appreciate you sharing those memories of the good times," Jay compliments. "Remember that you were once in love and there were probably plenty of good times. It's just when the marriage deteriorates that we tend to focus on the negative and forget the good times. But they were there. Let me ask you what you would need to hear from your co-parent for communication to begin to improve."

"What I would need to hear is that the children would come first and the kids would not be involved in our disagreements," volunteers Danielle.

"I'd like to hear Chris say that he's getting help with his temper because he realizes he has a problem," Mary Anne says.

"Ike needs to acknowledge that he is equally at fault for things going wrong between us," says Janelle. "He needs to admit he needs therapy, too."

Julia chimes in disdainfully, "Bruce couldn't say anything that would help at this point. I've heard his words before. What I need are actions. He needs to show that the children are a priority."

In the other room, the men are commenting on the answers they've written to these same questions. Bruce, for instance, says he would need to hear a sincere apology from Julia. "She should genuinely apologize for spiteful, vindictive behavior toward me."

Ike says that his communication could get better with Janelle if she would say she was sorry and begin to work on raising their son with him — rather than going about it separately.

Chris offers, "What I really need to hear from Mary Anne is that she isn't going to drink in front of the children any more and that she's ready to be responsible when it comes to handling money."

When the men and women come together, more video clips of family interaction are shown. The discussion, as in week two, is of the ways parental conflict interferes with children's adjustment. When this discussion is finished, Jay discusses "I" messages and reflective listening. "By avoiding blaming and finger-pointing and detaching yourself when you respond to your co-parent, you'll be making a conscious effort to defuse conflict. That's important for your children."

With this as the instructional part of the program, the leaders direct co-parents and their coaches to return to the task begun in Session Two. "Work with your coaches to settle on the three conflicts you and your co-parent want to work on for the rest of this series."

Four couples who had begun working with coaches find different spots in corners of the room and they and their coaches continue to work on negotiating an agreement on their three conflicts.

Ike and Janelle are the first to reach agreement. The three conflicts they choose are

1. Communicating without using their son and without negative remarks about each other
2. Keeping a focus on the best interests of their son
3. Not sharing personal issues with their son

Each of them writes down the agreed-upon conflicts and signs each other's forms.

Danielle and Phil are the next co-parenting couple to find common ground. They decide their most important conflicts are

1. Communicating without involving the children
2. Money issues
3. Protecting the children from their conflicts

They, too, sign each other's conflict forms.

For the other two couples, agreement isn't easily reached. For instance, the coaches for Mary Anne and Chris get a real workout shuffling back and forth between the co-parent they are representing and each other. They readily agree that their first conflict, child support, is indeed a contentious issue. They come to terms on conflict number two by setting aside specific issues each wants to build into a list of conflicts and instead settle on this more general wording: "Direct communication between co-parents." However, conflict number three isn't going to be so easy.

Mary Anne wants to get agreement on a conflict that says that Chris is too rigid and punitive with the children. Chris wants more time with the kids and argues that one of their conflicts is that she is too controlling about sharing time with the children. He also tells his coach Mary Anne is an alcoholic and she shouldn't drink around the children. After much discussion and negotiation, late in the second and final hour of the third session, the coaches convince them to agree that conflict number three should be "Co-parents drinking in front of the children."

Neither Chris nor Mary Anne is completely happy with this definition of the problem. "It makes it sound like both of us drink in front of the children," Chris says. "There are other issues I want to get as part of our three conflicts," Mary Anne adds. "However, I can see that if it's a big issue for him, maybe I should just accept it without getting too upset. When we talk about resolving these conflicts in a couple of weeks, then we can discuss this in more detail."

Couples who have not started working with coaches have a few minutes to begin to acquaint their coaches with the conflicts they have listed. However, time runs out and it's time for the quiz and the homework for next week. And thus Session Three ends on an upbeat note: Four couples have hammered out agreements on their three conflicts with the help of other parents acting as coaches.

❖ ❖ ❖ ❖ ❖

The fourth week of ADEPT

Session Four begins with the women asking what is on the agenda for the meeting with the men today.

"There will be further work with coaches to settle on your conflicts," Jay answers.

"Then what?" Mary Anne asks.

"Then, if we have time, you'll begin working on constructing 'I' messages in order to begin practicing with your co-parent."

"What do you mean practicing?" Mina asks.

"We'll have you using 'I' messages and reflective listening statements with your co-parent."

"I can't do that," Mary Anne says. "As you can see, I'm already breathing heavy." The other women laugh.

In the men's group, they're going over the homework given at the end of the previous session. The homework requested they identify the most frequent issues that lead to conflict with their co-parents.

Chris raises his hand. "Her drinking," he says. "When she's drinking around the kids it endangers them. I can never accept that."

"The next question is what do you do to either start this conflict or keep it going?" Renee asks Chris.

"I don't do anything," Chris retorts angrily. "It's not my fault she drinks around the kids."

"That's not exactly what we're asking you, Chris," she says. "You may not have anything to do with her drinking, but what do you do to start conflicts over this issue?"

"I confront her," he snaps belligerently. "I do that and I'll do it every time. Wouldn't you?"

"Maybe," she says. "But do there have to be conflicts and fights over it? Could there be another way to handle it?"

"What else can I do?" Chris inquires helplessly and throws up his hands.

"Have you tried talking to her without getting mad and yelling?" Rod asks him from across the room.

"You don't expect me to be nice to her when she could hurt our kids, do you?" Chris asks. "That's what you want me to do, isn't it? Be nice to her. Well, I can't!"

In the other room, Mina is saying that the issue causing the most problems at present is Randy's refusal to help pay for a private school for their two children.

"And what do you do to cause this conflict or keep it going?" the leader asks.

"Nothing," Mina responds predictably. "We haven't talked in two years." The other women titter. "I can't change him or talk to him or get him to agree with anything. He just takes me to court whenever there's an issue. We can't settle anything."

"Well, that's why you're here," Jay explains.

There's further discussion of the agenda for the day with Jay's encouragement to work diligently with the coaches to get conflicts settled with the co-parents.

In the room with the men and women together, coaches are assigned and co-parents meet in different parts of the room with their coaches. After Chris and Mary Anne work with their respective coaches for about twenty minutes, the coaches ask for a consultation with the leaders.

"We have a real problem," Russell, Chris's coach, says. Janelle, who is Mary Anne's coach, nods her head in agreement.

"He wants to put her drinking down as a conflict, and she wants to say that any drinking she does is purely social and appropriate," Russell explains.

"Let's look at it this way," Jay clarifies. "If he sees this as a conflict, whether she thinks it's an issue or not, it is a problem. Now the thing for you to do as coaches is to get them to agree on a wording they can both live with."

"You mean we could call this a lifestyle difference?" Janelle asks.

"Hey!" Jay says, "That's good. See if they'll go along with that. Call the conflict a lifestyle difference and see where you get with it."

The coaches go back to their respective co-parents. After consultations with co-parents and then with each other, the coaches give the leaders a thumbs-up signal. Chris and Mary Anne agreed on "Lifestyle differences" as their third conflict.

Sharon and Adam are also working with coaches, and they eventually settle on their three conflicts. They are

1. Disagreement about boundaries for the children and parenting practices
2. Communicating adult personal issues to the children
3. Parents punishing the children as a way to get back at each other

Both Adam and Sharon say they're happy with the choice of the three conflicts. They initial a copy of the conflicts for each other.

Renee and Jay ask co-parents who've agreed upon their three conflicts (and who aren't coaching) to begin constructing "I" messages related to those conflicts.

At 8:55 p.m., all parents take a quiz that asks questions about "I" messages and reflective listening. Then, as they leave, each takes a homework assignment for the coming week.

❖ ❖ ❖ ❖ ❖

The fifth week of ADEPT

At the beginning of the fifth session, Renee and Jay, in their respective single-gender groups, go over the quizzes from Week Four after handing them back. The quizzes ask questions about "I" messages and reflective listening and are designed to test whether co-parents have a basic concept of the skills involved with both techniques.

Leaders ask co-parents to construct an "I" message to the following situation:

You're upset because your co-parent would like you to help pay for summer camp, but your co-parent didn't talk to you about sending your child to camp or splitting the cost ahead of time.

Wendy writes the following "I" message: "I feel frustrated when you don't give me proper notice because I need time to plan my budget. I need you to tell me about things related to our child ahead of time."

However, Mary Anne writes this "I" message: "I feel that you don't talk to me ahead of time because I have an equal say in what happens to our children. I need you to be more assertive in your communication."

The leader asks the rest of the group to point out to Mary Anne how she might improve her "I" message.

"You left out a feeling," Danielle offers.

"And you seem pretty vague about what you're asking for from him," Mina says.

With help from the group, Mary Anne rewrites her "I" message in this way: "I feel annoyed when you plan events with our child without consulting me because often such events have an impact on my life. I need you to discuss plans ahead of time so we can make decisions together."

In the men's group, some of them are grappling with creating "I" messages that are direct without being hostile.

Phil writes: "I feel angry that you never talk to me ahead of time because then you want me to help pay for something I had no say in deciding. I need you to stop being so secretive."

With help from the other guys, he's able to reshape his "I" message.

But they also have problems with reflective listening. The quiz had an item where co-parents were to construct a reflective listening statement to the following remark: "You had no right taking our daughter to a therapist without consulting me. You do this kind of thing over and over!"

Adam writes: "I feel it was important to our daughter to take her to therapy, and I have every right as a parent to do so because it was in her best interest."

"Whoa," says Renee. "That sounds like you were to trying to give an 'I' message and defend yourself at the same time. Let's take it again and try to mirror back what is being said."

With help from other group members, Adam develops the following reflective listening statement: "You're angry because I took our daughter to a therapist without talking to you first. You feel like I do this all the time."

"That," says Renee, "is simply letting your co-parent know that you heard what she said. Remember, you don't have to defend yourself. What you should be trying to do is to defuse the situation."

After reviewing communication techniques in both single-gender groups, the men and women get together. The leaders notice that the men are on one side of the room with the women on the other side.

They show a video that demonstrates how parents can hold their anger in check and still confront their co-parents over an important issue related to their children. A second video explains how various communication blocks, such as sarcasm, demanding, advising, put-downs, and hostility, escalate anger and lead to unproductive arguments and fights.

The task for the night is to make sure every co-parenting couple has selected three conflicts and that everyone constructs "I" messages based on those three conflicts and begins practicing those communication techniques with each other. The leaders get everyone involved in one of the three tasks and act as consultants to help them. Several parents need assistance in writing appropriate "I" messages.

With time running out in this session, Sharon and Adam volunteer to be the first couple to practice communication. They are seated back to back with a leader supervising closely. Other parents watch the demonstration as Sharon reads her first "I" message.

"I get upset when you get so angry and yell at me when we're trying to talk about our daughters," Sharon communicates, "because I get too nervous. What I need is for you to keep your anger under control so we can communicate better."

Adam responds: "Sometimes I do get angry . . . "

The leader immediately stops him. "Adam, just say back to her what you heard her say, not what you'd like to say back. Okay?"

"I hear that you are upset when I holler at you because you want to communicate better."

Again, the leader intervenes. "You left out a couple of things. So I'm going to have Sharon read her 'I' message again, and this time just say back exactly what you hear." He nods his head indicating he will try.

Sharon reads her "I" message again, and Adam tries again. With only one prompt from the leader, Adam produces a pretty good "I" message. Sharon confirms that he understood what she was trying to say. It's now Adam's turn to give her one of his "I" messages and for Sharon to try to reflect back what he says.

She, too, has some difficulties. But the leader has them go back over it until she gets it right. Then, they switch roles again. After they each have several turns, others who were watching get the idea of what is required in this exercise. It's then time for others to try. After all couples get to practice, time runs out. The co-parents take the quiz, collect their homework, and leave.

❖ ❖ ❖ ❖ ❖

The sixth week of ADEPT

As people meet in the single-gender groups, they are aware that the series is rapidly coming to a close. After tonight, there will only be two more sessions.

"Are we actually making fast enough progress?" Chris asks.

"Yeah," echoes Phil. "It seems like we should have accomplished more by this time."

"Every group moves at its own pace," Renee comments calmly. "We think most of you are doing well. And you'll see that we'll try to move things along quickly in our last three sessions."

There is anxiety, although of a different kind, in the women's group.

"What's on our agenda tonight?" Danielle asks.

"Will we be alone with our co-parents?" Mina wants to know.

"You know we'll never do that to you," Jay reassures her. "But let me tell you specifically what's on our agenda for tonight."

He pauses and looks around the room and he notes that the women are anxious. Danielle is smiling nervously. Mina leans forward and looks intently at him.

"Here's what we'll be doing," he says. "First, Bruce and Julia are the last couple left to select their three conflicts. They've got to work fast and get that done tonight. Then, I think everyone else is ready to do more communication practice with their co-parents."

"Will we be sitting back-to-back?" Mary Anne asks.

"Yes, definitely, and one of us will be there to coach you."

"What if he says something that's cruel?" Mina asks.

"That's why we're here. Our job is to keep people within the boundaries of respectful communication."

"And what do we do after that?" Danielle wants to know.

"We move on to solving the conflicts," Jay explains.

"How can we do that when we haven't talked in two years?" Mina asks.

"Well, let's talk about the process so you know what to expect."

Jay goes on to explain that a traditional conflict resolution approach will be used. "With coaches helping out," he says, "each of you will brainstorm three possible ways to solve your first conflict. Then you will discuss those ideas, giving both the positive and negative aspects of the idea. If you both agree an idea has merit, you'll keep it. If it doesn't have enough merit, you'll discard it. When you have discussed all the ideas, you'll look at those you kept and work together to put those together in a compromise solution to the conflict. When you have agreed on the wording, you'll both write it down and countersign each other's form. Then you'll go on to the next conflict."

"But how do we solve a problem like the one we have?" Mina asks again.

"Which one is that?" Jay asks.

"It's the one we have the most trouble with. Whether the kids will stay in a private school or go to a public school."

"It might be a difficult conflict, but every conflict can be solved by reasonable people. You begin by brainstorming some possible solutions..."

"But there aren't any for this one," Mina protests.

"Sure there are," Jay replies. "For instance, one idea would be that the kids stay in a private school. Another is that they switch to a public school. Another is that the kids be consulted about what they want. And one more would be that you get a psychological or educational evaluation and let a third party decide what's best."

"We'll never agree on this one," Mina says.

"Don't be so quick to say that," Jay cautions. "You'd be surprised what people can work out."

"I don't know," Mina says, getting in the last word.

At this point, it's time for the women to join the men in the other room.

The leaders quickly tell the whole group the agenda for the evening and say that, in the interest of time, there will be no preliminaries. They will get everyone busy at one task or another.

Renee takes Julia and Bruce to one corner of the room, along with their coaches. She tells them they needed to catch up to everyone else and select their three conflicts. They both scowl.

The other leader begins to organize co-parents to practice their "I" messages and spontaneous reflective listening comments. He has Danielle and Phil sit back-to-back.

"Now," Jay says to them, "one of you will start with an 'I' message and the other will respond to it. So which of you would like to start?"

"Let her," Phil says politely.

"Okay," agrees Danielle, and she takes a deep breath.

"I get angry when you leave nasty messages on my voicemail at home because it is disrespectful. What I'd like is for you to leave only messages related to a concern about the children."

"Okay," the leader says looking at Phil. "Now reflect back what you heard her say."

"I don't leave bad messages any more," Phil says defensively.

"That may be, but the idea here is to let her know that you heard what she said. You don't have to defend yourself. Okay, try it."

"I hear that you are angry when you think I leave bad messages and I'll stop doing it."

"Okay, nice try, Phil. But I want you to try it again and repeat back exactly what she said. Danielle, you say your 'I' message again."

Again she gives the same message. And Phil tries his reflective listening statement: "What I hear you saying is that you're angry when I leave bad messages on your voicemail and you want me to stop it."

"Is that right?" the leader asks Danielle.

"Yes," responds Danielle. "Exactly."

"Very good, Phil. Now it's your turn to give an 'I' message and we'll see how Danielle does."

After Danielle and Phil have several chances to practice, the leaders invite more couples up to the two chairs to practice. The leaders direct all of the co-parents to go over their "I" messages or reflective listening statements — sometimes several times when they don't have them just right.

Jay looks to the corner where Julia and Bruce are trying to select their three conflicts and he frowns. They're sitting right next to each other. "Oh, oh," he says to himself. "That looks like trouble." He quickly looks around the room for Renee, who has been working with them. She is now coaching another couple, preparing them to practice their communication.

Later, as everyone is busily engaged in the evening's quiz, he asks her what was up with Bruce and Julia.

"You won't believe this," she says, "but we pretty quickly came up with an agreement on the three conflicts they wanted to select as their conflicts to work on here."

"Yes?" Jay says skeptically.

Renee further describes Bruce saying, "You know we've been fighting for almost four years, and I don't know about Julia but I'm tired of it. Why don't we just start talking and settling things?" So they moved over next to each other and started talking about their first conflict.

"You're right; I find it hard to believe. They are supposed to be our impossible couple in this group."

"I know," she says. "Sometimes people just have to be forced to come together in a nonadversarial setting — and they can afford to let go of some of their anger and bitterness."

❖ ❖ ❖ ❖ ❖

The seventh week of ADEPT

With only one more week remaining after this session, co-parents' anxiety seems to be rising.

"What if we haven't made enough progress?" Wendy asks. "Will we have to come back for another eight weeks?"

Mina raises another question. "Shouldn't we be further along? I mean I and my co-parent can't even agree on our three conflicts, and some people here are starting to resolve their conflicts."

Mina brings a smile from everyone when she opens a plastic bag and dumps eighteen Hershey chocolate bars on the table. "This is to help reduce our anxiety," she proclaims.

In the meantime, in the room where the men are gathered Bruce is making a confession of sorts.

"I know I shouldn't have done it, but one day this week I was thinking about my kids and I was working near their neighborhood, so I just stopped over."

"Really?" Renee says raising her eyebrows.

"I know it wasn't right," admits Bruce. "Julia was there and she was outside with some neighbors and the children. She was friendly and smiling and she introduced me to her friends and said I could spend some time with the kids in the backyard. But I shouldn't have done it."

"Probably not," Renee agrees. "But what's done is done. You'll probably want to talk to Julia about that tonight, and consider thanking her for her kindness."

"I know."

Both the men and the women are curious about the agenda for the evening. Although the leaders review the agenda, when everyone's together the leaders reiterate the tasks ahead of them in the last two sessions of this eight-week program.

"First, we have people at different stages," starts Jay. "Some of you still haven't finished your communication practice, and others are ready to get on with resolving conflicts."

Renee takes over the explanation. "So what we'll do tonight is have everyone busy and working at one of these tasks. We have a lot to do before we end next week."

"Exactly," continues Jay, "We want everyone to have resolved at least one conflict by tonight, and it would be great if some of you have resolved all three of your conflicts and gone on to design and sign a co-parent agreement."

"What's that?" inquires Phil.

"That's simply an agreement between co-parents about how you're going to work together to be great co-parents for your children. But we're getting a bit ahead of ourselves. You'll get the form as homework tonight, and then you can read it over and think about it during the coming week, and hopefully you'll get a chance to discuss it with your co-parent at our last session."

Again Renee takes over, shifting the focus. "But now, it's movie time. Tonight we are going to show some of the parents who were fighting in earlier videos resolving their conflicts."

The video shows two couples talking about and resolving conflicts related to their children. When the video is over, Renee says, "I hope you noticed how important their use of "I" messages and reflective listening was in settling disputes they had."

"We've really been promoting communication techniques and now you've had a chance to see them in operation," Jay chimes in. "In good conflict resolution, several important things take place.

"First, you have to find a good time and place to talk — preferably away from the kids. Second, someone starts by giving an 'I' message. Just as you saw in this video, when the woman said, 'I get very concerned when you work late and then pick the kids up late because it throws off everyone's schedule. What I need is for you to call if you're going to be late or to work it out with your boss so you aren't late'.

"Then, the other co-parent follows this up with a reflective listening statement. This restates the first parent's concern and shows that the parent not only cares about what's troubling his co-parent but, in fact, heard what she had to say.

"The next step is to move toward brainstorming some ideas to solve the problem. After several ideas are out on the table, you have to negotiate until you've found one or more ideas that you can put together into a win-win solution, in which both of you feel you've come out winners.

"What we're going to do here is to give you an opportunity to practice these important conflict resolution steps. If you can resolve one or more problems here, then you will prove to yourself and to each other that you can do this outside of here."

With that explanation and after giving co-parents a chance to ask questions, the leaders divide everyone up into one of two groups representing the two stages that people are at. Russell and Paula, as well as Randy and Mina, Rod and Wendy, Adam and Sharon, and Phil and Danielle are in the group ready to practice communication sitting back-to-back. Bruce and Julia and Chris and Mary Anne are ready to move on to conflict resolution. But first, Bruce and Julia need to talk about him stopping over unannounced. There is a leader with each group of co-parents.

Bruce is as apologetic and contrite to Julia as he was in the men's group earlier.

"I'm sorry, Julia, I know it was the wrong thing for me to do, stopping over like that."

"You're right," she says. "It was stupid. You always do things like that and then you apologize afterwards. That's why we had a personal protection order."

"I know," he says. "I really am sorry and I won't let it happen again. I also appreciate how nice you were about it in front of the kids and the neighbors."

"Oh, I've heard that before," Julia proclaims. She isn't giving an inch to him.

"Can we get beyond this?" the leader supervising this exchange asks. "He's apologized and said he knows it was wrong."

"I don't see why I should overlook this," Julia says adamantly.

"I'm not asking you to overlook it," Bruce pleads. "I'm asking for forgiveness for something I did that was wrong."

There is silence until the leader looks at Julia and asks, "Well?"

"I don't think I should forgive him. If I do, it will just keep happening over and over again. That's his pattern."

Bruce begins to lose his patience. "I'm tired of begging you." He leaps to his feet, pushing his chair back. "You're so high and mighty. You never do anything wrong. Well, I'm out of here!" Bruce turns around and stomps out of the room. Everyone in the room watches him leave. Jay follows him out in the hall to talk: "Take a few minutes to cool down, Bruce."

"I'm sorry," Bruce says, "I know I shouldn't let her get to me, but I do."

"I realize it's frustrating," Jay says.

Bruce nods, "I think I'm ready to return. I think I can keep it under control with Julia." Jay walks back into the room with him.

At the same time, in other parts of the room, Rod and Wendy are sitting back-to-back giving "I" messages and reflective listening statements. The co-leader with them corrects them and asks them to do parts over so they can get it right. Other co-parents are sitting nearby so they can learn from this interaction.

In another corner of the room, Chris and Mary Anne have decided to work on their first conflict. The conflict is over child support payments. Mary Anne has dreaded this confrontation and is very nervous about it. Recently in court, she blew up in rage and called Chris the worst name she could think of. The judge threatened her and finally ordered her out of the courtroom.

But they are both calm this evening, and they each suggest three ideas to resolve the conflict over child support. With urging by a co-leader, they discuss the six ideas they came up with and both agree that several ideas are good ones. After about fifteen minutes of discussion, the leader says, "Now take all those good ideas and mold them into a win-win solution."

"I'll defer to Mary Anne," Chris offers. "She was the journalism major." Mary Anne nods and starts writing. After several moments she looks up and says, "I've got something."

"Okay, here goes. We agree that child support payments will be made on time and the mortgage payments will also be made in a timely fashion. We will communicate by email if we have questions or concerns about child support. We will share statements from the mortgage company with each other to ensure that mortgage payments are being made on time."

"That sounds good," says Chris. "Read it again slowly so I can copy it down."

Mary Anne does. And when both have written it down, they exchange conflict resolution forms and initial each other's.

The leader compliments them. "I think you're ready to go on to your second conflict." They both agree.

After practicing communication, Rod and Wendy ask if they can begin conflict resolution. "We're both going to be on vacation next week," Rod says. "If we could resolve our conflicts, then we wouldn't have to come back and make up the last session."

The leader agrees. They sit down across from each other at a table, and with another parent as coach, begin to brainstorm ideas for their first conflict. A half-hour later, Jay checks in with them.

"How are you guys doing?" he asks.

"I can't believe this," Wendy says sounding surprised. "We're talking. We haven't done this in three years. Can you believe this, Rod?"

"No, but I'm glad we're doing it,' Rod says. "This needed to be done."

"I know," she agrees.

"We could have done this on our own," Rod says.

"Maybe," Wendy replies. "But it took a program like this forcing us to get together before we actually did it."

Before they leave, they discuss and agree on a co-parenting plan.

In another corner, with the help of two persistent coaches, Russell and Paula have finally agreed on their three conflicts. "We picked the really important ones," Paula says. "These were problems that had been bugging me for years."

But Mina and Randy start out the evening right where they had left off the week before. "I won't agree on anything unless we can include her false accusations against me as a conflict," Randy says adamantly.

Several tables away, Mina tells the leader: "There's no way I'll ever agree to that!"

With persistence and the co-leader working with them, Randy agrees to drop his demand in exchange for an agreement from Mina to move on to communications practice. The leader has them sit back-to-back and use "I" messages and reflective listening. To their own and everyone else's surprise, they do this without rancor. Even more surprising, they move next to conflict resolution and begin discussing the most knotty problem they face: Whether the kids will stay in a private school or move to a public school. Although they don't reach agreement, they are talking.

"That's more talking than we've done in several years," Mina says as she leaves at the end of the session.

Like everyone else, Mina does her quiz for the night and takes the co-parenting agreement homework home with her.

❖ ❖ ❖ ❖ ❖

The eighth and final week of ADEPT

"I can't believe it's the eighth week already," exclaims Chris in the men's group at the beginning of the eighth session. "It's gone by fast."

"And I have to admit I learned some things," Phil adds. "I know I had a hostile attitude in the beginning, but it's been good for me."

In the women's group, Mary Anne says that no matter whether or not she and Chris have an improved relationship after ADEPT, she is definitely going to continue to use the communication techniques they've been practicing. "I don't know whether you said this or not," she says looking at Jay, "but I think it keeps down hostility between us if I can remember to use reflective listening and 'I' messages."

"I agree," adds Julia. "I've been using them with my kids."

Danielle perks up and seems to want to say something. "You know another thing is that I used to think I was the only one who had this bad relationship with my co-parent. But being with you guys has helped me to realize that I'm not so bad and I'm not alone. There are lots of us who have to work on getting along with our co-parent for our kids' sakes."

"I found out a friend's child has leukemia this week," Sharon says joining the conversation. "We complain about our co-parents and other things, but it's really important that we put things in perspective. Our kids are healthy. And it's our job to keep them that way. All we have to do is talk more to our co-parents."

There is a chorus of "Yeahs" around the room.

Jay tells them about the agenda for the evening and urges them all to get as much accomplished as possible in this last opportunity to work with their co-parent with supervision. With that, the women leave to join the men in the larger conference room.

Jay and Renee make just a few introductory remarks before setting out the task for the evening. However, while they thank everyone for participating and putting forth effort, they indicate they're always available to help them in the future. Anytime they have a question or concern, they can call or email.

The leaders continue, "The task tonight is simple. We want all of you to resolve as many of your three conflicts as possible. Then, if you have time, go on to discussion of the co-parenting plan that was your homework. That plan is an agreement between the two of you that you will put aside bitterness and resentment so you can work together from now on in the best interests of your children."

Renee and Jay assign co-parenting couples to different parts of the room, and move from couple to couple to make sure they're using the approach and format for discussing conflicts. They emphasize the need to focus on coming up with win-win solutions.

Russell and Paula choose the issue that has been most difficult for her — his getting a job so he can provide child support. The leader who's coaching them asks them both to come up with three brainstormed ideas to resolve this conflict. "You could just take any job that is available," suggests Paula immediately.

"I could update my resume and send it out more often," Russell offers. "And I can do more networking."

"That'll be the day," Paula says, rolling her eyes sarcastically.

"Do I have to put up with that sarcasm?" Russell asks with a pained expression on his face.

The coach looks at Paula and says: "Paula, you know the rules about sarcasm. It's not going to help resolve anything."

"I know, but I think he should prove that he's sending out more resumes," Paula adds defensively.

"Let's just stick to brainstorming ideas," the coach directs. "Then if you want to critique the ideas you can."

Paula and Russell come up with six ideas. Russell quickly says he can agree with all of Paula's ideas except the one where he would have to prove that he was making renewed efforts to get a job. "There's no way I can prove this and I don't think I should have to."

Paula continues complaining, "But you've been saying for years that you're going to get a job and you never do. This is ridiculous. If we just let him say he's going to do something, he won't do anything."

"Is that right?" the coach asks Russell.

"No," Russell assures her. "If I agree to a solution here, I'll follow through."

They work on a solution statement. They agree on: "Russell will redouble his efforts to obtain a job. He will revise his resume and send out more copies, and he will accept any job, no matter what the job, as quickly as possible." They both sign each other's copy of this solution statement.

In another part of the room, Chris and Mary Anne are talking with each other and are busily engaged in brainstorming ideas for their second conflict. They agreed earlier to work on having more direct communication with each other. They come to a solution for this conflict and move on to their final conflict: drinking alcohol in front of the children. They follow the process, keep their dialog on a business-like basis, and resolve that conflict, too.

Mina and Randy aren't quite having the same success. However, they're talking to each other without a coach present. When one of the leaders checks in with them, Mina gives an update of their progress. "We came to an agreement on the medical bills, and he has agreed to share the cost of all medical expenses."

"But when it comes to where the kids go to school, we are at an impasse," Randy says, sounding discouraged. "We just agreed to disagree for the time being."

Jay asks them if this is the best they can do at this time. They both say yes. He congratulates them on their progress, and wishes them well as they deal with other issues in the future.

Although Julia and Bruce are not making much progress resolving their conflicts, they are keeping their anger in check. Renee points out that that in itself is progress

Danielle and Phil, in contrast, are making significant progress. They come up with equitable solutions for their communication conflict, their arguments concerning money, and their desires to shield the kids from any further conflict. "If nothing else," Phil says, "we realize that our fighting in front of the kids has been hurting them. We have agreed never to do this again."

Danielle nods her head in agreement. "Our kids are too important for us to let our emotions get in the way of their happiness."

As it's approaching 9:00, the participants fill out class evaluation forms, and the leaders ask everyone to be honest in giving feedback. As the co-parents finish the evaluation, they turn it in, say goodbye to the leaders and to each other, and leave.

On his way out, Chris tells the leaders, "Any time you want me to come by and talk to new recruits or help out as a coach, just call me. I believe in this program."

Russell shakes the leaders' hands and says, "You guys are doing a good job; keep it up. I wish Paula and I could have made more progress, but at least we sat down together in the same room. That hasn't happened for a long time."

"This program has made a big difference for us," Danielle says as she's leaving with Paula and Julia. "I think our kids are going to be better adjusted people as a result."

❖ *In Conclusion*

ADEPT is a unique group program for high-conflict divorce couples. Its effectiveness derives from several factors.

1. It is a group program. Couples entrenched in high-conflict relationships are accustomed to fighting with each other — but mostly in private. In a group and public setting, they are less inclined to display their anger, bitterness, and hostility. There are two reasons for this. One is the power of peer pressure. Most individuals in a public forum (even one like ADEPT, which brings together high-conflict couples) wish to be seen as reasonable and kind. They would like the world to see that it's their co-parent who's unreasonable and abusive. Second, there is a natural sense of comparison and competitiveness that operates in a group setting. If one couple acts badly, other couples compare themselves to that couple and wish to be seen as "better" and more "normal."

2. It is a confidential program. By judicial agreement, nothing that happens in ADEPT (aside from attendance) can be reported to the court or used by either party in their dispute. Since the ADEPT interactions won't be seen by the court, couples have less need to show up the other person or "pretend" to be cooperative. The confidential nature of the program facilitates parents' willingness to put forth their best efforts.

3. Men and women are separated for a part of each session. This gender-separation aspect of the program serves several purposes. First, it allows same-gender individuals to bond with each other and work together. Second, it reduces the opportunities for face-to-face expression of hostility between couples or just between men and women in general. Third, by placing an opposite sex group leader in the single-gender groups it reduces the "men-bashing" or "women-bashing" that might go on in the early sessions of the program.

4. *It includes peer coaching.* Peer coaching not only enhances bonding between individuals, but it leads men and women to work together. This cooperation may not necessarily be apparent in the early sessions with one's co-parent. Peer coaching sets an example for co-parents. Each co-parent can see that the co-parent is able to work in a reasonably cooperative and productive way with other people in the group — both men and women. Furthermore, the use of peer coaching requires that every individual learn the techniques of communication and conflict resolution to be able to coach and instruct others. By having coached others in the fine points of a technique, each is thus more motivated to show that, having taught the method to others, he can actually do it himself with his co-parent.

5. *Expectations are high.* Every individual is expected to take some measure of responsibility for communication failures in the relationship. In addition, each set of co-parents in ADEPT is expected to agree on three conflicts to work together on during the eight weeks. They must learn and practice communication skills under supervision as well as learn and practice conflict resolution methods. Every couple is fully expected to solve all three of their conflicts and to discuss and agree on a basic co-parenting plan. These high expectations are communicated at the first class and are continually emphasized throughout the program.

6. *The leaders use important counseling and therapeutic principles and techniques.* Both leaders make concerted efforts to form a relationship with each person in the single-gender group. As part of this effort, the leaders listen attentively and use reflective listening and "I" messages as a normal way of communicating with the parents in the program. Furthermore, the leaders don't reinforce parents' anger, negative perceptions (of their co-parents, attorneys, judges, or others in the judicial system), hostilities, or vindictiveness. The leaders provide emotional support and consistency. They don't over-respond to co-parents' crises or emotional outbursts. They also don't take sides or play one parent against another. As indicated previously, they steadfastly maintain a positive attitude and support even minor efforts to bring about improvements in co-parent relationships. They work to ensure that each parent leaves the program feeling successful.

These six factors, we believe, make the ADEPT program both effective and a model for other court programs. There are, however, some contraindications for the program. For instance, when co-parents have personal protection orders against each other, have recently been assaultive to one another, or are unable to control their anger, they perhaps should not be in this group program. In addition, co-parents entrenched in conflict for several years may need much more than an eight-week program to begin to resolve their conflicts.

The ADEPT program will be successful for many co-parents, but it won't meet every high-conflict couple's needs. As you will read in the next chapter, other approaches that don't rely on a group approach can be effective as well.

16

The High-Conflict Treatment Team

There are times when parent coordination and family therapy are unsuccessful. Despite an experienced professional's best efforts, sometimes mediation techniques and collaborative methods just don't work to reduce interparental conflict.

❖❖❖❖❖

Ricardo and Chantelle provide an example of a couple experiencing high conflict who had failed to respond to every program and approach to which they had been referred. They were stuck on their anger toward each other, which stemmed from his numerous affairs with female co-workers and her explosive temper that led to physical attacks on Ricardo.

❖❖❖❖❖

Like many other high-conflict couples, Ricardo and Chantelle failed to benefit from previous interventions. Also like other co-parents with ongoing conflict, the intense challenge they presented for mediators, parent coordinators, and therapists was related to some or all of the following reasons:

❖ One or both of the co-parents refuse to speak with the other.
❖ The co-parents will meet together, but one or both are rigidly fixated on a particular description of the past that doesn't allow for cooperation or forgiveness (e.g., violence, affairs, emotional abuse, or the other's decision to divorce is unforgivable).
❖ One co-parent is unable to adjust to the other developing a new relationship.
❖ One or both feel wronged in the financial settlement or in the negotiations for the settlement of the divorce.

❖ One co-parent is angry at or frightened of the other (e.g., because of substance abuse, mental illness, physical abuse, or other behavioral problems).

When these reasons apply, despite excellent mediation skills on the part of the professional, the co-parents themselves continue to define the situation as adversarial. The professional can spot a case that's heading this way by such indicators as either or both co-parents

❖ refusing to be in the same room as the other
❖ exhibiting rapid emotional escalation despite no troublesome topic having been broached
❖ leaving the room precipitously
❖ rapidly moving to threaten court action whenever the other doesn't agree with a proposed solution
❖ dogmatically refusing to negotiate for a common solution
❖ being unwilling to accept any solutions other than those he or she is proposing

If you are the professional faced with these conditions, you don't necessarily have to give up on helping the couple find a peaceful solution. However, you will certainly conclude that this is a more challenging situation. This conclusion will be inescapable regardless of whether only one of the parents seems angry, intractable, or responsible for the impasse. You can safely assume that the other parent is intimately involved in the struggle — whether her part is visible or not. All resistant impasses involve at least two people and neither should be assessed as "innocent."

With these opening remarks as a backdrop, in this chapter we present a treatment team and systems therapy approach to working with the most daunting and challenging high-conflict co-parents.

❖ *Fundamentals of the Treatment Team Approach*

The room. The ideal arrangement for a high-conflict treatment team requires two offices with a one-way mirror between them. A sound system must be in place with microphones capable of picking up whispers to communicate the dialog to the next office. It is ideal to have a video camera in the therapy room and a monitor in the observation room. The sound through the video system may be enough to hear clearly, but a more specific sound system is often needed.

Sessions are videotaped so the co-therapists can review each session, and co-parents are clearly told that these tapes will be erased shortly after they have been reviewed so they don't fear they will be used as evidence against them in court. A local line on a telephone system or an intercom that functions like a telephone is needed so that the team members can communicate during the session. Some therapists like a "bug-in-the-ear" — an earphone worn by the therapist in the room. Others recommend against this choice as it interferes with the therapist's nonverbal communications with the clients. A ringing phone merely stops the action temporarily, which resumes once the therapist has listened.

The clinical structure. Two therapists are used for a high-conflict treatment team. Additional therapists may be present behind the mirror for specific consultation methods that are presented later in this chapter. One therapist observes and calls observations in to the therapist in the room with the client(s). The other therapist is the primary therapist while in the room and has final say on the actions he will take during the session. The therapists may reverse positions and roles throughout the session based on a variety of needs, or the therapists' roles can remain fixed.

The following models are a few of the most common methods used in live consultation, but the potential is limited only by the level of creativity of the professionals involved.

❖ The Consultation Model

When using the consultation model, there is typically one therapist in the therapy room and one consultant behind the mirror. The purpose of the consultant is to be an impartial pair of eyes who can provide perspective and ideas to the primary therapist. The locus of power remains with the therapist in the room. The goal is to augment the skills of the therapist while not distracting unduly from the therapy. The minds of the clients should remain in the room with their therapist as much as possible. Ideally, they pay little attention to the consultant.

When using the consultation model, it's unusual for the therapists to reverse roles. The therapy is simply enhanced by the ideas and observations of two therapists. Approximately three-quarters of the way through the session, the therapist steps out to consult with the observer and explains this to the family. The therapist and consultant formulate a plan using their combined knowledge and that approach is then presented to the clients. The plan usually consists of one of the following:

1. *Directions as to what to do to solve the problem during the period until the next session.* These directions will be straightforward and clear, such as a direction to meet on Sunday evening at 8:00 p.m. and agree on an exchange schedule for the following week.

2. *Indirect directions as to what to do, the purpose of which will remain unclear to the clients.* This method is used when clients are more highly oppositional.

> An example of this is when in a session, the therapist made a request to Josh to continue trying to convince his co-parent to change her mind through persuasion. Josh believed he was being told to try harder, but in fact he was being asked to continue to do what hadn't been working for him already. The therapist hoped Josh would conclude that he must act differently. It was also expected that Josh would become more frustrated during the next week. This would allow the therapist to request a different set of actions on Josh's part in the next session, since the current approach wasn't working.

3. *Directions that the therapists believe will open the clients' eyes to a reality that they are overlooking, thereby changing their behaviors.* This approach presupposes a reasonable level of cooperation from the clients.

4. *Along with directions, insights that make it more difficult for the clients to continue a counterproductive set of behaviors.*

> For example, Jocelle almost always yelled at Vernon, her co-parent, whenever they spoke on the phone. It was inevitable that Vernon would say something that offended Jocelle. The therapist can redefine her angry outbursts as "playing right into his hand" by allowing Vernon to describe her outbursts to the court as proof of her lack of self-control. If the therapist has a playful demeanor with her client, as Jocelle's therapist had with her, she could comment, "How kind it is of you to make his case for him."

5. *Helping co-parents reach an agreement on an issue, and having them sign a document to that effect.* Furthermore, after signing the agreement, they are directed to shake hands on the agreement or at least state to each other that they agree and voice to each other what they agree to.

6. Leading both parents by attributing attractive characteristics to them and attaching certain behaviors to those attributions.

The therapist told Vernon and Jocelle that both were so passionate about several issues because they love their daughter so much (when they both appear to, in fact, be vindictive). The therapist went on to tell them that, in light of this ardent love for their daughter, they both certainly know that it's damaging to her for them to argue in her presence. She also said that since they're both intelligent and insightful they will certainly want to stop any such arguing and refrain from disagreements until the next session.

The Greek Chorus and Reflecting Team Model

The Greek chorus (Papp, 1980) and reflecting team (Anderson, Goolishian, and Winderman, 1986) approaches require a group of therapists behind the one-way mirror. There must be at least two therapists behind the mirror and more than two is preferable. The locus of power in this approach is in both the therapy room and the observation room. For the Greek chorus, the family understands that comments will regularly be sent into the room with the therapist obligated to read them verbatim. These comments may be similar to the insights discussed above in the consultation model, but they have much greater clinical latitude.

For example, a portion of the group behind the mirror may present one position and another portion may present a different position. The males in the group might align with the female in the room, and the females in the group might align with the male. The males may join together to attempt to sway a male from an unfortunate sexist position, and the females may do likewise with the female in the room. The group can split itself by race, gender, educational level, socioeconomics, or any other factor that is present in the struggle between the co-parents.

For instance, you may recall Marta and Gregor from chapter fourteen. Gregor believed Marta was maliciously doing whatever she could to keep the children from him. The therapists, in this approach, would try to help him understand that Marta was frightened for the safety and well-being of their children. Also, she experienced separation anxiety when not close to her children. In order to create doubt about Gregor's certainty, the Greek chorus might send in a message stating that, of the men in the group, thirty percent of them agree that she is hateful and being obstructive and he should never trust her. However, seventy percent of the men in the group see a frightened young mother who has never really been separated from her children and faces the prospect of having to deal with separation from her "babies" years before she would ever have had to do so if there hadn't been a divorce.

Using the reflecting team approach, some or all of the therapists behind the mirror enter the room late in the session and hold a conversation between themselves in front of the family. This discussion is typically metaphorical for the struggle between the parents and may have many of the characteristics indicated in the Greek chorus. However, this method allows the parents to identify with professionals as they discuss something that is deadlocked in the session and then watch the professionals reach a solution. The parents may be swayed by discussions they hear or recognize the foolishness of positions they've taken when watching someone else dramatize these positions. Again, creativity allows for endless options when using a reflecting team.

❖❖❖❖❖

Jeb and Lily were co-parents in a family who required the high-conflict treatment team. The therapists decided on a reflecting team approach when it became clear that Jeb and Lily, having shared legal and physical custody, would never agree on which school their 5-year-old soon-to-be kindergartener would attend. Jeb said that Lily was letting her feelings interfere with acknowledging that the school he preferred had better test scores. Lily said Jeb only wanted their son to be closer to him. As Lily and Jeb became stuck in their rigid positions, the reflecting team asked to join them in the room to discuss a problem they were having.

The reflecting team members had planned a dialogue in which Zach, a social worker, and Loretta, a psychologist, discussed their disagreement over whether the therapist, Marissa, was being too hard on the couple. Zach argued that Marissa was being overly emotional and losing her objectivity. Loretta argued that Marissa was being impatient and wanting the couple to change and decide too quickly. As Loretta and Zach debated their differences over Marissa, they gradually listened better to each other's points and finally agreed that there was some validity to each of their concerns, but overall Marissa was doing a good job.

❖❖❖❖❖

The Strategic Mediation Model

❖

The strategic mediation model was developed by Thomas Blume and Jerome Price (Blume and Price, 1993) out of a desire to merge the skills of an experienced mediator with an experienced family therapist to treat cases that neither was successful with alone. Strategic mediation is intended for cases that traditionally are unsuitable for mediation due to accusations of past violence, substance abuse, child abuse, and other more serious conflicts. It also can successfully treat couples who haven't agreed to cooperate with each other, whereas mediation can only be used when there is a clear desire to cooperate.

In strategic mediation, treatment begins with the mediator in the treatment room and the therapist in the observation room. As in all mediation, the mediator works with a vision toward creating stability for the couple through negotiation, discussion, and agreement. The mediator works in his usual way with occasional calls into the room from the therapist with observations. In high-conflict cases, it's inevitable that the mediation process will break down when a high-conflict topic or ritualized struggle emerges. When the mediator concludes that he can go no further, he leaves the room and the therapist enters the treatment room and takes over.

The role of therapist is one of destabilization rather than stabilization. The couple has become stable in the sense that they have once again embedded themselves in their unchanging ritualized struggle. Such consistency and predictability is quite stable. The therapist's job is to destabilize the stuck cycles with challenges, probing into motivation and feelings and use of indirect interventions — if necessary — such as the use of paradoxical interventions. When the therapist succeeds in creating more of a sense of openness in the couple and a willingness to cooperate, he leaves the room and the mediator returns to continue the mediation process.

The article by Blume and Price cited above offers specific techniques and methods for use by the mediator and the therapist in the strategic mediation process. This chapter won't go into extensive detail about how to carry out this process, but you might seek out the article (Blume and Price, 1993) to learn about this approach.

High-Conflict Case Example with Clinical Commentary

❖

The following high-conflict case uses elements of the consultation model along with a kind of redefinition such as might be used in the Greek chorus model to bring about change in a painfully stuck case.

❖❖❖❖❖

Raja and Tarak sat across from each other in the waiting room. She was a slight, dark-haired woman in her mid-forties who initially appeared rather meek. She looked worn and drawn. He, on the other hand, was large and seemed quite imposing. He also seemed quiet, but his presence alone was quite powerful judging from the way Raja glanced over at him frequently to see how he was reacting. They scheduled what the therapist thought was going to be a session for their teenage son, Jag, but Raja provided little information on the telephone as to the nature of the problem.

They arrived without their son, and when they entered the therapy room Raja and Tarak moved immediately to separate corners, like boxers getting ready for the big fight. Despite Jag being their stated reason for seeking help, this looked a lot like many other couples who have sought help for their troubled marriages. As they spoke, both used vague references to the problems with their son's behavior. They used phrases like, "we can't communicate with him" and "we don't get along with him" — as if this would explain everything that Marian, the therapist, might need to know. When Marian tried to clarify why they had come in for therapy, Raja and Tarak continued to speak in abstractions about their son, with Raja doing most of the talking. Thirty minutes later, Marian still didn't have any idea why they had come to therapy but, considering that they never looked at or spoke directly to each other, her clinical intuition told her this was a family in need of help.

Finally, Marian jumped in and asked them to be more specific about why they came in. She went on to wonder with them if they were having marital problems. Raja suddenly erupted, shrilling, "What, be married to him? Are you crazy? I've been trying to divorce him for two years and I just want to never have to deal with him again. But we have a son. Tarak won't cooperate with anything I try to do for Jag's sake!"

Raja's voice became shriller — almost to the point of a scream — as she continued. Tarak sat impassively, staring off into space as his wife continued to berate him for his lack of cooperation both in the marriage and in the impending divorce. Marian listened intently as she tried to figure out what she was dealing with. Was this a child case, a marriage case, or a divorce case? What was this drama that was unfolding? The atmosphere was charged in the room and this seemed to make it impossible for either Marian or Tarak to interrupt Raja. Tarak continued his passive withdrawal.

❖ ❖ ❖ ❖ ❖

Although the decision is usually made in advance to convene a high-conflict treatment team, Marian made the call on the spot that this was a high-conflict case that required a treatment team approach. She had a colleague step behind the mirror after getting Raja and Tarak's permission to proceed. The co-therapists began to conceptualize what was happening and what needed to be done.

On the one hand, Raja and Tarak had spent the first portion of the session acting like most any couple who might be in conflict about their child and had sought help. On the other hand, they'd been in the divorce process for two years. Why was this case so confusing?

It was confusing because, like many couples who are legally divorced or seeking legal divorce, Tarak and Raja were still emotionally married. In their case, this emotional marriage made it difficult to get the legal divorce. In some instances, a couple may have been legally divorced for many years and have the same problem.

The struggles that bound Raja and Tarak together hadn't really changed despite the decision to divorce and having spent two years going through the divorce process. So, what should the therapist address next? Would it be wise for Marian to crack open this emotional powder keg and discuss why they were so upset with each other? Might it be better to see them separately to figure out why the emotional intensity between them was so high and to clarify the issues they needed to resolve regarding their son?

Marian opted for the latter. As the tale unfolded from each of their accounts, the factors that kept them emotionally married became progressively clearer. The first factor had to do with attachment.

Attachment. Attachment can be best judged by how strongly the divorced couple seems drawn back together on a regular basis.

Remaining overly attached can take the form of constant anger or loose boundaries in which neither acts married. Anger is a separation factor discussed later in this chapter. Loose boundaries can be seen in regular activities such as going out to dinner and the movies, taking vacations together, and even continued sexual involvement.

It's always helpful to wonder with the couple about whether either one must call ahead or knock on the other's door before entering the other's home. Who has keys to whose house? The therapist can consider the following questions:

* ❖ How long has the couple been divorced?
* ❖ Do they act like a couple who has settled into healthy divorce routines for the number of years or months they've been apart? (For instance, what is their level of friendliness or affection for each other?)
* ❖ Are they establishing outside relationships?
* ❖ Is there a clear schedule for parenting time, or do they simply come and go?
* ❖ Have all marital possessions been divided up?
* ❖ Are there clear financial agreements that are carried out?
* ❖ Do they have separate rituals for their children's birthdays, Mother's Day and Father's Day, and other holidays?

The answers to these questions will reveal if this may be a couple who is overly attached. In the case of Raja and Tarak, Raja still drove Tarak to doctors' appointments and brought him soup when he was sick — despite the fact that they no longer lived together. She had a new circle of friends, but he hadn't moved on to finding others to share his life. They spoke on the phone every day. Because the divorce wasn't over, Tarak's possessions were still stored in the marital home where Raja was living. Clearly they were still attached.

Reactivity. Reactivity is measured by the intensity of each person's emotional reactions to the other. The content of the upset isn't important in this factor. As long as a person is having strong emotional reactions, she remains emotionally bonded to her spouse or ex-spouse. This distinction is important because strong negative emotions about someone give the angry person the illusion that she is truly finished with her former partner. Others may keep interacting like a couple while understanding themselves to be doing so for their children's sakes.

Judith Margerum (Margerum, 2005) suggests the following questions be used to measure co-parents' level of emotional reactivity to their ex-spouses. She asks co-parents to fill in the blanks with scaled scores from 1 (hardly a twinge) to 5 (highly or all the time). She asks the person scoring to include distress caused by frustration, anger, and hurt. Clearly this scale can be used for those divorcing as well as those already divorced.

1. When my ex rolls his/her eyes at me I am _____ distressed.
2. When my ex is fifteen minutes late I feel _____ distress.
3. When my ex calls during my parenting time I experience _____ distress.
4. When I see my ex to exchange the children I feel _____ distress.
5. When my children tell me how much fun they had with my ex I experience _____ distress.
6. When my ex does not agree with me I generally experience _____ distress.
7. When I see my ex with his or her new partner I feel _____ distress.
8. When I hear about any success my ex is having I feel _____ distress.
9. When my ex makes a mistake in regard to the children I experience _____ distress (for example, gets them to school late).
10. When my ex handles a parenting issue differently than I would have I experience _____ distress.

As you might expect, the higher the score, the more emotionally married the respondent remains.

Judging by the reactions of Raja and Tarak, the therapist could safely assume that they would score very high. With Raja shrieking and Tarak with his arms crossed and a deadpan expression on his face, both were reacting highly emotionally. The paradox was in Raja screaming that she wanted nothing more than to be divorced from Tarak. Yet that very emotional intensity was the proof that she was in fact ambivalent about letting go of her attachment.

Betrayal. When either partner has been betrayed by the spouse, the betrayal binds them together more tightly than a simple divorce in which people have straightforwardly concluded they can't get along. One parent may also view the divorce itself as a betrayal. If a woman has been physically abused by her husband, her hurt over the abuse and violation of her trust makes the divorce harder to get over. Her mind will continually go back to the past, and she may conclude in advance that her co-parent will do similar things to the children.

If a husband finds that his wife has been having a relationship with another man and seeks a divorce, the hurt of this betrayal leaves him struggling to let go of his need to seek justice or vengeance. He may conclude that the children aren't safe because their mother isn't to be trusted and will most likely be having group sex in front of them. When the divorce itself is seen as a betrayal, this context again binds the couple together through the anger and bitterness of the betrayed spouse and the indifference of the spouse who sought the divorce.

❖ ❖ ❖ ❖ ❖

For Raja and Tarak the sense of betrayal was palpable. Tarak had not only had an affair, but had squandered a great deal of the couple's life savings on his mistress. As they tried to divorce, any lapse in Tarak's cooperation with her led Raja to feel violated and revictimized, particularly if he was withholding or dishonest about his handling of the situation. His guilt over what he'd done led him to be depressed and withdrawn. His withdrawal appeared to Raja as indifference and she concluded that he didn't want to cooperate. In fact, any time he moved toward her emotionally to cooperate with the divorce, he became overwhelmed with guilt and shame and withdrew in depression. To Raja this was a revictimization because he was now having an affair with whatever was going on inside his own head. The feeling component for her was very much the same as the affair.

❖ ❖ ❖ ❖ ❖

Passion and sexual attraction. Divorcing people refuse to allow themselves to be conscious of the fact that a man or woman they wanted, had been turned on by, and had slept with repeatedly is most likely someone they still feel some attraction to. They also may feel a need to reconstruct the past and conclude that they never felt anything for their ex-spouses and never really loved them in the first place. The only couple we ever believed had never really loved each other was an Indian couple who, when we challenged their assertion that they never felt anything for each other, said, "You have to understand, our marriage was arranged."

❖ ❖ ❖ ❖ ❖

Passion and drama clearly continued with Raja and Tarak. Tarak, in fact, was so distressed about what he'd done to Raja that he had attempted to hang himself in order to get her the insurance money to replace what he had spent. Tarak's attempt to kill himself was nearly lethal and he spent a long time hospitalized after the attempt. The passion in this act led to Tarak gaining sympathy and protectiveness from their son. Jag criticized and yelled at his mother whenever she spoke ill of Tarak or became angry at him. Tarak's apparent depression continued to be a looming threat of impending suicide, which terrified Jag. Jag's criticism of his mother's expressions of pain added to Raja's emotional intensity and sense of betrayal.

❖ ❖ ❖ ❖ ❖

Tarak's passion was so intense that he was willing to die for his wife. This is a graphic example of the continuation of a love that some divorcing and divorced people still have for each other. Passion can exist in a pure form, as we believe it did for this couple, or it can be embedded in the denial that there is still a sexual attraction. If you've seen enough couples, you can attest to the number of them either during divorce or years later who fall back into each other's arms.

Anger. Anger is the great disguise. As long as people are angry at each other, the anger acts as a smoke screen that disguises the continuation of love, attachment, and passion. As mentioned earlier, people believe that if they are angry at their spouses or co-parents, this is evidence that they no longer love those people. In fact, anger and rage may be the pure evidence that love, passion, attachment, and, in some cases, attraction are still strong.

Why would one parent be angry and jealous when the other finds a new love if not for passion, love, and attraction? In cases where there is little reactivity and attachment, the spouse who hasn't found love is happy for the other because he hopes the new spouse will mellow his co-parent and make her easier to deal with. Logically, a happy, satisfied co-parent, who has moved her love and passion elsewhere, should be much less trouble to deal with because she can be much more businesslike in her dealings about the children.

As was discussed above, Raja was enraged at Tarak for being unfaithful and wiping out their finances. Tarak had been angry at Raja for a long time. Otherwise he would never have had the affair in the first place. He'd become depressed because any awareness of his anger was at war with his shame over his behavior. He couldn't, in his mind, be justifiably angry at a woman who he had so wronged. Therefore, the pattern in their marriage continued on into the divorce. Raja was critical and Tarak was withdrawn. The reasons were different, but that doesn't change the drama.

Treatment — session one. The first step in treatment is to make this covert drama overt. The therapist told Raja and Tarak what she thought was happening, despite the likelihood that they would reject the understanding. Once a covert drama has surfaced, it becomes harder to maintain.

❖❖❖❖❖

Marian simply stated that she thought that they were still quite attached to each other despite the decision to divorce. She shared that she felt there was still a great deal of love in this relationship. Neither challenged Marian's assertion at this point. Otherwise, why would Raja be so overwrought with passionate emotion months after the betrayal? Likewise, why would Tarak be so overwrought with shame and have to be so withdrawn? In fact, she told them, it seemed to her that they were acting in much the same way they had acted while they were married. Therefore, she doubted whether they really wanted to be divorced. It should be noted that both the therapist and the treatment team felt strongly that anyone in Raja's position who wasn't enraged would have to be crazy. They weren't challenging the validity of her anger. They were challenging the relentless intensity of it, and they challenged her to move beyond it and proceed toward the divorce and a better future.

Marian's comments brought an immediate emotional reaction from both of them. Raja cried, "Do you call this a good marriage? I don't want to be married to him. He keeps hurting me just like he did when we were living together. He withholds everything!" Marian challenged further by saying that she appreciated Raja's strong feelings about this, but the very strength of her passion supported her assessment that they were still sufficiently in love and emotionally attached that she doubted their true commitment to divorce.

Raja again cried, "I've never done this before. Tell me what I have to do and I'll do it." Marian said she wasn't yet convinced and, surprisingly, Tarak came to Raja's rescue by making one of his first clear statements. He sat forward for the first time and angrily blurted, "We don't have to convince you of anything!"

Marian and the treatment team were struck by Raja's statement. She had made another covert script overt. She had pretty much labeled them as emotionally still married. They could remain so for years beyond a legal divorce if the emotional drama remained unchanged. Marian's position allowed her to wisely remain neutral on whether they should or should not be divorced. She simply described what she saw.

Raja and Tarak had been unable to cooperate on any of the steps needed to work out the financial settlement. So Marian challenged them further by saying that, if they were indeed ready to let go of each other emotionally, they should be able to pick one settlement issue that remained unresolved and complete it in the following two weeks.

❖ ❖ ❖ ❖ ❖

Treatment — session two

❖ ❖ ❖ ❖ ❖

Tarak and Raja walked into the next session dramatically altered. Raja said, in a conversational tone, that they'd been working on their divorce and began listing financial issues that she and Tarak had addressed. Tarak agreed with a much more open and warm tone. Raja remembered something that Tarak needed to pursue with his accountant and when she mentioned it, Tarak promptly took out a pad and pen and jotted himself a note to take care of it.

The overt understanding that their love stood in the way of divorce brought about a transformation. Both were more in touch with their feelings of kindness toward each other and were pursuing the divorce nevertheless. If they had come back saying they had decided not to divorce, the therapist would have supported this decision as well and offered to help them reconcile. Despite the direction of their decision, the therapist helped Raja and Tarak become a couple who were acting congruently with their stated intentions.

❖ ❖ ❖ ❖ ❖

Treatment — subsequent sessions

❖ ❖ ❖ ❖ ❖

Each session after that was spent addressing two topics. Marian first celebrated with them the steps they had completed toward divorce and honored these accomplishments as evidence of their true intent to divorce. She then discussed the struggles they were still having as evidence that they were still ambivalent about letting go of each other.

At each session, they accomplished more of the items they needed to complete to be ready for the court date, and Marian spent more time appreciating their true commitment to cooperate and divorce. She spent less time in each session punctuating the evidence that they were still emotionally married.

The date for court and finalization of the divorce came between the sixth and seventh therapy sessions. Raja and Tarak were ready to complete the divorce on that date, and therapy was terminated a few sessions after the finalization of the divorce. Both Raja and Tarak, as well as their son Jag, came in periodically over the next two years for counseling sessions geared toward helping everyone adjust emotionally to the divorce and succeed in becoming a cooperative postdivorce family.

❖ ❖ ❖ ❖ ❖

The Dilemma of Emotional Marriage

The dilemma of being emotionally married isn't restricted to those seeking divorce. Many times therapists see cases — and not infrequently these are high-conflict divorce cases — in which co-parents have struggled with emotionally divorcing for years beyond the legal divorce. They often damage their children horribly by keeping them embroiled in the marital struggles that led to the divorce in the first place. Understanding that emotional divorce is a serious factor to be addressed has ramifications for the treatment of many troubled children and teens, as well as the divorced couples themselves.

The High-Conflict Treatment Team in Summary

The high-conflict treatment team as described in this chapter, particularly in the case of Raja and Tarak, uses the creativity of the team to effect change in treatment situations where one therapist alone finds herself struggling. A family is also put on notice that something more dramatic is happening when they know they've been referred to the treatment team. This knowledge creates a greater expectation of changes in their minds.

As with any family in which terrible symptoms have been found to be intractable in traditional treatment, high-conflict divorce relationships require methods that go beyond the everyday approaches of talk therapy. There is considerable information available about the live supervision and consultation models in family therapy that we've discussed in this chapter. We strongly suggest that if you are interested in pursuing the high-conflict treatment team approach, you explore this literature, which will help you be more effective in working with high-conflict divorce cases (Madanes, 1984; Selvini and Palazzoli, 1991; Haley, 1996).

A Final Word on Working With High-Conflict Divorce Couples

In the chapters you've just read, you've had an opportunity to be exposed to a number of programs and strategies for working with high-conflict divorce couples. You've walked through a plethora of cases that demonstrate both the problems you'll face and the solutions you'll need to be successful with this most contentious clientele.

That's the point — you now have those strategies to draw on as you plunge into your work with these families. Now it's time to feel hopeful. Yes, these couples can be treated successfully. However, you won't apply one strategy or program we've offered and just turn these cases around. You'll need to apply a full range of strategies and deal with a number of the systems with which couples are involved.

You'll deal with the court, attorneys, and the children. You'll provide therapy to the family, and even send some of these couples to visit their clergyperson before you may see a measurable improvement. So be patient. Brief therapy for these cases is rarely brief — as we've found. These couples tend to move more slowly because of the numerous problems involved in each case.

We hope you have been inspired and encouraged in these pages to explore the range of dilemmas that therapists, lawyers, judges, court counselors, and other professionals face. Testing, parental alienation, parent empowerment, group treatment, parent coordination, high-conflict treatment teams — we're all in up to our ears! We hope that you enjoy the challenge these cases present.

As you have seen in the preceding chapters, working with high-conflict couples is not for the faint of heart or the timid. It is extremely hard work that calls for guts, determination, and sophisticated clinical skills. It's not an activity that any young, naïve therapist can jump into. It is therapeutic work that calls for the therapist's adroitness, flexibility, self-confidence, emotional stability, and tolerance for putting up with conflict.

Because of the emotionally taxing nature of treating bitterly conflicted couples, this is not work you should take on in a vacuum. That is, you need to have trusted co-workers with whom you can consult, and on whose shoulders you can occasionally cry. It's invaluable to have professional colleagues — not to mention supportive family members — who will help you put your professional life, your expertise, and your feelings about yourself in perspective. As a group, couples entrenched in high-conflict divorces are among the most challenging clients you'll ever encounter and, as a result, work with this difficult therapeutic population will frequently lead you to feel frustrated, discouraged, and sometimes doubtful of your professional competence.

However, some of the more negative feelings associated with this kind of work can be minimized if you coordinate your efforts to help couples in high-conflict divorces with other clinicians, as well as attorneys and judges. You need to collaborate with as many other professionals as possible so that you have in your corner others who are trying to help these couples. Furthermore, the more colleagues with whom you collaborate, the more resources and points of view you'll bring to your work with each unique high-conflict divorce case.

And that's one of the most important points we've tried to make in this book. By working together with other professionals within a clinical or judicial system, you can be successful and you can help the couples who are embroiled in high-conflict relationships.

When professionals do work together, it is possible to put into place interventions that reduce high conflict. Working cooperatively is in everybody's best interest — especially the children who will be affected by co-parents learning to get along better.

By helping these high-conflict couples, you are ultimately going to be helping children. If you can keep this goal in mind, it will keep you going when you're faced with the frustration of co-parents who can't seem to work out their conflicts.

To be at your best in working with high-conflict couples, you must not give in to the natural tendency to look at conflict in terms of win-lose. If you do that, you'll repeat what high-conflict couples are already doing. And then, everybody loses. And, furthermore, you just perpetuate the conflict.

With the tools we've provided, you will have greater ability to keep your objectivity and maintain your professional posture. Keep working, creating, and enjoying the difficulties that come from working with high-conflict divorces. It can be very rewarding to see a family that has been stuck begin to cooperate in a more productive fashion so they can move on to a new stage of life.

After reading this book and understanding the processes we've described, you are grounded in some approaches that will help you to begin truly changing these families. We expect that you and other professionals will continue to develop methods to expand and improve upon the approaches we've presented here. This is a very young field of practice which is fertile ground for your creativity. Enjoy the opportunity to wade into the flow of a young stream that holds deep mysteries and great promise.

Bibliography

Ackerman, M. (1995). *Clinician's guide to child custody evaluations.* New York: Wiley.

Adelmann, P.K., Chadwick. K. and Baerger, D.R. (1996). Marital quality of black and white adults over the life course. *Journal of Social and Personal Relationships*, 13, 361–384.

AFCC Task Force on Parenting Coordination (2003). Parenting coordination: implementation issues. *Family Court Review*, 41 (4), 533–564.

Ahrons, C. (1994). *The Good Divorce: Keeping your family together when your marriage comes apart.* New York: Bloomsbury.

Amato, P. and Keith, B. (1991a). Parental divorce and well-being of children: A meta-analysis. *Psychological Bulletin*, 110 (1), 26–46.

Amato, P. and Keith, B. (1991b). Parental divorce and adult well-being. *Journal of Marriage and the Family*, 49, 327–337.

American Association for Marriage and Family Therapy. (2001). AAMFT Code of ethics. Alexandria, VA.

American Counseling Association. (2005). ACA Code of ethics. Alexandria, VA.

American Psychiatric Association (1994). *Diagnostic and Statistical Manual of Mental Disorders, Fourth Edition.* Washington, DC: American Psychiatric Association.

American Psychological Association. (2003). Ethical principles of psychologists and code of conduct. *American Psychologist*, 57 (12), 1060–1073.

American Psychological Association (1994). Guidelines for Child Custody Evaluations in Divorce Proceedings. *American Psychologist*, 49, 677–682.

Anderson,H., Goolishian, H. and Winderman, I. (1986). Problem determined systems: Towards transformations in family therapy. *Journal of Strategic and Systematic Therapies*, 5, 1–4.

Arbuthnot, J., Kramer, K. and Gordon, D.A. (1997). Patterns of relitigation following divorce education. *Family and Conciliation Courts Review*, 35, 269–279.

Association of Family and Conciliation Courts (2006) *A History of innovation and conciliation.* [on line] Available at: www.afccnet.org/about/history.asp

Benjamin, M. and Irving, H. (2001). Money and mediation: Patterns of conflict in family mediation of financial matters. *Mediation Quarterly*, 18(4), 349–361.

Benjet, C., Azar, S. T. and Kuersten-Hogan, R. (2003). Evaluating the parental fitness of psychiatrically diagnosed individuals: advocating a functional-contextual analysis of parenting. *Journal of Family Psychology*, 17(2), 238–251.

Blume, T. W. and Price, J. (1993). Strategic mediation: Strategies in service of family empowerment. *Journal of Systemic Therapies*, 12 (4), 53–65.

Booth, A. and Amato, P. (1991). Divorce and psychological stress. *Journal of Health and Social Behavior*, 32 (4), 396–407.

Bow, J. N. and Quinnell, F. A. (2004). Critique of child custody evaluations by the legal profession. *Family Court Review*, 42, 115–126.

Boylan, S. M. and Termini, A. M. (2005). *The psychotherapist as parent coordinator in high-conflict divorce: Strategies and Techniques*. Binghamton, NY: The Haworth Clinical Practice Press.

Bryner, C. L. (2001). Children of divorce. *Journal of the American Board of Family Practice*. 14 (3), 178–183.

Buchanan, C. M. and Heiges, K. L. (2001). When conflict continues after the divorce ends: Effects of post-divorce conflict on children. In J. Grych and F. Fincham (eds.), *Interparental conflict and child development* (pp. 337–362). New York: Cambridge University Press.

Buchanan, C., Maccoby, E. & Dornbusch, S. (1991). Caught between parents: Adolescents' experience in divorced homes. *Child Development*, 62, 1008–1029.

Camara, K.A. and Resnick, G. (1988). Interpersonal conflict and cooperation: Factors moderating children's post-divorce adjustment. In E.M. Hetherington and J.D. Arasteh (Eds.), *Impact of divorce, single-parenting, and stepparenting on children* (pp. 169–196). Hillsdale, NJ: Erlbaum.

Camara, K. and Resnick, G. (1989). Divorced parents: Effects on child behavior and adjustment. *American Journal of Orthopsychiatry*, 59(4), 556–575.

Child Abuse Prevention and Treatment Act (P.L. 93–247). Amended as Keeping Children and Families Safe Act of 2003 (P.L. 108–36). U.S. Code 42, 67.

Coontz, S. (1997). *The way we really are: Coming to terms with America's changing families*. New York: Basic Books.

Cummings, E.M. and Davies, P. (1994). *Children and marital conflict: The impact of family dispute and resolution*. New York: Guilford.

Cummings, E. M. and O'Reilly, A. W. (1997). Fathers in family context: Effects of marital quality on child adjustment. In M. E. Lamb (Ed.), *The role of the father in child development* (3rd ed., pp. 49–65, 318–325). New York: John Wiley.

Depner, C.E., Cannata, K.V. and Simon, M.B. (1992). Building a uniform statistical reporting system: A snapshot of California Family Court Services. *Family and Conciliation Courts Review*, 30, 185–206.

Derogatis, L. R. and Spencer, P. M. (1982). *The brief symptom inventory (BSI) administration, scoring and procedures manual: I*. Baltimore, MD: Clinical Psychometric Research, Johns Hopkins University School of Medicine.

Ehrenberg, M.F., Hunter, M.A. and Elterman, M. F. (1996). Shared parenting agreements after marital separation: The roles of empathy and narcissism. *Journal of Consulting and Clinical Psychology*, 64(4), 808–818.

Ellis, E. M. (2000). *Divorce wars: Interventions with families in conflict.* Washington, DC: American Psychological Association.

Elrod, L. (2004). Reforming the system to protect children in high conflict custody cases. *William Mitchell Law Review,* 28 (2), 495–551.

Emery, R. E., Matthews, S.G. and Kitzman, K.M. (1994). Child custody mediation and litigation: Parents' satisfaction and functioning a year after settlement. *Journal of Consulting and Clinical Psychology,* 62, 124–129.

Emery, R. E., Sbarra, D. and Grover, T. (2005). Divorce mediation: Research and reflections. *Family Court Review,* 43 (1), 22–37.

Fincham, F. D., Grych, J.H. and Osborne, L. N. (1994). Does marital conflict cause child maladjustment? Directions and challenges for longitudinal research. *Journal of Family Psychology,* 8, 128–140.

Firestone, G. and Weinstein, J. (2004). In the best interests of children: A proposal to transform the adversarial system. *Family Court Review,* 42(2), 203–215.

Furstenberg, F. and Cherlin, A. (1991). *Divided families: what happens to children when parents part?* Cambridge, MA: Harvard University Press.

Fyfe, B. J. (2003). The unfinished promise of parenting coordinator. *The SCP Forum.* Retrieved on May 23, 2006 from www.Coloradopsychologists.org/newsletters/newslet2.pdf

Gardner, R. (1987). *Parental alienation syndrome and the differentiation between fabricated and genuine sexual abuse.* Creskill, NJ: Creative Therapeutics.

Gardner, R. (1989). *Family evaluation in child custody, mediation, arbitration and litigation.* Cresskill, NJ: Creative Therapeutics, Inc.

Garrity, C. and Baris, M. (1994). *Caught in the middle: Protecting the children of high-conflict divorce.* San Francisco, CA: Jossey-Bass.

Geasler, M.J. and Blaisure, K.R. (1999). 1998 nationwide survey of court-connected divorce education programs. *Family and Conciliation Courts Review,* 37 (1), 36–632.

Gilmour, G.A. (2004). *High-conflict separation and divorce: Options for consideration.* Family, Children and Youth Section, Department of Justice Canada, 2004-FCY-1E.

Glod, M. (May 13, 2002; p. B1). For father and child, time to get acquainted; Daughter returns after nearly 8 years. *Washington Post.*

Goodman, M., Bonds, D., Sandler, I. and Braver, S. (2004). Parent psychoeducational programs and reducing the negative effects of interparental conflict following divorce. *Family Court Review,* 42 (2), 263–279.

Grych, J. and Fincham, F. (1993). Children's appraisal of marital conflict: Initial investigations of the cognitive-contextual framework. *Child Development,* 64, 215–230.

Guidubaldi, J., Cleminshaw, H.K., Perry, J.D. and McLoughlin, C.S. (1983). The impact of parental divorce on children: Report of the nationwide NASP study. *School Psychology Review,* 12, 300–323.

Haley, J. (1991). *Problem-solving therapy,* (2nd. Ed). San Francisco, CA: Jossey-Bass.

Haley, J. (1984). *Ordeal therapy.* San Francisco: Jossey-Bass.

Harrist, A. and Ainslie, R. (1998). Parental discord and child behavior problems. *Journal of Family Issues,* 19, 140–163.

Hauser, B. B. (1985). Custody in dispute: Legal and psychological profiles of contesting families. *Journal of the American Academy of Child Psychiatry,* 24, 575–582.

Hetherington, E. M., Cox, M. & Cox, R. (1985). Long-term effects of divorce and remarriage on the adjustment of children. *Journal of the American Academy of Child Psychiatry,* 24, 518–530.

Hetherington, E. M. and Stanley-Hagan, M. (1999). The adjustment of children with divorced parents: A risk and resiliency perspective. *Journal of Child Psychology and Psychiatry,* 40, 129–140.

Hopper, J. (2001). The symbolic origins of conflict in divorce. *Journal of Marriage and Family,* 63, 430–445.

Johnson, H., LaVoie, J.C. and Mahoney, M. (2001) Inter-parental conflict and family cohesion: Predictors of loneliness, social anxiety and social avoidance in late adolescence. *Journal of Adolescent Research,* 163 (3), 304–318.

Johnston, J.R. (1994). High-conflict divorce. *Children and Divorce,* 4 (1), 165–182.

Johnston, J. and Campbell, L. (1988). *Impasses of divorce: The dynamics and resolution of family conflict.* New York: Free Press.

Johnston, J. and Roseby, V. (1997). *In the name of the child: A developmental approach to understanding and helping children of conflicted and violent divorce.* New York: Free Press.

Kelly, J.B. (1996). A decade of divorce mediation research: Some answers and questions. *Family and Conciliation Courts Review,* 34, 373–385.

Kelly, J. B. (2000). Children's adjustment in conflicted marriage and divorce: A decade review of research. *Journal of the American Academy of Child & Adolescent Psychiatry,* 39, 963–973.

Kelly, J.B. (2003). Parents with enduring child disputes: Multiple pathways to enduring disputes. *Journal of Family Studies,* 9 (1), 37–50.

Kelly, J.B. and Johnston, J. R. (2001). The Alienated child: A reformulation of Parental Alienation Syndrome. *Family Court Review,* 39 (3), 249–266.

King, V. and Heard, H. E. (1999). Nonresident father visitation, parental conflict, and mother's satisfaction: What's best for child well-being? *Journal of Marriage and Family,* 61, 385–396.

Kitzman, K. M. and Emery, R. E. (1994). Child and family coping one year following mediated and litigated child custody disputes. *Journal of Family Psychology,* 8, 150–159.

Kline, M., Tschann, J. and Johnson, J. (1991). The long shadow of marital conflict: A model of children's post-divorce adjustment. *Journal of Marriage and the Family,* 53, 297–309.

Kramer, K., Arbuthnot, J., Gordon, D., Rousis, N. and Hosa, J. (1998). Effects of skill-based versus information-based divorce education programs on domestic violence and parental communication. *Family and Conciliation Courts Review*, 36, 9–31.

Kranitz, M. (2000). *Getting Apart Together: The couple's guide to a fair divorce or separation*. Atascadero, CA: Impact Publishers.

Kraus, D.A. and Sales, B.D. (1999). The problem of "helpfulness" in applying Daubert to expert testimony: Child custody determinations in family law as an exemplar. *Psychology of Public Policy and Law*, 5, 78–99.

Kressel, K., Jaffe, N., Tuchman, B., Watson, C. and Deutsch, M. (1980). A typology of divorcing couples: Implications for mediation and the divorce process. *Family Process*, 19, 101–116.

Lamb, M.E. and Kelly, J. B. (2001). Using the empirical literature to guide the development of parenting plans for young children: A rejoinder to Solomon and Biringen. *Family Court Review*, 39 (4), 365–371.

Lovenheim, P. (1996). *How to mediate your dispute*. Berkeley, CA: Nolo Press.

Maccoby, E. E. and Mnookin, R. H. (1992). *Dividing the child*. Cambridge, MA: Harvard University Press.

Mackey, R.A. and O'Brien, B.A. (1998). Marital conflict management: Gender and ethnic differences. *Social Work*, 43, 128–141.

Madanes, C. (1981). *Strategic family therapy*. San Francisco: Jossey-Bass.

Margerum, J. (2005). *Emotional divorce quotient*. Unpublished manuscript.

Markan, L. K. and Weinstock, D. K (2005). Expanding forensically informed evaluations sand therapeutic interventions in family court. *Family Court Review*, 43, 466–480.

Marlatt, G. A., Blume, A. and Parks, G.A. (2001). Integrating harm reduction therapy and traditional substance abuse treatment. *Journal of Psychoactive Drugs*, 33 (1), 13–21.

Mathis, R. D. (1998). Couples from hell: Undifferentiated spouses in divorce mediation. *Mediation Quarterly*, 16 (1), 37–49.

McIntosh, J. (2003). Enduring conflict in parental separation: Pathways of impact on child development. *Journal of Family Studies*, 9(1), 63–80.

McIntosh, J. and Deacon-Wood, H.B. (2003). Group intervention for separated parents in entrenched conflict: An exploration of evidence-based frameworks. *Journal of Family Studies*, 9 (2), 180–199.

McLoyd, V.C., Cauce, A.M., Takeuchi, D. and Wilson, L. (2000). Marital processes and parental socialization in families of color: A decade review of research. *Journal of Marriage and the Family*, 62, 1070–1093.

Melton, G. B., Petrila, J., Poythree, N. G. and Slobogin, C. (1997). *Psychological evaluations for the courts: A handbook for mental health professionals and lawyers* (2nd ed.). New York: Guilford Press.

Nakonezny, P.A., Shull, R. D. and Rogers, J. L. (1995). The effect of no-fault divorce law on the divorce rate across the 50 states and its relation to income, education and religiosity. *Journal of Marriage and the Family*, 57, 477–488.

National Association of Social Workers. (1999). *Code of ethics*. Washington, D.C.

Nicholson, J., Sweeney, E.M.. and Geller, J.L (1998). Focus on women: Mothers with mental illness: I. The competing demands of parenting and living with mental illness. *Psychiatric Services*, 49, 635–642.

O'Donohue, W. and Bradley, A.R. (1999). Conceptual and empirical issues in child custody evaluations. *Clinical Psychology: Science and Practice*, 6, 310–322.

Papp, P. (1980). The Greek chorus and other techniques of paradoxical therapy. *Family Process*, 19 (1), 45–57.

Parks, G. A., Anderson, B. K. and Marlatt, G. A. (2000). Harm reduction therapy with co-occurring disorders. *The Los Angeles Psychologist*, Jan/Feb: 3, 23.

Posthuma, A. and Harper, J. (1998). Comparisons of MMPI-2 responses of child custody and personal injury litigants. *Professional Psychology: Research and Practice*, 29, 547–553.

Retzinger, S. and Scheff, T. (2000). Emotion, alienation and narratives: resolving intractable conflict. *Mediation Quarterly*, 18 (1), 71–85.

Rudd, J. E. (1996). Communication effects on divorce mediation: How participants' argumentativeness, verbal aggression and compliance-gaining strategy choice mediate outcome satisfaction. *Mediation Quarterly*, 14 (1), 65–78.

Selvini, M. and Palazzoli, M.S. (1991). Team consultation: An indispensable tool for the progress of knowledge. Ways of fostering and promoting its creative potential. *Journal of Family Therapy*, 13 (1), 31–52.

Siegel, J. C. (1996). Traditional MMPI-2 validity indicators and initial presentations in custody evaluations. *American Journal of Forensic Psychology*, 14 (3), 55–63.

Siegel, J. C. and Langford, J. S. (1998). MMPI-2 validity scales and suspected parental alienation syndrome. *American Journal of Forensic Psychology*, 16 (4), 5–14.

Siegel, L. J. Welsh, B. C., and Senna, J. J. (2006). *Juvenile delinquency: theory, practice and law* (9th ed). Belmont, CA: Thomson/Wadsworth.

Sistler, A.B. and Moore, G.M. (1996). Cultural diversity in coping with marital stress. *Journal of Clinical Geropsychology*, 2, 77–82.

Smiley, G.W., Chamberlain, E.R. & Dalgleish, L. I. (1987). Implications of marital separation for young children. *Australian Institute of Family Studies*, (Working Paper No. 11). Melbourne, Victoria, Australia.

Stahl, P. (1999). *Complex Issues in Child Custody Evaluations*. Thousand Oaks, CA: Sage.

Stahl, P. (2000). *Parenting After Divorce: A guide to resolving conflicts and meeting your children's needs*. Atascadero, CA: Impact Publishers.

Stewart, J.W. (2000). *The Child Custody Book: How to protect your children and win your case*. Atascadero, CA: Impact Publishers.

Stolberg, A. L., Camplair, C., Currier, C. and Wells, M.J. (1987). Individual, familial and environmental determinants of children's post-divorce adjustment and maladjustment. *Journal of Divorce*, 11, 51–70.

Tippins, T. M. and Wittmann, J. P. (2005). Empirical and ethical problems with custody recommendations: A call for clinical humility and judicial vigilance. *Family Court Review*, 43, 193–222.

Trovato, F. (1987). A longitudinal analysis of divorce and suicide in Canada. *Journal of Marriage and the Family*, 49 (1), 193–204.

U.S. Census Bureau (2001). *America's families and living arrangements*. Washington, D.C.: Author.

Waldo, M.C., Roath, M., Levine, W. and Freedman, R. 1987). A model program to teach parenting skills to schizophrenic mothers. *Hospital and Community Psychiatry*, 38, 1110–1112.

Wallerstein, J. (1985). Children of divorce: Preliminary report of a ten-year follow-up of older children and adolescents. *Journal of the American Academy of Child Psychiatry*, 24, 545–553.

Wallerstein, J.S. and Kelly, J.B. (1980), *Surviving the breakup: How children and parents cope with divorce*. New York: Basic Books.

Wallerstein, J. S. and Lewis, J. (1998). The long-term impact of divorce on children: A first report from a 25 year study. *Family and Conciliation Courts Review*, 36 (3), 368–383.

Warshak, R.A. (2001). Current controversies regarding parental alienation syndrome. *American Journal of Forensic Psychology*, 19 (3), 29–59.

Weinstein, J. (1997). And never the twain shall meet: the best interests of the children and the adversary system. *Miami Law Review*, 79, 133.

Weir, K. (2006). Clinical advice to courts on children's contact with their parents following parental separation. *Child and Adolescent Mental Health*, 11 (1), 40–49.

Wingspread Conference Report (2001). High-conflict custody cases: reforming the system for children. *Family Court Review*, 39 (2), 146–157.

Zill, N., Morrison, D. and Coiro, M. (1993). Long term effects of parental divorce on parent-child relationships, adjustment and achievement in young adulthood. *Journal of Family Psychology*, 7, 91–103.

Index

The Practical Therapist Series®

Books in *The Practical Therapist Series®* are designed to answer the troubling "what-do-I-do-now-and-how-do-I-do-it?" questions often confronted in the practice of psychotherapy. Written in plain language, technically innovative, theoretically integrative, filled with case examples, *The Practical Therapist Series®* brings the wisdom and experience of expert mentors to the desk of every therapist.

Rational Emotive Behavior Therapy
A Therapist's Guide (Second Edition)
Albert Ellis, Ph.D. and Catharine MacLaren, M.S.W., CEAP
Hardcover: $24.95   176 pages   ISBN: 1-886230-61-7
Up-to-date guidebook by the innovator of Rational Emotive Behavior Therapy. Includes thorough description of REBT theory and procedures, case examples, exercises.

Metaphor in Psychotherapy
Clinical Applications of Stories and Allegories
Henry T. Close, Th.M.
Hardcover: $29.95   320 pages   ISBN: 1-886230-10-2
Creative collection of stories and allegories, and how to use them as teaching tools in psychotherapy, including metaphors for children.

Integrative Brief Therapy: Cognitive, Psychodynamic, Humanistic & Neurobehavioral Approaches
John Preston, Psy.D.
Softcover: $27.95   272 pages   ISBN: 1-886230-09-9
Answers the perennial therapist question, "What do I do now?" Integrates proven elements of therapeutic efficacy from diverse theoretical viewpoints.

Anger Management: The Complete Treatment
Guidebook for Practitioners
Howard Kassinove, Ph.D. and R. Chip Tafrate, Ph.D.
Softcover: $27.95   320 pages   ISBN: 1-886230-45-5
Research-based and empirically validated "anger episode model" presented in a desktop manual for practitioners. Offers a comprehensive state-of-the-art program that can be implemented almost immediately in any practice setting. *Also available on 2-DVD set, approx. 150 min., $69.95.*

Please see the following page for more books.

The Practical Therapist Series®

The Soul of Counseling: *A New Model for Understanding Human Experience*
Dwight Webb, Ph.D.
Softcover: $24.95   192 pages   ISBN: 1-886230-59-5
Practical, down-to-earth aids to integrate into professional psychotherapy practice to help deal with clients' issues of the human spirit.

Meditative Therapy
Facilitating Inner-Directed Healing
Michael L. Emmons, Ph.D. and Janet Emmons, M.S.
Softcover: $27.95   230 pages   ISBN: 1-886230-11-0
Guide to creating the conditions for natural healing and recovery. Help clients harness their inner resources for emotional, physical, and spiritual growth.

Creative Therapy with Children and Adolescents
Angela Hobday, M.Sc. and Kate Ollier, M.Psych.
Hardcover: $21.95   192 pages   ISBN: 1-886230-19-6
Over 100 activities for therapeutic work with children, adolescents, and families. Simple ideas, fun games, fresh innovations to use as tools to supplement a variety of therapeutic interventions.

How to Fail as a Therapist
Bernard Schwartz, Ph.D. and John V. Flowers, Ph.D.
Hardcover: $22.95   160 pages   ISBN: 1-886230-70-6
Well-researched strategies reduce dropout rates and increase positive treatment outcomes. This book details the 50 most common errors therapists make, and how to avoid them. Practical, helpful steps for avoiding not recognizing one's limitations, performing incomplete assessments, ignoring science, ruining the client relationship, much more.

Ask your local or online bookseller, or call 1-800-246-7228 to order direct.
Impact ✐ Publishers®
POST OFFICE BOX 6016 • ATASCADERO, CALIFORNIA 93423-6016
Visit us on the Internet at www.bibliotherapy.com • Write for our free catalog.

Since 1970 — Psychology you can use, from professionals you can trust